Chasing the Panther

Chasing the Panther

Adventures & Misadventures
of a Cinematic Life

Carolyn Pfeiffer

with Gregory Collins

HARPER HORIZON

Published by Harper Horizon, an imprint of HarperCollins Focus LLC.

Book design by Aubrey Khan, Neuwirth & Associates, Inc.

Any internet addresses, phone numbers, or company or product information printed in this book are offered as a resource and are not intended in any way to be or to imply an endorsement by Harper Horizon, nor does Harper Horizon vouch for the existence, content, or services of these sites, phone numbers, companies, or products beyond the life of this book.

This is a work of nonfiction. The events and experiences detailed herein are all true and have been faithfully rendered as remembered by the author, to the best of her ability. Some names and characteristics have been changed, some events have been compressed, and some dialogue has been re-created.

ISBN 978-0-7852-5541-3 (Ebook)
ISBN 978-0-7852-5518-5 (HC)

Library of Congress Control Number: 2022948236

Printed in the United States of America
23 24 25 26 27 LBC 5 4 3 2 1

For Lola, Shannon, Cassia, and Luce

As a woman I have no country.
As a woman I want no country.
As a woman my country is the whole world.

VIRGINIA WOOLF

Contents

CONTENTS

Author's Note

I never imagined that I would write about my life, mostly because my professional training was to protect the privacy of the people for and with whom I worked. That said, as a young woman, I witnessed moments of lasting cultural and historical significance. The people and events written about here—many of them, at least—are in the public record. But I was there, too, and I'd like to contribute my memories to that record.

CAROLYN PFEIFFER
Marfa, Texas

One

Beginnings, like endings, are slippery. Because everything exists in the middle. There was something before, and there will be something after.

I remember standing in a field outside my home in Madison, North Carolina. It isn't my earliest memory, but it stands out among them. In it, I jump from one rock to another, losing myself in concentration. As I do so, the sky falls away and the wind grows silent, and in the stillness of this trance, I feel something call to me. It's subtle but unmistakably urgent. And I feel the response within: a yearning, hungry and impatient.

I have always been average, but I have never been typical. Yet when I try to make sense of this idiosyncrasy, when I track its origins back through the tangled woods of memory, the trail disappears when I arrive at the happy oblivion of childhood.

The world seemed simple then. World War II was newly won, and my life was a colorful mosaic of tobacco farms and bamboo fishing poles. Beneath me was the mud of the Dan River, the pebbles from a dirt road caught between my toes. Around me was the culture of the South. Exaggerated respect for elders. Excessive hospitality. Relentless self-sufficiency. And total faith that the relationship between the sexes, between the races, and between man and nature were organized and ordained by God.

I was too young, jumping from rock to rock, to make sense of the stirring within me. I was of that beautiful age when a child is fully conscious yet still fully a part of all things. Until then, the impulse to stand apart, the knowledge of individuality and purpose, was still dormant. That moment when a child understands herself to be distinct in the universe was held at bay by the comfort and safety of my family.

Bill, my brother, was younger than me, but we did everything together. If he peed outside, I peed outside. If he took his shirt off to wade in the creek, I took my shirt off to wade in the creek. But one afternoon, my maternal grandmother—a handsome Southern woman with auburn hair mononymously known, even to us grandchildren, as Edna—instructed me to put my shirt back on even as Bill was allowed to keep his off.

"You're too old now," she said sternly.

It was a fence across the open field of my life. I resented the imposition of a boundary where none had existed before and where one need not have existed at all. It wasn't long before more fences were constructed, and while they were intended to bring order where chaos was perceived to reign, they instead caused me to look beyond them, to fixate on horizons I otherwise might never have noticed.

One such horizon was my Great Uncle Goat, so named because of his close-set, gray eyes and because he was more at home in the wooded countryside surrounding Madison than he was in town. Refusing to set foot indoors his entire adult life, he lived in a collection of canvas tents on a fenced-in compound where he kept his horses and cooked over an open fire.

2

I spent long summer days with Uncle Goat. We'd go fishing or we'd trap squirrels and rabbits for the Brunswick stew that took a week to prepare. And all the while, I'd study him closely. I was sure the horses and the land communicated with him, and I was sure that I understood him, that I was the kind of person in whom he could confide. Alas, he had as much use for words as he did for the indoors. When I pleaded with him to tell me about serving in the cavalry out West, for example, he'd just shrug and say, "It was all right, I guess."

Carolyn (center), Bill (far left), and Madison children
(Pfeiffer family archive)

If it were up to me, I would have lived in a tent next to his and never set foot in school. I was one of only two students in my class who didn't live on a tobacco farm. The other was David Spear, whose parents ran the local paper, the *Madison Messenger*, and whose grandfather was Sherwood Anderson, the author. Energetic and mischievous, David was always looking for a prank to pull. But there was also sentimentality in his energy. He saw things that I didn't: bird nests, spiderwebs, clouds of all different kinds. He saw the tracks of a deer where I saw dirt, the reflection of the sky where I saw a rain puddle.

David told me he was going to run the *Messenger* someday; I told him I was going to be president.

When I wasn't with Uncle Goat, I haunted Big Bill's stables in the center of town. Big Bill—not to be confused with my younger brother, Bill—was my grandfather and something of a dignitary in our little town. He had a long scar down his cheek that he'd gotten one night when a drunk came onto Edna. He'd intervened only for the drunk to unsheathe a Bowie knife and start slashing around like a maniac. But Big Bill sorted him out all the same.

Incorporated as a township in the early 1800s, Madison had begun as a rowdy trading center, a place where merchants and hog traders in flat-bottomed boats could do business and make merry as they shuttled between Greensboro and Roanoke. But the railroads, in rendering the river trade obsolete, had stripped Madison of the potential that once seemed to promise so much.

Tobacco now fueled the economy, and tobacco farmers from across the county were always gathered around the potbellied stove in the stables' office talking politics and tobacco prices. I loved being in their company. With jeans on under the dress I was obliged to wear, and with my hair in two braids, I'd listen to their banter and then slip away to whisper my hellos to the horses. The smoke from the farmers' cigarettes mixed with that of the stove's burning wood and with the deep, earthy smell of the horses. Breathing it in was breathing in the mysteries of the grown-up world, a world that was slowly drawing me into its orbit.

Edna and Big Bill were second cousins, not altogether unusual in those days. Both Cardwells, their marriage had consolidated the property of their family branches, and after church each Sunday, we—the extended Cardwells—gathered for lunch at an old antebellum mansion tucked into the hill of a sloping farm that had been in the family for generations. White pillars framed a spacious upstairs balcony, and rich mahogany trim gave the interior a stately feel. Edna's siblings, Uncle Tom and Aunt Caroline, lived in the house and managed the property and the Black sharecroppers who worked the land. Uncle Tom had been struck by lightning some years earlier and rarely spoke at all anymore. Aunt Caroline, who'd never married, raised an orphaned niece, Rosa B., and was a formidable cook who oversaw elaborate lunches of roasts, fried chicken, mashed potatoes, fresh vegetables, and homemade biscuits and pies.

After lunch, Bill and I would explore the farm and the surrounding acreage until the sun set over the green hills. Sometimes we'd meet up with the sharecroppers' children and spend hours wading in the creek, catching frogs, and playing tag until it was too dark to see and we had to go our way and they had to go theirs.

That they were Black and we were white was obvious enough, but it wasn't a distinction that registered as meaningful. I was drawn to Thomas, who was younger than me and who had eyes of conviction and the hands of an artist. With his parents and eight siblings, he lived in a two-room log cabin, and though we were from different worlds, we were nonetheless of some similar make. In the midst of a frenzied activity, I'd find him seated beside me. During hide-and-seek, we'd find the same hiding place. Or we'd lie on our backs talking and doing nothing while the others wrestled around us.

Thomas told me he was going to be a doctor. I told him I was going to be an explorer.

Then, before bed one Sunday night, Edna forbade me from playing with Black children.

"You're too old now," she said.

Up until then, I'd thought segregation was for other people. I'd assumed that my obligation to comply with it was because of real problems in the real world. A war, perhaps, or some other adult reality beyond my comprehension. It never once occurred to me that segregation was also, specifically, for me and Thomas.

Another fence stretched across the already bisected field of my life. There were so many things—more and more of them—that I accepted but that I did not understand. The way religion and respect could coexist so effortlessly alongside segregation. The way hospitality was only up to a point, for some people and not for others.

Whether to preempt any trouble I might have gotten into or simply to afford me new experiences, at the end of fourth grade, my parents began sending me to stay with my aunt and uncle in Washington, DC, for the summers. I liked Aunt Helen, my father's sister, but it was Uncle Frank, funny and energetic, to whom I grew attached. With warm brown eyes and Dean Martin eyebrows, he had a wonderfully uneven smile that could dispel the darkest of moods in an instant. He'd been in the army during the war, and despite Aunt Helen waiting impatiently at home, he'd stayed in Europe for several years to help with reconstruction. The tensions between them were thick, and it was clear that whatever pleasures Uncle Frank had indulged in overseas were unwelcome back at home.

World War II, Uncle Frank liked to say, was a waterfall in human history.

"There is a before, there is an after, and there is no going back," he'd explain. "Means you're growing up in a whole new world."

How I loved his stories. About the war but also about Europe itself: about Paris and its monuments and sidewalk cafés; Rome, with its fountains and basilicas; Warsaw, which he called *Varshava* with a perfect Polish accent. The cultures of Europe, he'd say, were so much older, the traditions so much richer. They'd had time to refine and perfect their customs and cuisines, their arts and their philosophies.

A devout Catholic, Uncle Frank was mesmerized by Notre Dame, which had given refuge to Quasimodo in Victor Hugo's novel and whose magnificent bells had been melted down and made into guillotines during the French Revolution. He was transfixed by Antoni Gaudí's *Sagrada Família*, a basilica in Barcelona that had been under construction for three quarters of a century yet wasn't even close to finished.

"I think," he sighed over popcorn and a game of checkers one night, "that I left my soul over there."

When I returned home at the end of each summer, Madison felt smaller and smaller. Main Street, once broad and crowded, was little more than a handful of shops and offices. Even the Cardwell farm, once sprawling, was now contained, every inch of it known.

But then, after lunch one Sunday, Big Bill called us to him.

"The two of you are growing up, aren't you?" he asked as he pulled me onto his knee and ruffled Bill's hair.

This sounded like the preamble to good news, and we volunteered an eager yessir in unison.

"Lemme ask you, then. Would you rather have"—he paused for so long that the silence became unbearable—"a bicycle?" Here he paused again, this time to give my brother's squeal of delight the full measure of time it required. "Or a horse?"

There was never a question, not for me. Horses occasionally arrived from Tennessee, and I lived for the moment the train came to a stop. I loved the sound of stomping hooves just before the car doors opened; the bewildered, ecstatic look in the horses' eyes as they emerged into the sunlight; the way a crowd gathered to guide the flow of animals down Main Street to Big Bill's stables; and most of all, I loved the quiet that followed when I could walk the stalls and make friends with the horses.

Miss Nancy, a sorrel mare, was plain and dignified. Though a gift from Big Bill, she was a bridge to Uncle Goat, who, unbeknownst to my parents or grandparents, would invite me to ride with him out to the white-lightning shacks that littered the countryside. That ours was a dry county made no difference to Uncle Goat, and I suppose he didn't know what to do except bring me along with him from time to time.

So I'd follow behind him through woodland trails I never knew existed, and I'd feel a part of Madison's peculiar charm.

It really was beautiful, in its way. But it was also haunted, a place laden with sadness and history lost to time. Farmers now grew corn and alfalfa in the fertile bottomlands where the Dan and the Mayo Rivers came together, but this was the same land that slaves had once worked and that the Saura people, for hundreds of years prior, had farmed.

Arriving at a white-lightning shack, we'd dismount, and I'd tether the horses and stay with them while Uncle Goat disappeared into the wooden structure. Every now and then a hard-looking, leathery man would enter or exit, and I'd stare, seeing my future in them. These men were creations of this land, tied to it in every way that a person can be tied to a place.

Eventually, Uncle Goat would stumble out, alcohol heavy on his breath, a jar of moonshine in his hand, and I'd follow him back through the woods conspiratorially.

With Miss Nancy, Madison became limitless once more. My best friend, Patsy Cox, lived on the edge of town. Her family kept a few horses, and I'd ride out to her house, and we'd set out to see what we could see. Now and then my cousin Nancy Lee would come along, and we'd ride up to Mayodan, the neighboring town, explore the surrounding woodlands, or follow the Dan River. Sometimes we'd find a field where we could work our horses up to a full gallop. There was no feeling more exhilarating than that of my feet against Miss Nancy's sides

Miss Nancy
(Pfeiffer family archive)

and the wind snapping my hair against my neck. For a moment the world around me would vanish as if it didn't exist at all. And then, as Miss Nancy slowed, it would return from wherever it had been, and I would listen to Miss Nancy's panting and puzzle over why I, too, was out of breath.

"What are you going to be?" I asked Patsy one afternoon as we rode back to her house.

"A professor. What about you?"

"A fashion model."

It was a recent notion, one animated by changes that, at least in their origins, were not external but internal. It had begun as a sensation; a tenderness within me that hadn't been there before. Then, gradually, the invisible had become visible. And as puberty cunningly doctored my hormones and redrew the lines of my figure, I inventoried its progress, obsessively registering the peripatetic fit of my clothing.

There arose around me a new emphasis on modesty and on formality. Affections from my father, Big Bill, and the men around me became briefer and more infrequent. Orchestrated by this unseen force, my body was reconfiguring itself for unknown reasons, and for reasons that were equally unknown, the world around me was reconfiguring itself in response.

This metamorphosis illuminated a million little things I'd never before noticed in the women around me. Eyebrows, meticulously shaped. Forethought in every neckline. Scents and sprays, not as fancy flourishes but as essential attire. From the nuances and variations within makeup and jewelry to those within hair, nails, and dress, I became aware of a vast code of symbols at play in the world and of the unique intelligence needed to decipher and master it.

Nowhere was this language on better display than in the movies I watched every Saturday at the Pivoti, the cinema in the center of town. Segregated, as all Madison's public spaces were, the Pivoti primarily showed Westerns and B movies, but every now and then we were treated to a first-run feature with recognizable stars. How vividly I remember the hushed anticipation, the lights turned down low, and the clickety-clack of the old dual projectors whirring into action. And then, as if by magic, the screen would transform into an open window, a portal through which I could slip away and escape Madison completely.

I developed favorite actors, and I began to understand them as individuals, as women distinct from the characters they played. I idolized Rita Hayworth, her lashes long, her hair immaculate, but I also loved Marlene Dietrich, who dressed like a man and was still supremely feminine, and Ingrid Bergman, who in *Casablanca* and then in Alfred Hitchcock's *Notorious* evoked a universe of adventure and intrigue.

Since the end of the war, the culture had undergone a profound shift. Televisions were now in every living room and motorized lawn mowers were in every shed. Advertisements and commercials were ubiquitous, each chanting the one-word slogan that reverberated across America: *buy.* This growing consumerism brought new comforts into our lives; however, I was less susceptible to the products being advertised than I was to the people advertising them. Just as I loved the actors on the big screen, the models in the pages of *Vogue* and *Harper's Bazaar* awakened some vital part of me. I studied them and copied their looks because they were visible in the way I wanted to be visible, alive in the way I wanted to be alive.

By my senior year, I had to contend with the fact that I'd lost the battle against a shrinking existence. There was nothing more I could do to push back Madison's limits. My friends all wanted to go to college or start a family, but I was restless. I didn't want to do with my life what others did with theirs simply because it was what was expected of me. If I did, the things inside me that were starting to glow would dim and, with time, would fade away.

The only person in whom I could confide was my mother. Unlike Edna, she was at peace with the world's complexities and contradictions. Maybe it was because of her early relationship with Edna, but where Edna drew a sharp line, my mother was happy to smudge it up as much as she could. She would later help Thomas with school fees, for example, and would make sure he had textbooks and medical encyclopedias with which he could prepare his applications for medical school.

With my father's support, my mother also owned and single-handedly ran a flower shop, The Flower Box, and she had a gift for handling with grace the stress piled onto her by those getting married, those celebrating holidays, and those burying loved ones.

"If you're spending money on flowers," I remember her saying, "probably it's 'cause you're drowning in one emotion or another."

While helping her fashion a floral manger scene the Christmas before my graduation, I was in agony over my future. Despite the cost, my parents planned to send Bill to Duke, an expensive university. But I was a girl, and though I was older, there was only enough to send me to Guilford, a nearby Quaker college. And the fact that marriage and motherhood was still understood to be the most reliable path to stability was at bitter odds with my dream of moving to New York City and pursuing a career in fashion.

My parents were resolute and insisted that I give college a try. I felt trapped. Our stop would come, the doors would open, and we'd spill out, eyes ecstatic and wild like those of the horses on the train to Madison. And then we'd find ourselves guided down Main Street and ushered into the town's stables. The doors would close and that would be that.

"Hon," my mother sighed sympathetically. "Your father and I only want what's best for you. And, remember, you're only seventeen."

"I know," I whispered.

We worked on the manger scene in silence for a long time, and then my mother turned to me.

"Here's what I think," she began. "I think it's easy to confuse rebellion with sabotage."

"What does that mean?"

"The way I see it, sabotage destroys but rebellion creates. Matter of fact, I tend to think every act of creation is also an act of rebellion. Even this"—she nodded at the half-finished crèche in front of us—"what we're doing right now."

"What is this a rebellion against?"

"Oh," she sighed. "Against ugliness, I guess. Against the cold of winter. Against the emptiness that some folks feel this time of year. But, hon, what I'm saying to you is that you only get the one life. You only get to live the one time. Rebel all you want. But don't sabotage it. That's all I'm saying."

Persuaded, I enrolled in Guilford, and I kept at it for as long as I could, but it was no use; it wasn't for me. And so I left and started making plans to move to New York. I loved Madison for the home it had been to me, for its wooded hills and open fields, for its deeply held notions of family, self-reliance, and respect for elders. These things would be with me always, but I also knew that there awaited something for me out in the world and that, if I did not pursue it, would extinguish my spirit entirely.

The 1950s were ending, and beneath the glossy surface of television and suburbia, a volatile energy simmered. Those who'd been excluded from society were finding one another. Communities were growing, as was discontent and an appetite for change. In San Francisco and Chicago young people were agitating, rubbing against one another and creating friction so strong that the sparks of music, art, and poetry were illuminating new cultural frontiers.

I needed to be a part of it. Or at least I needed to try. Because boundaries out in the world were falling, and I needed those within me to fall too. Somehow, the internal and the external were bound together. Knowledge of one lay within experience of the other, and it was only through radical exploration that I had a chance of erasing the space between them and easing the yearning that had plagued me since that day in the field so long ago.

Two

ew York City was the ocean into which all rivers emptied. I don't remember what the train was like or how much my ticket cost. Nothing about the countryside, which was gradually replaced by growing swaths of industry and suburbia, was particularly memorable. The moment I'll never forget—when I realized that my imagination was not too big at all; that, if anything, it had been much too small—came when I walked out of the cold granite chill of the old Pennsylvania Station and into a sunny spring New York City day.

Crowds swept around me in a current of languages I'd never heard before. Exhaust and the smells of trash and food were infused with sea salt and hung in the air. Taxis, endless streams of them, flashed by like flood waters, and the buildings, the tallest in the whole world, encircled everything around me, sealing the streets beneath a towering canopy of sky.

"Lemme guess," said my taxi driver as he smirked at me in the rearview. "Mississippi? One of the Carolinas?"

My room at the midtown YWCA, bland and dormitory-like, rented for five dollars a week. And while it didn't have a laundry or cafeteria, it did have an early curfew. This meant that the New York I'd come to experience, the downtown jazz and folk clubs that didn't get going until late at night, was off limits until I could find a more permanent place to live. To afford that, I needed a job as soon as possible. Eager to escape my quarantine, I developed a routine of taking the day's paper to the Automat on West 57th Street and looking through the classifieds. I'd then spend the evenings writing out my letters of inquiry and my mornings delivering them around the city.

After only a week of this I was invited to interview for a position with Helena Rubinstein, a cosmetic company known all around the world—even in Madison where its ads for makeup and beauty regimens had peppered the pages of the magazines I'd grown up reading. Helena Rubinstein, the company's founder, was a mythical figure. An émigré from Poland to Australia at the turn of the century, Madame—as she was universally known—had seen an opportunity in the cracked skin of Australian women. She'd then grown her company into a global empire and was now a cultural icon and one of the richest women in the world.

I showed up to the interview wearing white gloves and a pearl necklace. Though unaware that I'd packaged myself up as a curiosity from the exotic South, it must have worked to my advantage. Combined with a thick North Carolina accent and recherché etiquette, I was a hit with human resources. I didn't have clerical experience, but I was nonetheless hired as the executive receptionist. My duties were to answer the phone, take messages, and announce visitors to the executives working down the hallway.

After moving into an apartment with a few other girls in the fortress-like London Terrace building on West 23rd Street, my friend Franco, an architecture student I'd bumped into while staring up at what was then called the RCA Building (now known as 30 Rock), took me to the Five Spot Café, a jazz club in the Bowery, to celebrate my escape from the Y. Of Italian descent, Franco was burly with short brown hair and had a brotherly quality about him. When he invited me out, it was with the unspoken understanding that he was proposing friendship and not romance.

Franco loved poetry, jazz, and the blues almost as much as he loved architecture. He was convinced that the downtown clubs and coffee-houses, in providing experimental spaces in which these things were refined and reformulated and from which new sounds continually emerged, had lit a fuse that was now burning ever closer to an arsenal of cultural explosives.

When we arrived at the Five Spot Café, Thelonious Monk was at the piano surrounded by his quartet. I'd heard of Thelonious Monk, but I hadn't understood that he was one of the greatest jazz musicians alive. His music was seductive and hypnotic, and I slowly found its rhythms and settled into their cadence. All kinds of people crowded into the smoky room, and I couldn't help comparing it with the segregated the-ater in Madison, with the way an experience that was intended to be shared was undone by a venue that was decidedly unshared. As the night grew late, I felt a boundary that had been imposed a long time ago begin to melt away.

It wasn't until I'd been at Helena Rubinstein for a few days that Madame, all four feet eight inches of her, swooshed past my desk on the executive floor. In a flaming maroon trapeze dress—Yves Saint Laurent's daring update to Christian Dior's signature tight-waisted silhouette—she had a sixteen-strand ruby necklace around her neck and a feathery pink mohair hat cocked at an angle atop her tightly braided hair. Awestruck by her extravagance, I failed to respond when she nodded at me in greeting.

"Magnificent, isn't she?" asked a woman who'd materialized at my desk.

I looked up to see the serene blue eyes and knowing smile of someone who'd already experienced what I was now experiencing. She had an English accent, and I'd never met someone with an English accent.

"I reckon she is," I allowed.

As my eyes met hers, I could see that she'd never heard a North Carolina accent and that she was as intrigued by me as I was by her. It was obvious that we were unlike each other, but it was also obvious that we had one important thing in common: we were unlike the New Yorkers all around us.

"Penny," she said, holding out her hand.

"Carolyn."

Then, shaking my hand, she said, "Do you *reckon* we should be friends?"

"I do indeed," I said with a smile.

With a small but steady income, I enrolled in evening modeling classes. This, I'd heard, was the surest path into the industry. In our first class, we learned to "walk," which amounted to crisscrossing the classroom with books balanced on our heads. At first it felt foolish, like a child's dare, but the sincerity with which we practiced gave it an air of gravity. After getting the hang of "walking," our instructor, a rail-thin woman nearing fifty, sent us around the building, books still on our heads, to find stairs that we might gracefully ascend and descend. Future classes were devoted to crossing and uncrossing our legs, to standing up and sitting down—again with books on our heads—and to posing with one foot planted in front of the other in order to "slim the waist and lengthen the legs."

I grew comfortable in my routine of work and evening classes and was flattered when Madame's assistant, Patrick, invited me to a party at Madame's 625 Park Avenue apartment. This was a big deal to me, and as the uniformed doorman opened the lobby door for me, I felt a formidable sense of agency. Here I was, in New York City, on my way to a party that was sure to be attended by Manhattan's rich and famous.

A palatial triplex penthouse comprising the top three floors of the thirteen-floor building, Madame's penthouse was a museum, mansion, and resort all at once. Elaborate chairs like ornate seashells sat opposite tufted couches of such intricacy that they seemed to have been designed for royalty. Statues and sculptures announced themselves with ferocious intensity. With imperious eyes and jagged war paint, they suggested distant lands and islands across the sea.

Wandering through rooms filled with shiny people, I began to feel out of place. I felt like an imposter, and I began to wish that I hadn't come at all. My peripheral vision began to narrow, and my head began to spin. Passing a server, I reached out a shaky hand and managed to grasp a flute of champagne. At the nearest painting, I tried to take an interest.

"Do you like Dalí?" came a familiar voice.

I turned to see Penny, whose blue eyes and unbothered smile again suggested that she had plenty of experience with my present discomfort.

"I'm sorry?"

Clinking my glass with hers, she nodded at the painting.

"It's a Salvador Dalí. Powerful, isn't it?"

"Do you know all of them?"

"Not all."

"That one?" I pointed to a colorful mess of paint only barely hinting at a figure buried beneath its brushstrokes.

"De Kooning," she said. Then, taking my hand, she added, "Come. I'll show you around."

I followed her as she pointed out paintings by Picasso, Miró, and Modigliani. Her command of art was impressive, and the more we talked, the more I liked her. She put me at ease, and it felt natural when our conversation turned to my upbringing in Madison and to hers in England. I told her about growing up in tobacco country, and she told me about working as a London journalist but being unsure about what she really wanted to do in life.

"That makes two of us," I said. "But I still miss home sometimes. Don't you?"

"I don't know." She shrugged ambivalently. "My mum can be difficult."

"And your dad?"

"He died a few years ago."

"I'm so sorry."

"It's all right. It's a story for another time, perhaps."

Then, with a playful nod, she pulled me through an open door to Madame's bedroom. There I found myself looking at the most peculiar bed I'd ever seen. Elegantly curved, as if formed over a thousand years by underwater currents, it was made of a hard, translucent material and, magically, was lit up from within.

"Ever seen such a thing?" asked Penny.

"Is it beautiful or is it hideous?"

Penny laughed. "Both? Neither? I don't know!"

Just then I realized that I hadn't seen anyone else from the office.

"Penny," I said, looking around. "I don't see any of the other girls. Why—"

"It's because we're collectibles."

"Collectibles?"

"Don't you see? I'm the international woman of mystery, and you're the Southern belle from Dixie."

Penny and I were soon inseparable. When we weren't exploring the city together, I was exploring it alone. I was like a raft that, adrift on the open ocean, is reduced to a witness. What New York did, I did. What New York was, I was. I surrendered, held nothing back, kept nothing of myself and nothing for myself. I'd been detonated, exploded into someone I could never have been in Madison.

My first paid modeling gig was for an art class, a course on fabric. I was nervous and self-conscious. With the class of a dozen students gathered in a semicircle, I stepped onto the pedestal at its center and sat with my legs crossed in a way that allowed the fabric of my dress, a black taffeta maxi with a slit up one leg, to bunch and festoon.

"Ready?" asked the instructor.

He started his timer, and I was transported to another plane. How unexpected that this demarcation of time could have such an effect. The start and stop of it, the *apartness* of it, infused the minutes in between with a heightened quality, with a sense that *happening* was at that moment taking place. I became aware of my breathing and my swallowing. My saliva glands begged for instruction, but I had none to offer. In need of something to hold onto, my eyes found those of a young man with olive skin and dark, curly hair.

Impulsively, he looked down. I could feel his eyes traveling over me, searching for something that might prevent them from returning to meet my own. I could see the effort with which he kept them down, and I resolved that I would not look away if he looked at me again. Slowly, his eyes rose higher, from my thigh to my waist and then to my arms. Then, higher still, they wavered, uncertain how long to linger. When they again locked with mine, a dart of adrenaline shot harpoon-like between us. I tried not to smile but I know I did, and I remember thinking that it is impossible, when you are looking into another's eyes for the very first time, to not be completely and perfectly present.

It made me happy when he caught up to me on the street after class.

"I wanted to say thank you," he stammered.

"For what?" I said, laughing. "I'm the one who got paid."

"Yeah, but . . ."

He blushed as he fumbled for words. Already I could see that he was one of those boys who, though sometimes short on wit, has charm in abundance.

I nodded at the portfolio under his arm.

"Can I see?"

He showed me his drawings and I was surprised at how good they were. Seeing myself through his eyes turned his drawings into representations not only of me but of him, too, of us together.

"You're talented," I said. "Really."

He shrugged this off, and I could see that there was something else he wanted to say.

"Will you watch a play with me?" he asked.

"Okay," I said, confused by his wording.

"Well, not watch with me but . . ."

"I'm sorry?"

"What I mean is . . ."

Again, his wit fell short and his charm was on hand to compensate.

"See," he began, "I'm in this play. It's not a big part, but I figured, you know, since I got to stare at you maybe this would even things out."

His name was Tony and his acting was as good as his drawing. The play, Federico García Lorca's *Blood Wedding*, told a dark and beautiful story about obsession and murder. It was getting positive reviews, and I loved it unreservedly, not only because I was swept into the drama of the plot but because I knew someone in the cast.

We fell into a rhythm, Tony and I. After his performances, we'd walk for hours, prowling the downtown neighborhoods, him talking breathlessly about the power of art as he burned off the high of the nightly ovations, and me, enchanted, grateful just to absorb his energy. Tony loved the great masters, painters whose names I was beginning to recognize—Degas, Cezanne, Durer, Rembrandt, Klimt, Vermeer, Caravaggio—and he leaped around the globe and danced back and forth through time in a mad effort to make sense of technique and talent, of inspiration and influence. He talked feverishly, obsessively, and it was clear that he was still brilliantly unformed, still searching for his gods, still unsure of the altars at which he wanted to worship.

Once, after walking all night, we came to an outdoor market. The sun was rising over the East River, and the vendors, under the sleepy veil of early morning, were still setting up their stalls. Tony bought some coffee and pastries, and we sat shoulder to shoulder on the sidewalk.

"What is it?" I asked when he handed me a pastry.

He was quiet for a moment, a funny smile on his face.

"You know what you are?"

"What am I?"

"You're an uptown girl with a downtown heart."

"What does that mean? Why do you say that?"

"No, no reason. It's just, you know"—he nodded at the pastry—"it's a croissant. I dig that you don't know that."

And so, the thing with Tony became a thing of firsts. I'd never had a croissant before, had never known a real actor before, had never walked across the island of Manhattan before. But it was also loose, a playful mix of friendship and relationship. I saw other boys too. Franco had become one of my closest friends. His love of music was infectious, and we saw Duke Ellington and John Coltrane, Miles Davis and Mahalia Jackson. In the documentary *Jazz on a Summer's Day*, a concert film about the 1958 Newport Jazz Festival, we're in the audience, his arm around my shoulders. And if we weren't listening to jazz or blues, we were taking in the beat poets. We saw Gregory Corso and Allen Ginsberg, whose poems were relentless and raw, as if they'd opened up their veins only for words to spill out of them.

Music and poetry were finding each other, mixing together with transformational power, and every night the city roared with a pent-up energy that raged against the bloat of 1950s consumerism, against the facade of contentment and conformity that blanketed so much of popular culture.

"'Music is liquid architecture. Architecture is frozen music.' Know who said that?"

I was sitting across from Franco in a dive bar in Greenwich Village. He'd been accepted into an architecture program in Rome, and we were having a drink to celebrate his departure.

"I'm guessing either an architect or a musician?"

"Goethe," he said. "A writer."

That Franco and I could never have dated was decided by chemistry. Ours were parallel tracks that no amount of physical affection or emotional intimacy could bend toward romance. On park benches we linked arms and sat close together, but between his body and mine, there was an understanding, a truce engineered with long-term friendship in mind.

Still, it unsettled me that he was leaving New York. Not because it would be a traumatic separation but because New York was so immense I'd almost forgotten that a world existed beyond it. But now, as Franco talked about drinking wine in cobblestoned piazzas and living amidst *chiesas* and palazzos that predated the Empire State Building by millennia, I recalled my Uncle Frank's stories about the great cities of Europe.

When Franco left, I held ever more tightly to Penny. She was dating Burt Reynolds, the actor, who was still unknown and who still went by "Buddy," his childhood nickname. Theirs, like mine and Tony's, was a fun and flirtatious relationship, and we'd watch movies together and dissect everything that was wrong with Hollywood: the stilted acting; the tame, recycled plots; the conspicuous absence of young people on-screen; the studio system, with its aging stars and hefty contracts, teetering on the brink of collapse.

It wasn't love with Tony, but I really liked him. We'd kissed a few times, and one night I agreed to pose for him in his room on the condition that I could move my wine hand while he sketched.

When he showed me the drawing, I smiled.

"You made her prettier than me," I said.

"Not true. I couldn't if I tried."

"Liar."

Then he turned the page, and when he did that, the energy in the room changed. We were silent for a long time, and I was suddenly aware of his body, his hands, his breath.

At last, he spoke.

"I could draw you without your dress on."

He said this without looking at me. His eyes were down just as they'd been when I'd posed for his class. But then they rose to meet mine, and a dart of adrenaline again shot harpoon-like between us.

As I looked nervously at him, the pleasure of anticipation began to build.

"Is that what you want?" I asked.

A long moment passed, and when he spoke, there was a quiver in his voice.

"Not the drawing part—if I'm being honest."

"Okay," I said.

He put his charcoal and paper on the floor and lay beside me. What happened next was another first. It was gentle and sincere and it confirmed what I'd already known—that this wasn't love, that this wasn't a thing that would last.

What is it that makes some people temporary visitors in your life and others permanent fixtures? Penny, I already knew, was the latter. But the summer was ending, and she was finalizing her return to London. I went with her to the travel office, and as we sat on the subway, she slipped her arm into mine and leaned her shoulder against me. I felt a violent pang of sadness. Franco was already in Rome, and with Penny now leaving, New York would be empty.

"I can't bear it," Penny said quietly, her arm still in mine. "Visit me in London, Carolyn. Promise me we'll see each other again."

Franco had said something similar; he'd invited me to Rome, insisting that I could stay with him for as long as I wanted. I'd dismissed this as an option that wasn't available to me, but hearing it again from Penny, something within me was reset. I thought back to the first time I climbed onto a horse. Uncle Goat had insisted I learn to ride bareback before using a saddle, but he'd refused to help me onto the back of a gentle old mare. I was a child, though, and the mare seemed ferocious

Young Carolyn
(Photograph by Jens Peter Bloch)

and huge. I believed in my heart that climbing onto her was impossible. But as I stuck with it, as I negotiated my body against hers, I began to feel the impossible become possible. Then, on my next attempt, the possible was suddenly inevitable. My determination melted into terror because it was happening. I was gripping the mare's mane, swinging my leg up over her back.

On the subway next to Penny, two realizations slammed into me one after the other. The first arrived as our train pulled into our stop. *Yes,* came the thought, *maybe I can go to London. Maybe I can scrape together enough money for a passage to Europe.* And then, as we stood on the platform figuring out which exit would take us to the travel office, goose bumps spread across my skin because the possible was now inevitable. I could do it. I *would* do it. Even if I had to go alone, I would get myself to Europe.

Penny's departure, instead of a goodbye, was a gift. An unexpected future awaited me, and returning to the travel office, I bought a one-way ticket to the Port of Southampton on England's southern coast. I was booked on the Holland America Line's SS *Maasdam* and set to sail out of New York Harbor in the spring. I hadn't intended to buy a one-way ticket, but I couldn't decide on a return date, and I had no idea where in Europe I'd be returning from. All I knew was that I'd visit Penny in London and Franco in Rome. I'd have to figure the rest out later.

At first, my parents were wary. But they could see how much this meant to me and how seriously I was taking it. I needed to make and save money quickly, which meant getting out of New York and spending as little as possible. I had an aunt and uncle in Los Angeles who were willing to let me stay with them, and I'd found a job at an employment agency near their home. With this arrangement worked out, I put in my notice at Helena Rubinstein and was soon on a bus to California.

We took the southern route—Atlanta, Houston, Las Vegas—and then turned north to San Francisco before driving down the coast to Los Angeles. I remember crossing the Mississippi River in New Orleans, seeing the Gulf of Mexico, the oil fields of East Texas. The skies unrolled before us, and it was as if we were in an eternal wilderness. There were Native American settlements and farmland, countless small towns divided by as many Main Streets. We passed freight trains crossing the continent and, every now and then, passenger planes flying low over the earth. Finally, the Pacific Ocean prevented us from going any farther.

The time passed quickly. I spent nothing and saved all I could, and before long I was returning home to say goodbye. Madison had never felt smaller and my affection for it had never been greater. In keeping with the practical nature of our relationship, my father insisted on teaching me to drive a manual transmission before I left for Europe.

"Just in case," he reasoned.

In my mother's flower delivery truck, he patiently coached me as I pushed the accelerator down with my right foot and let the clutch up with my left. For the first thirty minutes, I released the clutch too quickly, causing the truck to buck forward and stall, or else I didn't push the accelerator down with sufficient pressure, which again resulted in the car bucking forward and stalling. But I slowly began to feel the moment of tension when the accelerator rises up to meet the clutch, when the engine engages and the car eases forward.

When I got the hang of it, my father smiled.

"Attagirl," he said.

Over the following week, I bucked my way around Madison to say my goodbyes, stalling at stop signs and waving bashfully at the cars behind me. David Spear, Patsy Cox, Nancy Lee, Uncle Goat, Edna, and Big Bill—I hugged them all and promised to write all the time. At the station, my father was uncharacteristically emotional, and he held me close. When the whistle screamed, my mother, who was coming with me to New York, pulled me into the carriage. The train lurched into motion, and my brother ran beside us to the end of the platform, laughing and waving dramatically.

In those days, goodbyes contained within them the threat of finality. The world was bigger then, and the unknowns were more abundant. Who knew what storms awaited my undersized ocean liner or what violence was simmering beneath the surface of European politics? What if something happened to Edna or Big Bill and my parents couldn't reach me? Long-distance phone calls were astronomically expensive, which meant communication was only possible by mail. News from home, like starlight that reaches earth years after it is emitted, would be calibrated by delay.

In New York, I was proud to introduce my mother to the city I'd come to love. We window-shopped and talked fashion, and at night we went to clubs and parties. She endured all of this graciously, and the gay nightclub I dragged her to the night before my departure was no different. She shook hands and smiled the same way she did at the nursing home where she volunteered.

Back in our hotel room, with everything packed, we looked for things to say that were worthy of the occasion.

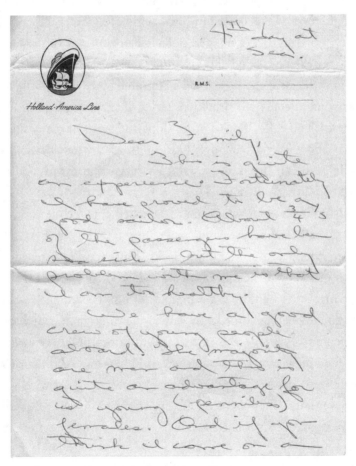

Letter from the ship
(Pfeiffer family archive)

"Sugar," she said. "We've taught you right from wrong, and I know you'll make good decisions."

"Yes, ma'am," I replied.

The next morning, another sunny spring New York City day, we took a taxi to the harbor. People were hugging and taking pictures. Dozens of handkerchiefs in outstretched hands fluttered from the pier, and dozens more fluttered back from the ship's deck in response. What is it that happens when strangers share an experience? Inhibitions slide away and emotions synchronize. My mother rarely cried, but now she broke into tears, which caused my own elation to splinter into a sobbing half-cry half-laugh. We hugged fiercely as people moved around us. Then I squeezed her hand and kissed her cheek.

From the deck of the ship, I had an uninterrupted view of the downtown skyline. I could see Brooklyn, Jersey City, Staten Island, and the Statue of Liberty. I could see other ships and boats of many sizes and tiny cars and trucks driving over bridges. It was a windy day and there was salt in the air. Looking down, I could see the crowd, and in the crowd, I could see my mother.

The ship pulled out to sea, and I watched the skyline sink slowly beneath the horizon. The wind picked up and the other passengers began to disappear into the lower decks. But I stayed longer to watch the water slide by. I thought of my mother, and I wondered if she was still crying, if she had the same anxious knot in her stomach as I did.

Despite my nerves, I made my way to the dining room. It was large and open and everyone was in their evening best. Old men in tuxes, young men in jackets, women in jewels and hats and such flourishes as class allowed. In a navy skirt and pale blue sweater, I sat with a group of Norwegians. They were older, midtwenties maybe. But after a friendly exchange in broken English, they reverted into their native Norwegian.

In my cabin, I took out pen and paper to reassure my family and myself that I was fine. "We're making good time," I wrote in messy cursive. "I'm already making friends." And then I turned off the light and slipped into bed. I felt expansive, more alive than ever before. But then the hum and vibration of the engine and the sometimes reassuring, sometimes nauseating rhythm of the ship brought me back into myself. And I felt small. The depths of the ocean below and the emptiness of the sky above were overwhelming, and I pulled the blankets tightly around me, cocooning myself within them.

I awoke early in the morning and went up to the deck. Salt filled my lungs as I squinted at the sun. I looked back to where New York had been, but it was gone. And so was the rest of the world.

Three

While Penny placed my suitcase in the back seat of her cream-colored Morris Minor, she explained that the two most famous ships to sail out of the Port of Southampton were the *Mayflower*, in 1620, and *Titanic*, in 1912. *How surreal*, I thought—not only that Southampton had such history but also that I'd made it. I'd crossed the Atlantic and Penny was standing right in front of me.

A week at sea had turned walking on solid ground into a balancing act, and I was grateful to climb into the passenger seat and be off my feet.

"What's all the construction?" I asked as Penny pulled into a roundabout.

"The Nazis bombed Southampton to kingdom come," said Penny matter-of-factly.

My stomach churned. As it had been for Penny, World War II was the backdrop against which I'd grown up. It was an immense evil that had demanded immense sacrifice, and there was nothing in America that the war hadn't touched. But it was also something that had happened in faraway places, in Europe and in the Pacific, and I was unprepared to see actual evidence of it.

We entered London and Penny talked about Hitler's Blitzkrieg, Germany's all-out assault early in the war intended to swiftly defeat Britain just as it had France and Poland. London had endured weeks on end of nightly air raids, a brutal, systematic demolition that had reduced entire city blocks to rubble and sent countless Londoners fleeing to the countryside. As Penny pointed out several new road and housing projects, I felt naive and sheltered, aware that I would never comprehend all that had happened here.

Penny lived with her mother, Iris Ashley, on Chapel Street, between Hyde Park and Buckingham Palace Gardens. With bouquets of fresh flowers in the main rooms and large oil paintings hanging on the walls, theirs was an elegant townhouse with high ceilings and handsome wainscoting.

"Penny says you're planning to tour Europe all by yourself?" Penny's mother said as she poured tea for us.

She struck me as kind without being warm, polite but also remote.

"Yes, ma'am," I said. "After Penny and I go to Paris, I'll go on to Rome. A friend of mine from New York is living there."

"What then?"

"I'm not sure. I've always wanted to visit Barcelona. Warsaw too."

"She'll need to find work at some point," interjected Penny.

"Yes, well," said Ms. Ashley, "I've arranged for you to meet with Irwin Shaw and Ginette Spanier in Paris. I assume you're familiar with them. Irwin's very well connected. He's quite close with Dorian Leigh."

Not only was Dorian Leigh a supermodel before the supermodel era, she was also said to be the inspiration for Holly Golightly, the heroine of Truman Capote's novel *Breakfast at Tiffany's*, which would be adapted for film the following year. With numerous lovers and a life of international intrigue, Dorian had founded her own modeling agency with offices in New York and Paris. This was to say nothing of Irwin Shaw himself, who, blacklisted by the FBI and living in self-imposed exile, was a literary giant. It was also to say nothing of Ginette Spanier, who, as director of the House of Balmain, was a major player in the fashion industry.

Realizing that Penny's mother had arranged for us to meet with such important people, I had a sense of the social position their family must occupy. In New York, it had just been the two of us, Penny and me. There'd been no Madison and no London, no parents and no families. We were free to be ourselves, and I'd gotten to know her as someone who was grounded and down to earth. But now there were expectations and appearances, a way of doing things.

When tea was over, Penny grabbed my hand.

"Where are you girls off to?" asked her mother.

"We're going to pop over to the Palace for a quick hello," answered Penny.

"Penny!"

Buckingham Palace was a few streets over, and it was one of Penny's great pleasures to needle her mother's sense of propriety by pretending that Her Majesty, the Queen was a casual friend.

We walked up to Wellington Arch and looked in at the gardens behind Buckingham Palace. Without New York's height or density, London was also without its chaos and congestion. In their place was restraint and composure, a feeling that there were hierarchies to mind and norms to abide.

"Your mother's nice," I said, hoping to draw Penny out.

"She's certainly English, if that's what you mean."

Penny explained that her mother was from an aristocratic family and that she'd become estranged from them when she chose to pursue a career in theater, which was considered beneath the family's station.

Even as she became a famous journalist—she was so well known that her photo was sometimes in advertisements on the sides of buses—she wasn't accepted back, and as a consequence, she had a hardness about her that never fully thawed.

"Anyway," said Penny, "I found a flat with a friend. I'm moving out soon."

"Who's your roommate?"

"A model, actually. You'll meet her."

Penny introduced me to her circle of friends at a dinner party in a Regency townhouse. We were seated, boy-girl-boy-girl, at a long table in an oversized dining room. The evening had an exaggerated, formal quality, as if we were reenacting scenes from a bygone era. After dinner, the men discussed the blues over cigars and brandy while we women gathered in tucked-away rooms to talk fashion.

I connected with Penny's roommate-to-be, Grace Coddington. She had pale skin and fiery red hair, and her modeling career was already beginning to blossom. Tessa Kennedy, a blonde woman with large eyes and a magnetic nonchalance, told us about being in Havana with her new husband, Dominick Elwes, during Castro's revolution and escaping Cuba on a raft.

They were all was so young, but their ambition gave the evening motion, a sense of forward momentum. Big changes, if they weren't already happening, felt inevitable. Indeed, somewhere in London, Mick Jagger had already met Keith Richards, and somewhere in Liverpool, John Lennon had already met Paul McCartney.

A week later, we loaded into Penny's car and set out for Paris. In Dover, we pulled into the belly of a ferry, and then went up to the deck to enjoy the sun and sea. The French coast was visible on the horizon, a strand of dark hair separating the blue of the sky from the blue of the sea, and I felt as light as a leaf on the breeze.

"Come with me," I said to Penny.

"What, to Rome? What on earth would I do there?"

"You'd grow."

"Thank you, no. I did quite enough of that in New York."

To say that Paris is merely a city is to say that the Louvre is merely a museum or that Notre Dame is merely a church. How many cities have modeled themselves—their boulevards and monuments, their garden parks and public transportation systems—after Paris? Driving into its spiderwebbed center, I could feel that it was without New York's pulverizing density yet also without London's dignified restraint. In their place, a comfortable grandeur radiated outward.

We checked into the inexpensive Hotel Saint Jacques, down the street from the Panthéon, before setting out on foot for the Arc de Triomphe. Heading north, we stopped at the Seine to admire Notre Dame. Then, crossing the river at Pont Neuf, we passed the Louvre and the Place de la Concorde, and finally reached the mighty Avenue des Champs-Élysées.

At a cinema, we stopped to look at the posters of forthcoming movies. Penny nudged me. I turned to see a maroon convertible, its top down. In it were two men waving and beckoning for us to join them. Seeing our indecision, they jumped out of the car. After some awkward flirting—the majority of it simple hand gestures and very small words—we figured out that they worked for *Paris Match*, France's equivalent of *Life* magazine. As such, they were the cowboys of the journalism world.

One of them introduced himself as Jean-Pierre and kissed me on the cheek. I blushed and turned away.

"It's okay," Penny said with a laugh. "It's their custom."

"*Oui*," Jean-Pierre said. "Our custom."

I was in a whimsical mood, and when they again gestured toward the convertible, I nodded to Penny.

"Let's," I said.

"Yes?"

"Yeah."

Penny took the front seat, and I sat in the back with Jean-Pierre. The sun slowly set, and we were treated to a chauffeured night tour of the city. We sped past lighted monuments and crowded sidewalk cafés. It was enchanting. Paris was every bit the glittering city of lights I'd imagined it would be.

Then, as we circled the roundabout at the Place de la Bastille, Jean-Pierre shifted in his seat to face me.

Slipping his hand onto my thigh, he said, "Equally, *this*. Our custom."

I laughed and moved his hand away just as it started to rain. What started as a sprinkle turned into a downpour, and we were immediately soaked. We shouted at our cowboys to put the roof up, but it was broken and wouldn't budge. At this, Penny and I leaped from the car, wet and happy, and made our way back to our hotel via the metro, a dryer—if less exhilarating—mode of transportation.

The next morning, we awoke early for our brunch with Irwin Shaw and Ginette Spanier. As Penny needed to return to London, she packed her things so she could leave from the meeting. I was nervous about being left alone in Paris but I was even more nervous about meeting Shaw and Spanier.

Though much younger than Helena Rubinstein, Ginette had a similar no-nonsense quality. She understood the beauty economy and she understood the position of power she held within it. Irwin Shaw was no less intimidating. In a navy blazer, he had close-cut hair and full eyebrows. He was difficult to read, and I couldn't tell whether our shared Americanness worked to my advantage or against it.

When they asked about my modeling experience, I told them about the gigs I'd had in New York, and I mentioned an interest in runway and magazine work. The conversation seemed to be going well, and Shaw offered that, though Dorian Leigh was out of the country, I should stay in touch with him.

My appetizer of fresh asparagus arrived, and I cut a stalk into sections. I was lifting a piece to my mouth on the tines of my fork when Shaw stopped me.

"My dear," he said curtly. "Fresh asparagus is eaten with one's fingers."

I froze, feeling my face turn red.

"Of course," I whispered.

How was it so obvious to him that I didn't know what I was doing? Was it my accent? My outfit?

On our way back to the car, Penny nudged me with her shoulder.

"You all right?"

"Fine."

"You sure?"

"Penny, what's your secret? How does nothing ever bother you?"

She looked at me suspiciously, eyes narrowing.

"What, the asparagus?"

I looked away and she put her arm around me.

"Caroline," she said, changing the final syllable from *in* to *een* in her best French accent. "Come now. You were marvelous."

At the car, we stopped. Peugeot motorcycles darted around speeding Renaults and Citroens, and a group of boys sprinted through a flock of pigeons, scaring them into flight.

"So, this is it?" Penny said with a sigh.

"I guess it is."

She took my hands in hers.

"You'll come back to me, won't you? If the Romans are terrible to you?"

"I'll come back even if the Romans are nice," I said.

She got into her car, and I waved as she drove down the street. When she disappeared around the corner, something cold shivered through me. I was suddenly alone. I didn't know anyone in Paris, and I didn't speak a word of French. I hurried back to the hotel, but as I arrived at my room, I saw that the door was cracked open. I was sure I'd locked it. My heart began to pound. I carefully pushed the door open and gasped when I saw that the contents of my suitcase were scattered across the floor and the drawers of the desk were open.

Missing from my belongings was some family jewelry that my grandmother had given me. It wasn't valuable, but it was irreplaceable. I thought of calling the police, and maybe I should have, but I didn't. I couldn't even bring myself to go out for dinner that evening. Instead, as night set in, I put a chair in front of the door and left the light on. Fully clothed, I lay in bed feeling helpless and afraid. By sunrise, I hadn't slept at all, and it wasn't until daylight filled the room that I drifted into an uneasy sleep.

It was late in the morning when I awoke. Looking out the window, the street below seemed to teem with hostility. Even if I did venture out, what would prevent the thief from coming back? From waiting for me in the closet or under the bed?

One thing the thief hadn't stolen was *Europe on 5 Dollars a Day*, a first-of-its-kind travel book my Uncle Frank had given to me before I left. Written by Arthur Frommer, a young army corporal, it was enormously popular and had gone a long way to upend the commonly held notion among Americans that Europe was affordable only to the elite. I now pulled it out and began to make an itinerary, to map out exactly how I would get from one place to another. Thus armed, I willed myself to the train station, where I bought a baguette sandwich and a ticket to Rome for the following evening.

Though I barely slept that night, I awoke early to see the city. I went to the Eiffel Tower and to the Sacré-Coeur Basilica, to the shopping district at Marché des Enfants Rouge and to the colossal shopping center, Galeries Lafayette. Most of all, I loved Sainte-Chapelle's soaring arches and the brilliant blues and indigoes of its exquisite stained-glass windows. And then I was on my way to the train station.

There is something inherently transformational about travel, about transitioning from one location to another. I already had a sense of the way that different places and different people could transform someone from one person into another. The Madison version of me, tomboyish and confident, was different from the New York version of me. And she, in her ambition to pass as cosmopolitan, was different from this American-in-Europe version that was still coming into being. The train snaked slowly through the Paris suburbs, and I had, perhaps for the first time, a sense of being without any identity at all, of at that moment being between identities.

A wave of exhaustion crashed over me, and I tumbled into a fitful sleep. Pulled into the train's hypnotic rhythm, I slipped in and out of consciousness. The roar of the engine and the rumble of the wheels faded into white noise as long stretches of darkness were interrupted by villages and small towns, clusters of light dispersed as quickly as they'd formed.

I was in this state of happy delirium when we pulled into Roma Termini, Rome's massive train station. There, waiting for me on the *binario*, was Franco.

"You made it," he said as he lifted me off the ground in a hug.

"I made it."

Outside, the sun was enormous, its heat unrelenting. Despite the bustle of traffic and pedestrians, the air had a quiet, empty quality. When Franco disappeared to arrange a taxi, I looked around. *So, this is Rome*, I thought. *So this is the Eternal City.* How alive it was—not as a city is alive but as an organism is alive: breathing, sensing, desiring.

"I hope you don't mind the couch," Franco said apologetically as the taxi pulled away from the curb.

"Of course not," I said, squeezing his hand.

Eager to share his knowledge of Rome, Franco rattled off trivia. Its founding in 700 BC. The she-wolf that adopted and nurtured its founders, Romulus and Remus. That, in 50 BC, Rome was the first city in the world to have a million inhabitants and that, after its sacking four hundred years later, the population had dwindled down to a meager thirty thousand. As he talked, I gazed up at the stone pine trees towering overhead, and I marveled at the ancient ruins that seemed to be strewn liberally along the streets.

Franco was explaining that Rome was only half the size of Paris when I interrupted him.

"Is that—"

My voice was sharp.

"That's it," Franco said.

Seeing the Colosseum for the first time happens only once. What's so unexpected is how familiar it is as a photograph, as a history lesson. I needed a moment to reconcile that it was real and that it was right in front of me.

"Unbelievable" was all I could think to say.

Franco's flat, which he shared with a roommate, was on the Piazza di Santa Maria in Trastevere, a cobblestoned pastiche of colorful buildings. When we arrived, I got out of the car and Franco settled up with the driver. The Santa Maria Basilica, one of the oldest churches in Rome, blocked out the sun and cast the entire piazza in shadow. Children played around the fountain at the piazza's center while groups of women draped in black lined the perimeter. Men, skinny and sinewy, sipped beer and wine at sidewalk cafés.

The flat itself was small, but it had high ceilings and oversized windows. Brightly lit, there was a living room and kitchenette off one end and two cozy bedrooms off the other. Franco brewed espresso, and as we sat across from each other at the little kitchen table, I told him about the voyage and about London and Paris.

It was still early in the afternoon, but I was exhausted and couldn't keep my eyes open. When I yawned a second time, Franco suggested that I lie down.

"Rest," he said. "I need to go to the market for dinner."

"I'll go with you. I don't want to be a bad guest."

"Seriously, rest. I insist."

I lay down on the couch and fell dead asleep. I don't know how long I slept, but I was awakened by the muffled sound of voices that seemed to be coming from a galaxy away. One was Franco's but the other, lower and more assertive, was unfamiliar. Blinking my eyes open, I couldn't be sure if it was evening or morning. Soft light came in through the open window and a cool breeze had replaced the oppressive daytime heat.

As the room came into focus, so did the man to whom Franco was speaking. He was dark and muscular, and though he was seated, I could tell that he was fit and broad shouldered. Dragging myself over, Franco introduced him as his roommate, Paul, a fellow American also studying architecture.

An open bottle of wine stood between them, and Paul lifted it up to me.

"Wine?" he asked.

I remember that there was something calculated in the way he spoke to me. Something not quite innocent, as if the two of us had been alone in the room.

"None for me," I said.

Sitting next to Franco, I listened absently as they talked about their classes and about this and that, and then I slipped my hand into the crook of Franco's arm and rested my head on his shoulder. Music and voices drifted up from the piazza outside. Mothers scolding, children squealing, men shouting at each other in their affectionate way. A sense of elation welled up in me and, with it, a tranquility that all was as it should be.

Somewhere in the room, a mosquito buzzed. I tried to follow the sound with my eyes, but it was no use. Then, as I swept a strand of hair behind my ear and settled into Franco's shoulder, I could feel Paul's eyes on me. It wasn't a gaze of seeing but of looking, and even without meeting his eyes, I could feel that it was also a look of wanting. This language of pursuit, with its maneuvering and its complexities, didn't come naturally to me, and I felt blood come into my face. For a long time, I did nothing.

And then I squeezed Franco's arm and closed my eyes.

Four

——————————

As I lay awake in the darkness, the voices of drunk and happy men drifted up from the piazza. Already I could parse out a handful of phrases from the slur of their sentences. And I could almost see their gesticulations: hands, like a conductor's baton, orchestrating symphonies of words. When at last their cries and footsteps faded to silence, nothing took their place. There was only the city—its breathing quiet, its heartbeat slowing to an even, unhurried nocturnal rhythm.

The weeks had passed quickly. Already I had seen so much of Rome, and already I knew my stay here would be far longer than I'd anticipated. On my first weekend, Franco and Paul had taken me to Ostia, Rome's only beachfront neighborhood, and I was surprised not only by how unlike the deep blue of the Mediterranean was from the gray-green waters surrounding Manhattan but also by the way beach culture, vibrant and colorful, rippled inland toward the city center. But, after that first weekend, Franco had gotten busy with his studies, and Paul had taken it upon himself to show me Rome proper. The Colosseum, the Pantheon, Palatine Hill, the Roman Forum. Everything old; everything important; everything infused with narrative about how the present had come to be.

Another narrative now unfolding was the one between Paul and me. He was so arrogant and so aggressive, so relentlessly alpha. But he was also attractive and obviously interested in me. For a while, this unsettled my friendship with Franco. He wasn't interested in me romantically, but there was nonetheless a question mark between the three of us. And, between the two of them, there was something that felt like competition. I wished this weren't the case because my loyalty to Franco was unchanged. At the same time, my feelings toward him were without the physical attraction that was so present in my feelings toward Paul.

At the Trevi Fountain, I pretended not to notice how he used the crowd of tourists as an excuse to stand close to me, his chest pressing lightly against my back. As we toured the cavernous atrium of Saint Peter's Basilica, I could feel his intentions in the way he slipped his hand around my arm to lead me from station to station. I loved it. I loved this language of touch, communication by action instead of by sound.

But at Michelangelo's Pietà, I resisted his pull.

"Wait," I whispered.

The Pietà is a marble sculpture depicting a crucified Jesus lying in the arms of Mary, his mother. But Mary is young, a girl in her teens, and Jesus—a grown man—is small in her arms. Christ's body is limp, and his every muscle is so realistically rendered that I could feel in the marble the agony of his crucifixion, the defeat of his death. And in Mary—her countenance peaceful and her ample robes flowing lifelike around her—there was such astonishing power that I found it difficult to speak. Why had Michelangelo chosen to make Mary so young and Jesus so small? Was he suggesting that Mary never aged? Or was it that, at the moment of Jesus's birth, Mary already knew, and had already accepted, that she would one day hold her child's lifeless body in her arms? Maybe the Pietà didn't depict an event that had already happened but one that hadn't yet taken place.

I wanted to discuss this with Paul, but he was more interested in the dimensions of the building and the ingenuity of its architects. He was taken by the grandeur the basilica represented; I was taken by the meaning it contained. The truth is that, in any other situation, I wouldn't have fallen in with Paul. He wasn't really my type but I quite liked that I was his. Besides, this was Rome, a dream, and, even as I lay in the darkness listening to the sleeping city, I couldn't stop myself from straining to hear every sound that came from his room.

There it was: the rustle of his covers; the soft padding of his footsteps nearing his closed door. When he emerged into the living room, my heartbeat was thundering in my ears. It could be that he wanted a glass of water, but it was more likely that a glass of water was a way to engineer a late-night interaction that was shielded from the clear-eyed reason of daylight.

Standing above me, he whispered, "Did I wake you?"

"I'm awake."

"Is everything okay?"

"I'm just listening."

"To what?"

"To the night. To the city."

He padded into the kitchen and soon returned with a glass of water. He again stopped and stood over me.

"Should I leave you to your listening?" he asked.

He wasn't one for subtlety, but in the beguiling trance of the midnight hours I didn't mind. I could have not taken the bait; I could have not followed him into his room, and I could have not slipped under the covers beside him. But I did. Because two people who want the same thing almost always take the most direct route to it. As our bodies negotiated how it would be, I thought of Tony, of his tenderness and timidity, of the fragility he presupposed. This was the opposite. Even in this, Paul was arrogant and aggressive, relentlessly alpha.

He pulled out as he came and, as etiquette allowed, I rushed to the bathroom. The pill wasn't available and my contribution to birth control was to sprint to the bidet. These may seem like half measures, but unlike in the world ushered in by the pill, they at least gestured at the sharing of responsibility.

The next morning, Franco was sitting alone at the kitchen table. I poured an espresso and sat across from him. When he looked up at me, I peered into his eyes for a long time. Deep within them was something wounded, something hurt, as if something had been taken away from him and given to Paul.

"You like him?"

There was an accusatory note in his voice.

"But I love you."

His eyes softened, and he looked down.

"Be careful," he said. "Paul is . . . Well, I know you know."

"Yeah," I said, reaching my hands across to take his in mine.

The weeks that followed transformed us from roommates into a household. Now we shopped together, cooked together, took day trips together. How thrilling to have two men devoted to me, each in his own way. Franco was cerebral and warm, with a love of art and music. Ours continued to be an intimate relationship but without any spark of romance. In contrast, Paul was entirely of the body—a man obsessed with possession and passion. In this, there was much to enjoy. Waking up to a rose on my pillow. Being pinned against a wall because his kisses couldn't wait. Feeling his greedy hand under the table of a darkened trattoria.

For a time, we were a happy threesome. Franco and Paul introduced me to a network of expatriates. Young Americans, Brits, and Scandinavians formed a society that existed parallel to the Italian one surrounding us. We spoke English and gathered in each other's flats, had dinner parties, and listened to American music. I went along with all of it because it was fun in the way that a vacation is fun: untethered, somehow, and underaffected by the real world.

But this expatriate bubble sealed me off from the culture and people of Rome, and I soon grew tired of it. I no longer enjoyed Paul's *us* versus *them* mentality, and as the infatuation of being in a passionate relationship in a faraway city wore off, I began to think beyond Paul. I'd already written home to let my family know that I was going to stay in Europe a while longer. My money was holding out and there was still so much to see.

Distracted by thoughts of what else I might do, an icy terror crept over me when I realized that six weeks had passed since my last period. I was late. Not only that, but for the last two days, my appetite had been finicky and I'd woken up with an unfamiliar tenderness in my breasts. I made a doctor's appointment but only as a formality. I already knew that I had stumbled into a merciless new world and that consequences of immeasurable severity awaited me.

That night, as Paul's hand traveled up my chemise, a scout on an exploratory mission, I was blind with fear. Trembling, I turned to face him.

"I'm pregnant," I whispered.

He paused, and withdrew his hand.

"You can't be."

"I think I am."

He sat up and turned on the light, and I could see the contempt in his eyes.

"Have you been to a doctor?"

"I have an appointment."

"So you might not be."

"But I'm pretty sure I am."

Paul didn't come with me to the appointment, and when I told him that the doctor had confirmed the pregnancy, he made it clear that he wanted nothing to do with it. He wanted the problem to go away, quickly and quietly. And I wanted, I don't know . . . I wanted to not be alone. But, for him, the connection between sex and conception was academic at best, and he washed his hands of it and me. He acted annoyed, and his refusal to acknowledge any responsibility made me feel that the pregnancy was something that happened to me alone, something that implicated me alone. So, in the way that biology allowed of Paul but not of me, he walked away while I became a would-be parent.

The fear and shame were more than I could bear. Because there was no escape. At least if you murdered someone, you could hide the body and cover your tracks. If you stole or coveted or lied or committed adultery, there was always the possibility of getting away with it. But not with this; not with pregnancy outside of marriage. This was the one thing where the evidence was internal and where it was just a matter of time until everyone found out.

To be pregnant and unmarried, even with a boyfriend, was to risk losing friends and family, employment and reputation. To be pregnant without a boyfriend was far worse; it was to be a pariah, perpetually guilty, entirely at the mercy of a judgmental society. So I did what so many in my circumstances have done: I kept my secret and I took my chances. Through an expat friend, I was put in touch with another doctor. I told Paul of my appointment and asked him to at least go with me for the procedure. But he declined. There was an architectural conference in Milan, he said, and he would be out of town.

What I remember about the doctor is that there was something cruel about him, as if his services were administered not out of care but out of vengeance. He seemed to take a perverse thrill in meting out this sort of punishment. But unable to communicate, I had no way of asking even the most basic questions. How long would it take? Shouldn't I be anesthetized? Would that which was within me feel anything?

I lay on my back and obediently put my heels in the raised stirrups. And then I turned my head to the side and closed my eyes. To trust like this, to be vulnerable like this, it was breaking some innocent part of me.

The doctor readied his instruments and I remember hating myself completely. I hated that there was so much prey in me and so much predator in Paul. I hated that I was so curious about the world and that, without family or friends, my warning systems had been drowned out by the thrill of the present. Most of all, I hated that I'd known all along that something like this would happen. On some level, I'd known that my naivety had been willful, and on some level, I'd known that Paul had only ever been a poor imitation of the person I'd made him out to be.

My knees were together, but the doctor roughly pulled them apart, and I let them fall away from each other. After an uncomfortable insertion of cold metal, the pain began in earnest. I tried to breathe but the pain was searing and raw. There was scraping and tearing and I thought I would faint. My eyelashes were wet, and I didn't know what to do with my hands. Tears welled in my eyes, and when I blinked, they slid down to my ears. It seemed to go on and on, and I resolved only that I would not cry out, that I would hold on to this inconsequential shred of dignity. And then I gave myself over to the pain and I prayed that the intensity of it would somehow cleanse me of my guilt.

In the taxi on the way back to our flat, I was numb. At our building, I got out slowly and walked carefully up the steps, stopping halfway because my head was spinning and because I thought I might collapse. Inside, I held my stomach and eased onto Paul's bed.

Franco arrived and I could hear him preparing dinner in the kitchen. I don't know what he knew. For all our intimacy, sex and what went on between Paul and me were off limits. After a time, he knocked on the door and stood hesitantly in the doorway.

"Are you hungry?"

I did my best to shake my head.

"I'll save some for you."

He turned to leave but then stopped.

"Are you sure everything's okay?"

My eyes found his. They were full of kindness, and I beckoned him over to the bed.

Sitting down, he took my hand and squeezed it.

"You warned me," I said weakly.

"About what? What are you talking about?"

"We're breaking up."

He was quiet, giving me as much time as I needed.

At last, I spoke.

"I need to move out."

Five

hadn't eaten in two days, or maybe it was three; I couldn't be sure. After finishing the pasta I'd brought with me, I'd survived on a wedge of Asiago. That, too, was gone now, but I didn't care. I'd stopped feeling hungry and the thought of eating no longer interested me. Still, as I lay on a mattress and stared up at the ceiling, I knew I had to get out of the flat. If I didn't, the impulse to leave at all, like the impulse to eat, would disappear completely.

How long had I been in this empty place? Two weeks already? More? Long enough, certainly, for time to become abstract, a distant awareness of light slowly draining from the day and then stealing back before dawn to dispel the night. In this glacial pulse of sunlight, I could almost convince myself that Paul wasn't real and that my suffering was the aftershock of a terrible nightmare. But shards of pain still tore through my abdomen, and the bleeding had not yet stopped. And these two things, pain and blood, were my only tether to reality, unwanted reminders that the body is a reliable thing, true as nothing else is true.

Had I been able to, I might have gone to London to be with Penny. Or I might have quit Europe and returned home. But travel was out of the question, and anyway, I could never have faced Penny and I could never have faced my family. The shame was too much. Thankfully, I'd found a flat not far from the Spanish Steps, which, except for a mattress on the floor and a few forgotten pots in the kitchen cupboards, was unfurnished. But a month's rent, combined with the looming expenses of food and furniture, had depleted my savings. My fear of running out of money was now acute.

In the bathroom I gently washed and tried to summon a reserve of strength, a measure of fight with which to face the outside world. But I had none, only the desire to return to bed, to let the world continue on without me. As I brushed my teeth, I caught a glimpse of my reflection, but I didn't recognize the face looking back at me. The joy was missing from the eyes, and the smile that was always there had been replaced by a line of such sorrow that I couldn't stand to look at it.

How dangerous it is to be alone with shame.

In the hallway I was met by my neighbors returning to their apartment. Romano was a journalist, warm and exuberant in his affections, while Zenia, an American with dark ringlets, was withdrawn but no less friendly.

"*Ciao*, Carolina," Romano said, beaming. "*Come stai oggi?*"

"*Sto bene*, Romano," I managed politely. "*Grazie.*"

But he eyed me dubiously.

"*Ma non*, Carolina. You're not *bene*," he said, turning to Zenia and asking rhetorically, "She isn't *bene* at all, is she?"

I assured them I was fine, but it was no use. They insisted I have dinner with them, and while I made a show of not wanting to impose, I gratefully accepted. The interaction sent a shaft of light into the depths of my malaise, and down on the street, I inhaled deeply. Oxygen rushed into my limbs, and as I looked around, it occurred to me that the street on which I now lived, Via delle Quattro Fontane—Avenue of the Four

Fountains—was quite beautiful. Narrow and lined with faded lemon- and salmon-colored buildings, it hosted a collection of shops and restaurants that led from its namesake four fountains at one end to an obelisk towering above the Spanish Steps at the other.

Animated by the beauty surrounding me, I took my time shopping. At the *panificio*, I chose bread carefully. I thought of the ingredients and the labor present in each loaf of *casareccio* and focaccia. At the *salumeria*, I bought burrata and a portion of fresh tagliatelle. At the *fruttivendolo*, I marveled at the rich display of produce. Taking a tomato in my hand, the feel of its taut and perfect peel against my skin felt somehow important, as if it could restore me if only I held it long enough. At the *vineria*, I bought a bottle of Montepulciano to bring to dinner.

Turning toward my flat, the cobblestones caught the afternoon sun and an old man smiled at me. These things, so simple and so inconsequential, warmed me unexpectedly, and a wave of something that felt like hope rose up within me.

Over dinner with Romano and Zenia, I drank wine and, for the first time in weeks, I laughed. They were planning a party for the following weekend and handily conscripted me into cohosting with them; rather than a small get-together in their flat, we would open up our adjoining units for the night and have a proper bash.

Romano's sister, an actress finding her way within the Hollywood on the Tiber movement—the flurry of Rome-based coproductions that had produced recent hits like *Roman Holiday* and *Ben-Hur*—wanted to bring some movie people along. A brush with the glittery, glamorous world of film had never occurred to me as something that Rome might offer, and the possibility of it revived my love of movies and brought back memories of passionate New York conversations with Tony, Penny, and Burt Reynolds.

I spent that week introducing myself at businesses and storefront photography studios. I desperately needed money and hoped I might find modeling work, but I also knew that my best chance of employment would be as an English tutor. My problem was that if I dipped into the money I needed to purchase my return passage to America, then I would strand myself in Europe. But if I didn't dip into it—and if a job didn't materialize very quickly—then I would have no choice but to spend my savings on a ticket home.

Still, the upcoming party was important to me, and at the *parrucchiere*, I spent some of my remaining money on a haircut. Weeks of isolation had left my hair in need of a trim, and I emerged from the salon feeling just a little bit better about myself.

The next day, I treated myself to one final extravagance: a movie. Italian neorealism, a movement that sprouted up during the war and stretched into the early '50s, had captured the world's attention. A counterpoint to Hollywood, these gritty films were shot on location, used unknown actors, and explored themes of poverty and economic hardship. Out of this movement, a cadre of highly esteemed directors— among them Luchino Visconti, Federico Fellini, and Roberto Rossellini—had emerged and were now leading Italy's cinema into an era of unparalleled artistic ambition.

If there were going to be movie people at our party, I wanted to have demonstrated at least a rudimentary interest in the country's cinema, and so late one afternoon, I walked into a theater where a screening of Fellini's *La Dolce Vita* was about to begin. From the opening sequence, in which an oversized statue of Christ is helicoptered across Rome, I was rapt. What I noticed immediately was that its storytelling was unlike that in the Hollywood movies I'd seen.

There were no good guys or bad guys, and there was no question of who would win in the end. Instead, the narrative unfolded slowly, organically, without concern for convention as I understood it. This, combined with my limited Italian, made the story difficult to follow. It had to do with religion and opulence, with a search for meaning.

Marcello Mastroianni and Anita Ekberg in La Dolce Vita
(United Archives/Hulton Archive © Getty Images)

I liked being in the company of the film's stars, Marcello Mastroianni and Anita Ekberg. He was smooth and easygoing, immediately likable, and she was overwhelming, impressively physical. And I liked that I recognized many of the film's locations: Saint Peter's Basilica, Via Veneto, Piazza del Popolo, the Trevi Fountain. On-screen, these places were somehow *more* than what they'd been out in the world. Not better or worse, bigger or smaller, or even different in any obvious way, but they had a quality about them that I can describe only as a quality of *more*.

When the movie ended and I left the theater, I entered a world that was forever changed. Evening had given over to a night that was deep and full, blue and black. Nothing was out of place or different in any obvious way, but it, too, had assumed a quality of *more*. The dam separating life and cinema had washed away, and I now walked streets that were not only steeped in history but also in art. In that moment, I longed to stay. I longed to not have to return to America. I wanted to stay in Rome, and I wanted to feel this feeling more deeply, to hold onto it as long and as tightly as I could.

On the day of the party, I started drinking early, in the happy antic-ipation of meeting new people and building new community. My hair looked good, and my smile once again came easily. It was the first time in a long time that I'd felt anything like myself. I'd invited Franco, as we'd stayed close, but a prior engagement prevented him from attend-ing. As it was, I only knew Romano and Zenia, and as guests streamed into my flat, I began to panic. There was too much noise and too many people. Feeling like I was about to drown, I waded through the rising tide of strangers and escaped onto the balcony.

Gulping in the evening air, I wondered what was wrong with me. I'd looked forward to this night. So why was I anxious? Why had I fled my own party? The answer dawned slowly. I was anxious because of how alone and how isolated I'd been. I'd been out of practice and forgotten the rhythm of human interaction, of human touch; people had become foreign.

This realization calmed me, and the panic began to recede. My com-posure returned and I was about to go back inside when Gianna, Romano's sister, appeared beside me.

"*Ciao*, Carolina," said Gianna gaily. "I want to introduce you to Anita."

Anita Ekberg, star of *La Dolce Vita*. There she was, right in front of me. I'm not easily starstruck, but I was stunned, undone once again by the quality of *more*, by the way actor and character differ and yet are the same.

Reentering the flat, I felt better. The guests were warm and talkative, and the despair that had been all-consuming a week earlier was no more. I toasted my neighbors repeatedly, and at one passing encounter, I found myself shaking the hand of a young man with blond hair and sky blue eyes.

"You're Carolina," he said, still holding my hand in his.

"How did you know?" I asked, wondering if our handshake was, perhaps, more than just a handshake.

"I saw you and I asked Romano."

Did all Italian men slip so quickly into the language of attraction?

"I'm Masolino."

"Masolino?"

"Short for Tommaso."

"Short, but with more syllables?"

"Short—it's the wrong word. *Mi dispiace*, my English, it's—"

His English was excellent, and it was clear that we were not talking merely for the sake of talking. An hour later, when he asked if he could take me out, I said I would love that, but that I would soon be returning to America.

"Why?" he asked.

I recounted my story, explaining that I had run out of money and that if I paid the next month's rent then I would not have enough to return home.

Masolino laughed.

"If you want to stay, stay."

"But I don't have a choice," I protested.

"*Ma*, Carolina, who decides, if not you?"

"Can't you see that it comes down to money?"

"To money? Tell me where to find this Money. I'll speak with him, and I'll convince him to let you stay."

As the night grew late, he became, for me, the only person at the party. And when people began to leave, I hoped he would seek me out, that he would find an excuse to linger. Maybe we could talk on the balcony. Maybe we could walk down the street to Piazza Barberini. We could splash around in the ankle-deep water of the Fontana del Tritone and imagine that, like Anita and Marcello in *La Dolce Vita*, we were beautiful and charismatic characters in an important moment of cinema. Or we could do nothing. We could just sit together and be close. Even that would be enough.

But he left with his friends and eventually my flat was empty. Romano and Zenia said goodnight and I went to bed. I was out of time.

If money didn't materialize within the next few days, I would have no choice but to pack up and head home.

I met Masolino late in the afternoon, and it felt like the first date of many. I saw him before he saw me. I was at the top of the Spanish Steps, and I saw him at the bottom, making his way through the tourists surrounding the Fontana della Barcaccia, the Fountain of the Boat. I took pleasure in watching him ascend the steps, knowing he was climbing them to see me. In dark trousers and a tucked-in linen shirt, he looked trim and, if I can use the word, beautiful. When he stopped to look up, our eyes met and we smiled. And then he was beside me, kissing me on each cheek in greeting.

We walked north and he pointed here and there and rattled off dates, events, and the names of architects as if it were all common knowledge. With carefully timed nods, I did my best to appear knowledgeable, but the more he talked the more I realized how little I knew about Rome. We climbed a steep ramp and turned around to see the entire city laid out below us. Then we continued on to Villa Borghese, a sprawling park with elaborate gardens. Tourists clustered around kiosks selling snacks and souvenirs, and I remember thinking how unbelievable it was that, for Masolino, this was just another day. For him, there was nothing special—nothing absolutely magical—about an afternoon walk through Rome.

At the Galleria Borghese, a majestic stone building, we stopped and Masolino pointed to the east.

"Over there, five minutes, is my home. Maybe we can go there together. You can meet my family."

"*Si, per favore.* I would love that," I said, feeling that the invitation had accelerated the thing now happening between us.

"And this?" I nodded at the Galleria Borghese. "What's this?"

"It's one of our best museums. Maybe we can go there some time as well."

"Can we go now?"

"Now?"

"Unless you don't want—"

"No!" he exclaimed. "I would have suggested it, but maybe it's too much."

"Of what?"

"I don't know. Of me."

"But Masolino," I said, "we've only just met."

One's whole life is spent studying the world, intently searching its patterns for the slightest flicker of meaning. Most of the time there is nothing, only accident and chaos. But now and then the presence of meaning is undeniable. It becomes a real thing—dimensional, measurable, indisputable. And it was this feeling that I couldn't shake—that things happened for a reason and that, if one listened closely enough, there not only existed profound meaning in the universe but also that my discovery of that meaning made me meaningful too.

It was this feeling that I saw manifested in Bernini's sculptures and in Caravaggio's paintings. Bernini's *Rape of Proserpina*—an astonishing marble sculpture depicting the god Pluto hoisting the goddess Proserpina onto his shoulders as he drags her down to the underworld—was nothing short of lifelike. It was violent and magnificent, and looking at it, my only thought was that *I feel so much*. At Caravaggio's depiction of a young David holding out Goliath's severed head, I couldn't take it anymore. The compassion in David's eyes. The grim acceptance of his fate as a weapon of the divine. I stared a dead stare, without any expression, without any thought. My body didn't exist at all, and I knew only that whatever this was—this place of total alignment—it was made from the same substance as the feeling that had visited me in the field in Madison so long ago.

Masolino put his arm around my waist and my head leaned against his. I didn't have words for what I wanted to express, and so I stepped away from him and looked into his eyes.

"Why do I feel sad, and happy, and beautiful beyond what I can describe?"

Masolino was quiet, his head down. Then he looked up and I held his gaze.

"Art is a panther, *cara mia*," he said, "with fur and teeth and claws. Sometimes, if you get too close, if you make it personal, it puts its claws in you and it doesn't let go."

Outside, we squinted in the sunlight and talked in low tones as we wandered south. We came out of the park at Porta Pinciana, multiple red-brick arches at the top of Via Veneto that Masolino explained had been entrances into the walled city of ancient Rome. There was something familiar to me about Via Veneto, though, and when I saw Harry's Bar, a restaurant bustling with outdoor dining, I stopped.

"Wasn't this in the movie? In *La Dolce Vita*?" I asked.

"Yes and no," said Maso. "It's in the movie but they didn't film here."

"They must have," I said. "I'm sure I recognize it."

He shook his head.

"They filmed at Cinecittà. They reconstructed Via Veneto there, in the studio."

"No," I protested. "That isn't possible."

Masolino laughed.

"Fellini's a clown, no? Clever, but a clown. My mother knows him well."

"What do you mean, your mother knows him?"

"I mean she knows him. They've worked together."

"But what do you mean?" I asked again. "What does your mother do?"

"She writes for the movies. You'll meet her. You'll see."

Masolino took my hand and I marveled at how masterfully Italian men deal in intimacy, how deftly they navigate its borders. I followed him down the crowded street, darting this way and that to stay together as what seemed like a million Vespas and Lambrettas sped past us. It was like walking with Tony, my New York artist, through lower Manhattan except that this had the quality of *more*.

As I tried to take in the spectacular uniformity of the stone buildings, each cascading with identical clay tiles, I also tried to take in Masolino, his searing intelligence. From what world did he come that his mother was a writer for the movies?

It was early evening when I arrived back at my flat. I was trying to open the door, but the lock was sticking. This went on for a long time and I was still struggling with the key when the phone in the apartment began to ring. I wanted it to be Masolino, for him to be calling me playfully even though we'd just parted. I forced the key harder. At last the lock turned and I dashed for the phone. But it wasn't Masolino. The voice on the other end was deep and masculine, and he introduced himself as a liaison for the Italian Air Force. He'd heard of my interest in teaching English and wanted me to begin lessons with a group of officers. The pay would be decent, and the hours would be flexible.

"I would be grateful," he said with military authority, "if you would work with us."

Six

---

found Via Giovanni Paisiello without difficulty, but as I entered the
old palazzo and closed the elevator gate behind me, I tightened my
grip on the bouquet of bluebells in my hands. The elevator creaked
upward. Stepping off, I found the flat with its oversized wooden doors
and paused to gather myself. Masolino had cautioned me that his father
could be intimidating, but in my experience, a man's good graces were
more easily entered into than a woman's. Especially Italian women,
who had protective, territorial relationships with their sons far beyond
adolescence.

It was for Suso, Masolino's mother, that I'd brought the flowers.

I knocked and the door was soon opened by a maid who spoke to me
in Italian. She took the flowers from me, pointed to double doors I
assumed led to the living room, and promptly vanished up a narrow
staircase. I stood motionless, uncertain what to do. In that stillness, I
felt the familiar fear of not belonging, of being an imposter. I'd felt it
in Madame Rubinstein's penthouse and again sitting across from Irwin

Shaw. But wasn't this different? Because I hadn't been invited as a collectible, as a mood piece for Manhattan's millionaires, nor was a famous writer deigning to meet with me as a favor; rather, I'd been invited to lunch as a friend—and maybe even as a girlfriend.

Just then the door opened behind me, and half a dozen people entered, sweeping me toward the living room. There was laughter and the clapping of hands on backs. My cheeks were kissed and my hand was shaken. Spilling into the living room, we found ourselves among even more people. However, even with all of the commotion, I immediately identified Suso. I didn't know what she looked like, but I knew that the striking woman seated on the couch across the room had to be her.

I steadied myself and was about to approach her when I felt a hand on my elbow. Masolino. A powder blue sweater covering everything but the collar of a white oxford saturated his eyes with color.

"*Vieni*," he said, "I'll introduce you."

Silvia and Caterina, his sisters, kissed me on each cheek and hugged me warmly. With multiple rings on each hand, Silvia was a few years younger than me and had an intelligent, sensible look about her. Caterina, the youngest, was freshly sun kissed and had a spirited twinkle in her eye. Both were comfortably and elegantly dressed, and they had an ease and openness that connected me to them. Masolino then interrupted a conversation between Lele, his father, and Nino Rota, the legendary composer whose film credits already included Fellini's *La Strada* and *La Dolce Vita*. Lele was as intense as Masolino had cautioned, but his face was also kind. After a brief conversation, we moved on, first to meet his uncle Dario Cecchi, a painter and production designer, then to an official from the mayor's office.

Each guest seemed more accomplished than the last, and when Masolino introduced me as a model who also taught English, it felt like an overstatement. Yes, I did some modeling and yes, I taught some

English, but I blushed self-consciously because I knew how fortunate I was just to be working. Still, at the mention of English fluency, eyes focused and glints of interest materialized. English, I would come to find out, was then in high demand within Italy's film community.

With short hair and soft curls brushed away from her forehead, Suso struck me as an old soul, wise and with a calming presence. She had just taken both of my hands in hers when the maid appeared and announced that lunch was served.

"You're welcome in our home, Carolina," Suso said.

I was seated between Masolino and the charming Nino Rota as the maid brought in a large bowl of pasta that had been lowered down on a dumbwaiter from the upstairs kitchen. Bottles of water, fizzy and flat, and wine littered the table.

"*Benvenuti a tutti,*" said Masolino's father in a loud voice.

This was met with a chorus of *grazies* and with the raising of glasses.

"We call this 'peasant pasta,'" said Masolino, leaning over to me. "Only olive oil, tomato, and garlic. Do you know in Italian, tomato?"

"*Ma certo. È pomodoro.*"

"*Pomodoro, si.* And oil?"

"*Olio,* no?"

"*Bene, si.* And garlic?"

"No, garlic, I don't know."

"*Aglio.*"

"*Aglio.*"

"But with your tongue: *aglio.*"

As the pasta disappeared, conversation turned to Rome's preparations for the 1960 Summer Olympics and to the heated topic of South Africa being allowed to compete despite its apartheid regime. The official from the mayor's office was being heckled for the mayor's handling of the event—a criticism that somehow extended to the mayor's blind allegiance to the Vatican—when conversation shifted to Sophia Loren.

Here the table grew impassioned. Sophia, the movie star and reigning ideal of Italian beauty, had fallen in love with Carlo Ponti, an Italian Academy Award–winning producer who had divorced his wife in Mexico so he could marry Sophia in Italy, where divorce was illegal. They were now being investigated for moral crimes, and their case had exposed a schism between young and old, traditional and progressive.

Silvia, the older of Masolino's sisters, addressed the politician in a confrontational tone.

"Does the mayor agree with the pope, that Sophia is a bigamist?" she asked. "Would he have her arrested now that she is back from America?"

The politician had no desire to trade fire with a fiery nineteen-year-old.

"Her husband . . . I mean, her . . . What I'm saying is that Ponti is already married."

"Only because divorce is against the law in this country."

"It's not the job of the mayor to make the laws."

Silvia stabbed the last of her pasta in disgust.

"So, you're saying yes, Sophia is a criminal and should be arrested?"

"I'm not saying what should or shouldn't happen. Only that the law is the law."

The pasta bowls were cleared, wineglasses topped off, and to my surprise, the maid arrived with a second course, a lamb dish. Suso, her hand on Silvia's forearm, brought up Vittorio De Sica's set of *Two Women*, rumored to be Sophia Loren's triumphant return to Italian cinema following her career's stagnation in Hollywood.

Lele, Maso's father, was dubious.

"She goes to America and now she's a star in Italy? It should be Italians who decide which Italian is talented and which should be famous. Not Americans."

A nerve was struck, and the table exploded into opinions about the image of Italy and Italians that Sophia Loren was projecting across the Atlantic. Words and syllables rained down like confetti, which I tried to gather up and to order into something comprehensible, but even with Masolino translating as much as he could, it was all I could do to keep up.

After eating so much pasta, finishing the lamb was a formidable challenge. I attacked it heroically, and when my plate was finally cleared, I exhaled in victory. But then, from the dumbwaiter, a salad course arrived. This, too, I forced myself to eat. But when it was finished and the plates had been cleared, the dumbwaiter descended once more, this time with platters of fruit and cheese. I watched as Suso took an orange and peeled it in one uninterrupted ribbon as Lele addressed me in English.

"Here we say that every Italian has a rich uncle in America."

"But for us it's the opposite," Masolino said with a smile. "We have a poor American living with us."

At this everyone laughed, and I looked down, unsure how to feel. Then I felt Masolino's hand on my shoulder, his voice in my ear.

"You see?" he whispered. "My family is now yours."

Having eaten too much, I excused myself. I thanked Lele, who held my hands in his, and then I hugged Suso, who instructed me to visit her soon. Outside in the heat, my head swam, and I leaned on Masolino to steady me. This he happily did, and when the episode passed and we started walking, he took my hand in his.

"What was the celebration?" I asked.

"What do you mean?"

"Lunch. So many people. So much food. What was the occasion?"

It took him a moment to understand the question.

"*Ma non*," he laughed. "There's nothing special today. No celebration. Every day is just like that."

He stepped toward me, and his arms closed around my waist. I put my hands the only place I could, around his neck, and I looked up at him. There is nothing quite so electric, nothing quite so vulnerable, as standing heart to heart with another human being for the very first time. In that simple acknowledgment of attraction, of desire, there is nowhere to hide.

"I lied," Masolino said. "It's not true that there's nothing special about today."

When he kissed me, his arms tightened around me and mine tightened around him. Passersby moved around us and a group of construction workers, waving origamied hats fashioned from the day's newspapers, shouted their approval.

Seven

Aided by the humbling reality that there was little else occupying my life, Masolino's family soon became the center of it. And, just as they'd done in the past, my Southern mannerisms came to my aid. The politeness and deference that had been so thoroughly drilled into me paired well with the hierarchy of Italian culture, and I was soon a regular at Casa d'Amico.

Most days I found Suso sitting on the end of the living room sofa, an Olivetti typewriter on her lap and an empty espresso cup on the table in front of her. Their cat, Modrone—who preferred the toilet to the litter box—was a gift from the director Luchino Visconti, a descendant of the aristocratic Visconti di Modrone family, and was often curled into a ball on a nearby chair.

When I first sat with Suso, she talked to me about her current project, an English coproduction that told the story of England and Italy facing off during World War II in Abyssinia, what is now Ethiopia.

But she soon turned her attention to me.

"So, *cara mia*, you're a model?"

"I'm trying."

"I couldn't do that. Not me."

"*Ma perché?*"

"Why not? Because I have my vanity," she laughed. "And I like pasta too much."

I smiled nervously.

"Listen," she went on. "This project, about Abyssinia. They want to cast a friend of mine, a well-known actor. He's a very funny man but his English is so bad. I want to ask if you will work with him. Will you do that? It will be a favor to me."

"*Certamente*," I said. "Of course I will."

"*Grazie, cara.* His name is Alberto Sordi. He's very funny. For many years he performed the voice of that American show. *Laurel and Hardy.* I think he was . . . Well, I don't remember. It was one of the two."

What I didn't fully understand was that the growing number of English and American coproductions brought with them coveted roles for Italian actors. Consequently, there was a rush to learn English. This meant that, if things went well, there would be no shortage of work and that I would be able to stay in Rome.

At the time, Masolino was taking a course in architecture, a field he took seriously and around which much of our early courtship revolved. From his building on Via Paisiello, we would choose a destination—the Colosseum, say—and we'd begin driving. Masolino would point out buildings, columns, and monuments. He'd tell me their names and some of their history and then, a few blocks later, he'd quiz me.

"Fontana di Trevi. Which period is it from?"

I racked my brain.

"The Renaissance?"

"Baroque," he'd correct me. "What about la basilica di San Pietro?"

"Baroque."

"Quintessential Renaissance, Carolina. This you have to know by now."

Sometimes the game would go on and on and what began as play would snap something inside me because the progress I thought I was making would come undone. How useless I would feel. How ignorant. More than anything it would be a stinging reminder that I was a foreigner and that I didn't belong in this place. About the history of Rome, I knew nothing. About empires and aristocracies, I knew nothing. I was just a simple girl from the South guessing my way, trying to impress, trying to pass—not as something else but as something more. Masolino, of course, had only good intentions, but it was humiliating. I hated the vulnerability of him seeing so plainly that there was a big space between the person I was and the person I was trying so hard to be.

Once, as he grilled me about the columns supporting the Pantheon's portico, I grew quiet. Were they Doric, Ionic, or Corinthian? From which part of Greece? From which order? I couldn't take it anymore and I started to cry silently. When he noticed, he pulled over. I tried to explain that it wasn't serious, only that I felt stupid, first for not knowing the answers and second for crying. He apologized profusely, and when I calmed down, he wiped my tears away.

"Carolina, you mustn't cry. If this were your home, what would I know of North Carolina? What do I know of Brunsw . . . what is it? The soup with the squirrels?"

"Brunswick stew," I sobbed.

"You see? Imagine if your uncle served me this stew. It would be me crying."

These words helped, but deep down the limbo of not belonging had become a purgatory from which I needed to escape. Masolino hugged me and I hugged him back, feeling that, in him, I held the possibility of belonging.

It was that time in a relationship when the other can do no wrong, when one's appetite for the other can never be satiated. If not for his school constraints and the constant presence of his family, we would

Carolyn and Masolino at Castiglioncello
(d'Amico family archive)

have tumbled into sexual intimacy much earlier. But, as it was, those appetites remained sublimated beneath a rising fire. At meals, we made the most of being seated next to each other. Feet kissed. Hands caressed. We snuck affections in his flat when no one was looking. We lay close together in the grassy nooks of Villa Borghese, testing the limits of public anonymity and of each other's sense of decency. From monuments to memories and from beaches to bodies, we made an obsession of exploration.

It happened that Suso, who had been in Naples to follow production on one of her films, returned to Rome, and that Masolino, Silvia, and Caterina were on break from school. The family decided to sneak in a trip to Castiglioncello, a fishing village on the Tuscan coast, where they had a villa. Set against the azure of the Mediterranean and surrounded by the scenic charm of the town, their villa would have been right at home on a postcard.

We arrived after dark and Masolino and I went for a walk on a stretch of rocky beach. What I noticed first was the silence. Gone was Rome's traffic. Gone was the constant drone of city life. And in its place was a gentle breeze, the soft splash of waves. Masolino took my hand, and when we came to a rock, he sat me down on it. He parted my legs so that he could stand between them, so that our stomachs and our foreheads touched. We kissed for a long time, his hands making their way under my dress to my hips, my sides, my breasts.

"Not like this, *amore*," I whispered.

"How, then? When?"

His voice was guttural, out of breath. I said nothing and only put my arms around his head, pulling it to my chest.

The next day I awoke to a quiet morning. I was sharing a room with Silvia but her bed was empty. Without getting up, I could sense that the house, too, was empty. I walked into the kitchen and found Masolino hunched over a newspaper. I stood behind him and leaned against his back. My arms wrapped around his neck. There was salt on his skin, and I knew he had already been to the water. I moved my hands to his stomach and then to the inside of his thighs.

"Maybe now?" I whispered quietly in his ear.

"Are you sure?"

"I'm sure."

Then he stood up and led me up to his room in the attic. When he kissed me, there were questions in his tongue. *Is this okay? Is this what you want? Is this where you are?* With mine I answered. *Yes, this is okay. Yes, this is what I want. Yes, right here, in this place with you, this is where I am.* We communicated like this for a long time. Then the questions were gone, and with hands, the urgent conversation of desire began. He touched my lips, my hair, the hem of my chemise. He brought it up so that my stomach was touching his. Naked now, there was nothing between us.

When evening came, the world was again changed. Again it had assumed the quality of *more*. Dinner was served on the patio where lights were strung overhead and the Mediterranean murmured in the distance. As I always did, I sat beside Masolino, but this time our feet didn't kiss and our hands didn't caress. The compulsion wasn't there because we had the comfort that soon there would be more.

When Suso sat down, she turned to me.

"*Cara* Carolina," she said. "I have another client for you."

"*Veramente?*" I asked. "Who is it?"

"Claudia Cardinale. You've heard of her, no?"

Of course, I'd heard of Claudia Cardinale; all of Italy had heard of her.

"La Cardinale wants me to teach her English?"

"In fact, it's her manager, Franco Cristaldi—you've heard me talk about him—he's the one asking. He wants to do with Claudia what Carlo Ponti did with Sophia. You know, make her into an international star."

"But why me?"

"To work outside Italy, La Cardinale must learn English. And who better to teach her than you?"

Eight

Claudia Cardinale was a falcon who'd been cast in the role of a dove. She lived on the outskirts of Rome with her family, and as I made my way out of the traffic-choked center in my blue Fiat 600, I was nervous. I wanted to make a good impression, not only because I needed the job but because Claudia intrigued me and because I liked her movies.

Driving in Rome was not for the faint of heart. Traffic laws seemed optional, general suggestions to take or leave. At first, I'd been terrified of doing something wrong, of unknowingly breaking the law, but I soon realized that Italy made more sense viewed through a lens of norms than through a lens of laws. The only time I was pulled over, for example, it had been for no reason at all. The officer had made a great show of his authority, had scrutinized my license with bureaucratic diligence, and then had showed up at my flat a few days later, flowers in hand.

Purchasing a car had been a decision I'd discussed at length in the letters I wrote home every week. My father, pleased that I'd be able to handle the car's manual transmission, had questions about mileage and the previous owner, and he urged me to find a good mechanic. To afford it, I'd emptied my savings, including the money I'd set aside for passage back to the States. It meant, for the time being, that I couldn't afford a ticket home. It also meant that I now lived in Rome. I was no longer visiting Italy and I was no longer touring Europe; I was living here and this was my real life.

Turning onto a nondescript street, it seemed like every car I passed was, like mine, a Fiat 600. With the front half resembling a Mini Minor and the back half resembling a Volkswagen Beetle, they were everywhere. As a car, the Fiat 600 was modest, but as a phenomenon, it was mighty. The war had reduced Italy's economy to rubble, but the reconstruction effort had been unbelievably successful. Streams of migrants flowed from the country to the cities, and the economy had picked up so much speed that what would become known as the Italian Economic Miracle was now in full swing. Once poor and predominantly rural, the country was on its way to becoming an industrial power, and the Fiat 600 was emerging as a powerful symbol of this transformation.

I arrived at the address Suso had given me and pulled into the driveway of a plain two-story house. I don't know what kind of house I thought La Cardinale would live in, but this, certainly, was not it.

"I'm here to see Claudia," I said to the woman who answered the door.

She had fair hair and doe eyes, and she invited me into the foyer and introduced herself as Claudia's sister, Blanche. She left to find Claudia and a small boy ran past me. He was chased by an older boy, and they were all giggles and energy. As I watched them race into the living room, I was struck by how ordinary it all seemed. How could this be the house of a movie star?

Suddenly, a husky voice was apologizing for keeping me waiting, and I turned to see Claudia, La Cardinale, descending the staircase. In that moment, I understood so many things. I understood that movie stars are people. That they have sisters and families and that they sometimes live in unexceptional houses. I also understood something of the one-way reality in which celebrities live. Because, like so many others, I knew Claudia Cardinale. I'd read about her in the papers, and I'd seen her in the movies. Yet this was her first time seeing me.

She smiled comfortably, though—a smile of recognition without recognition, of warmth without warmth. If my image of La Cardinale was somehow abstract, the woman in front of me was precise. Her face was open and radiant, darkly angelic. Her eyes were wide set, her nose small, and her lips and figure full. Most memorable was that, in her every expression and movement, there was something that echoed the Claudia of the movies, the Claudia I'd seen before.

We drank tea at the kitchen table and, despite the language barrier, were able to communicate. Like most people, I'd assumed that Claudia was Italian, born and raised. But, no, she'd grown up in La Goulette, a tranquil neighborhood in Tunis, the capital of Tunisia. As it was then a French protectorate, Claudia's first language was French and her second was Arabic. So, though her father was a Sicilian immigrant, her Italian was not much better than her English.

Happily, we got along well, and we agreed that I would drive out to meet her several times a week. Our lessons amounted to casual conversations in which I asked Claudia about herself and she did her best to answer. She told me about her first brush with film, how she'd appeared in a movie with a very young Omar Sharif, the Egyptian superstar, and how she'd shied away from cinema after that. But the producer Franco Cristaldi had "discovered" her at a beauty pageant just as Carlo Ponti had discovered Sophia Loren and just as countless other producers had discovered countless other starlets among the local and regional beauty pageants that were ubiquitous in those days. Success had come quickly.

She'd appeared in Luchino Visconti's *Rocco and His Brothers*, starring the French heartthrob Alain Delon, and she was increasingly being compared to Europe's reigning stars—Sophia Loren, Gina Lollobrigida, and Brigitte Bardot.

During those early lessons, I also got to know Blanche, Claudia's sister, as well as "Pit," short for Patrick, their much younger brother. Claudia and Pit were particularly affectionate, and I felt the pang of longing for my own brother and family.

Over tea one morning, I told Claudia about Madison, about my mother and about Miss Nancy, about the Cardwell house and about the endless miles of tobacco farms. Finally, I told her about escaping to New York and about coming to Europe.

"But why?" she asked. "It sounds so nice in your town. Why did you leave?"

"I left to see what I could see," I said. "And you? Why did you leave La Goulette?"

"For me, it was the same—just to see. But now, you know, there's this business of . . ." She paused, as if searching for the right word. "There's this business of La Cardinale."

"How do you mean?" I asked.

"I mean, Cristaldi," she continued. "He has high expectations. Specific expectations."

When I first met Cristaldi, I was again at Claudia's house. He was a short man with a long face and prominent mustache. He was pleasant enough, but I could see that he was the kind of person with whom disagreement could be consequential.

"Take this," he said to Claudia, handing her his empty espresso cup.

His voice had absolute certainty that she would obey, and she did.

"Carolina," Cristaldi said as he nodded for her to rejoin us at the table, "you haven't been letting Claudia speak any French, have you?"

"We only speak English," I assured him.

"It's a joke, Carolina. *Non preoccuparti.*" He pulled out a cigarette and lit it. Exhaling, he said, "*Ma guarda*, I want—and Claudia wants—to offer you a job."

"Another one?" I asked.

"It's like this," he said. "I want Claudia to speak English all the time. So I want you to help her with language, yes, but also with correspondence, with the press, with her fittings, with everything. *Hai capito?*"

I wasn't expecting to be offered a full-time job, and my mind raced at the thought of it.

"She needs you, Carolina," he continued. "She needs someone organized. Someone her age. A native speaker of English. What do you say?"

"Say yes, Carolina!" interjected Claudia.

I wanted to say yes, but it was a big decision, not one to be made lightly or by myself. And so I brought it up with Suso as soon as I could. Knowing next to nothing about the Italian film industry, her counsel would be invaluable. If she advised me not to accept the position, it would only be prudent to listen to her.

"You know," Suso said, "La Cardinale is in high demand. A lot of people want her. Already I know of two films Cristaldi is planning. One is with Jean Paul Belmondo and one is with Visconti. And if Visconti wants her, you can be sure there will be no shortage of work."

I nodded excitedly, already imagining what it would be like to go with Claudia to the set of one of her movies.

"It means travel." Suso's tone grew serious. "A lot of travel. Just as Claudia travels, so you will have to travel. It won't stop and it won't be easy. And you know"—she paused and leaned back—"that kind of thing has a cost."

It was a caution, a not very subtle reference to my relationship with Masolino, and I felt something inside me deflate. Suso had been supportive of our relationship and seemed eager to do what she could to help it last. If she thought this would jeopardize it, she could easily counsel me against accepting the offer.

"But," she said, raising her eyebrows and smiling, "I don't think you want to teach English forever. Do you, *cara*?"

I brought the matter to Masolino carefully, when my hand was in his. The current of our relationship was strong, but I worried that he would think the job was frivolous and disapprove. I told him how much I valued his perspective, and I explained that while teaching English had allowed me to stay in Rome, it wasn't what I'd come to Europe to pursue. It wasn't where my skills lay, and it wasn't what I wanted to do with my life.

"This opportunity calls to me, Maso," I said. "I'll have more money and our relationship will always come first."

He removed his hand from mine and walked a few steps ahead of me. When I caught up with him, he looked at me kindly.

"Of course, Carolina. Of course, you must accept this offer. I won't be someone who holds you back. I won't be someone who slows you down."

I think I'd always known that life would lead me to a career in cinema. How many times had I declared that I would be an explorer or the president or a dozen other things? And all along the movies had been right there, waiting for me. Far from a casual job, my position with Claudia would require all of me. And that level of commitment would transform my relationship with Masolino. Now, instead of drifting alone in the waters of young love, we were putting into port, docking in the harbor of the real world where other commitments and other adventures awaited.

The job wouldn't begin for a few weeks, though, and summer was just then blooming. The heat was still welcome and the colors, the blues of the Tyrrhenian and the dark greens of the city's stone pines, were at their brightest. With offices closing and families on holiday, Masolino and I decided to take a trip together. I still hadn't seen much of Europe, and we thought it would be fun to drive up and around the Mediterranean.

Living in Rome's *centro*, it was easy to forget the countless miles of beach, the silver lining, that all but encompasses Italy. As we drove north, we stayed close to the sea, stopping frequently to marvel at the vineyards that swept down from the Tuscan hills. Between towns and villages were sandy beaches so completely deserted that it felt like to witness them was also to create them.

One evening, we stopped where an old couple ran a restaurant out of their cottage. He fished every morning and she prepared the catch for dinner. We ate roasted mackerel as the sun set, mopped up its sauce with fresh focaccia, and followed it with crisp white wine. Afterward, we walked down the beach until we were alone with the sea. There, I slipped out of my dress and pulled him down. I remember the salt in my mouth and the sand on my skin. And I remember the silence of our suspended breathing, the nothingness that, for an instant, consumed us.

In Pisa, Maso laughed as I marveled at the famous leaning tower. By Genoa, Italian and French began to mingle together and, by Nice, there was no Italian left at all. We found a room in a small hotel and then wandered out to look for dinner. We were a proper couple, Masolino and I; he the flowering intellectual—his natural playfulness eyeing the gathering forces of professional ambition—and I, an American curiosity, uniquely a part of Italian society.

In Saint-Tropez, on the French Riviera, I introduced Masolino to Penny. She was on holiday with Richard, her strapping new boyfriend, and we'd planned to spend a weekend together. Penny was serious about Richard. He was an anthropology student at Oxford, spirited and passionate, and we laughed about both being involved with academics.

"So," Penny said to me as Richard and Masolino compared and contrasted their studies, "the Italians have got you, have they?"

"That one has," I confessed, nodding at Maso.

"Easy to see why," she said with a smile.

It was also easy to see why Penny had fallen for Richard. He was the special kind of person who drew out the shades of Penny's many colors. Committed to anthropology, he was planning a research trip to the Amazon, and he teased Penny in a futile attempt to get her to visit him on his Brazilian adventure.

In Arles, Masolino took me to a *corrida,* a bullfight, at the Roman amphitheater in the city center. I experienced this as violent and unexpectedly beautiful, a savage display of deeply human appetites. The appetite to gather in community; to participate in ritual; to pit brain against beast; and, finally, to enter fully into the presence of death, to see it plainly and to be reminded of its inevitability and its permanence.

The *corrida* itself was a *mano-a-mano* between legendary matadors Antonio Ordóñez and Luis Miguel Dominguín that had been promoted in newspapers throughout the region and had attracted a slew of dignitaries. Seated together in a ringside row below us were Pablo Picasso, the artist, and Jean Cocteau, the poet and novelist. They were down to our left, but I could still make out Picasso's bald head and Cocteau's angular profile. In my memory, Ernest Hemingway was there, too, on assignment for *The Dangerous Summer,* his book on bullfighting. Their celebrity fueled the collective effervescence of the crowd and, as the festivities got underway, I looked out across the amphitheater and squeezed Maso's hand in anticipation.

Then it began. For the entire afternoon, I was in a trance, unprepared for the violent and astonishing torture of bull after bull—for the operatic finality of the *estocada.* It was a display of blood and suffering and of the ferocious desire to live. When it was over, I left the amphitheater in a daze, feeling fragile and melancholy.

We next entered Spain, dry and windswept. In Barcelona, the architecture of Antoni Gaudí, rounded and natural, didn't look like the work

Jean Cocteau and Pablo Picasso at a bullfight in Arles, France
(Photograph by Edward Quinn © edwardquinn.com)

of humans but rather of the earth, as if Earth itself had evolved his designs out of its depths. Life molded from clay by the gods of old. The majestic *Sagrada Família*, which my Uncle Frank had told me about and whose bell towers, like anthills reaching up to the sky, were then already fully formed, was a work of incomprehensible ambition. If these were the ideas of the last century that were only now coming to fruition, then what were today's ideas that wouldn't be manifest until the following century?

In Pamplona, we met with Lucia Bosè, a friend of the d'Amicos. She'd been a famous actress and had only recently walked away from film to build a life with her new husband, Luis Miguel Dominguín, the matador we'd watched in Arles. Lucia was a gracious hostess and, as the Festival of San Fermín, with its annual running of the bulls, was looming, she introduced us, as if we were living for a few pages in Hemingway's *The Sun Also Rises*, to the bulls that would be loosed into the city's streets.

We returned home to a feeling of destiny. My work with Claudia was beginning and my relationship with Masolino had never been stronger. Everything seemed perfect.

Walking up the Spanish Steps with Masolino one evening, I impulsively stopped and hugged him tenderly.

In my ear he whispered, "You remember it was here that we had our first date?"

"I remember," I said.

He slipped his fingers behind my neck and held my head in his hands.

"When I saw you that night at the party, I hoped this moment would come."

I smiled and looked down, but he gently lifted my gaze to meet his. The blue of his eyes had never shone so brightly.

"When you chose to stay in Rome, I stopped hoping for this moment because I knew it would come." From his pocket he pulled a small garnet ring. "Marry me, Carolina," he said. "Stay in Italy, *amore mia*. Stay here with me."

Nine

Watching the final touches applied to Claudia's makeup was like watching the final brushstrokes applied to a Rembrandt or Botticelli. She was reclining on a burgundy chaise lounge, surrounded by assistants: one buffing her fingernails, another touching up her makeup, still another attending to the fiery bouquets of delphiniums and calla lilies carefully arranged around her.

When is it done? I wondered, *When is a vision complete?* The photographer, a tall Frenchman with a thin mustache, seemed to be weighing these very questions with the gravity I imagined Peter Paul Rubens or Diego Velázquez might have brought to their paintings.

How impressive Claudia was in this role. How easily it seemed to come to her.

"*Ma chére*," the photographer said, addressing Claudia. "Shall we begin?"

Claudia, her reflection smiling back from the mirror she held in her left hand, looked over at me.

"Caroline," she said, using the French pronunciation. "What do you think? Is it okay?"

I smiled.

"It's perfect. *C'est très belle.*"

As the camera clicked and as the photographer made his adjustments— *chin over here, chin over there*—the room was overtaken by the familiar feeling that art was now happening.

This wasn't our first visit to Paris, and in fact, I'd lost count of how many there'd been. The first time, a limousine had met us at Orly Airport. Claudia got in and I'd followed, pulling the door closed behind me. She began speaking to the chauffeur in fluent French and, just like that, the Claudia of halting English and imperfect Italian was nowhere to be found. She wasn't in the gravel of her voice, and she wasn't in the familiarity of her expressions. In the presence of this new Claudia, I had an idea of who she might have been as a girl as well as a sense of the long road she had traveled.

But on the path to fame, she had still further to go. Sophia Loren— curvy and visibly from Italy's Mediterranean center, as opposed to its Alpine north—embodied a new ideal of Italian beauty and had ushered in the *maggiorate fisiche*, a group of so-called "shapely stars," including Gina Lollobrigida, Silvana Mangano, and, until her retirement, Lucia Bosè.

Meanwhile, a transition was underway in the country's cinema. Italian neorealism, with its canonical films like Vittorio De Sica's *Bicycle Thieves* and Roberto Rossellini's *Journey to Italy*, was squarely in the rearview and a new genre of auteur-driven films was now entering the spotlight. Instead of the crippling poverty and moral injustice that characterized neorealism, filmmakers were beginning to imagine Italy's more distant past as well as its contemporary present. An increasing appetite for style and flourish fueled the race to find new talent.

In noting Carlo Ponti's role in Sophia Loren's ascent to fame, it was Franco Cristaldi who saw the *maggiorate fisiche* as a red carpet heralding

Claudia's arrival. In her, he'd found the raw ingredients for the perfect star; she was beautiful, relatable, talented, and eager. But there were two catches, neither of them small. The first, which I would not discover until later, was that Pit, her younger brother, was not who she said he was. The second, a more immediate challenge, was that Claudia wasn't Italian. She was from Tunisia, which was then a jewel in the crown of France's crumbling colonial empire. How, then, could Cristaldi ask a country so invested in its own identity to accept a French-speaking foreigner as a national treasure?

If this is a naive question, it's because I didn't realize that while some stars are born, many are made. For the public to embrace Claudia as Italy's answer to Brigitte Bardot, alterations were necessary and, for this, Cristaldi needed complete control. This required Claudia's entire family to move to Rome, which in turn meant that her entire family was now dependent on the success of her career. She knew full well that the consequences of any misstep would be exacted on her parents and her siblings, including Pit.

In indenturing herself to Cristaldi, she'd ceded her independence to him. He was the surgeon and she was the patient, entrusting to him the nature and extent of the operation. There was language to address, and myriad other personal and logistical details, but most importantly, there was an image to fashion, a narrative to spin. She needed to be introduced to Italy gradually, in a way that softened her past and facilitated the easy-to-make assumption that she was not merely Italian but quintessentially Italian. This meant activating the media and the many levers with which it shapes popular opinion: photo shoots, magazine interviews, and carefully selected movie roles.

When I began working with her, the talon of her tomboy temperament was still pronounced. Her celebrity was shiny and untarnished and the innocence of her life prior to fame was undiminished. This made for brilliant memories, in part because we were so young but also because neither of us understood that beginnings are frequently quiet,

Claudia and Carolyn at an Italian market
(Carolyn Pfeiffer archive)

whirlpool-like; that deep-water forces are always at work, and that the lazy outer orbit of the present and the churning inner vortex that lay ahead are interconnected elements of the same system.

Cristaldi's star-making objective infused those early days with meta-morphosis. In the mornings, I'd pick up Claudia from her home on the outskirts of the city. There she was a daughter, a sister, a wild spirit. While I drove, the transformation took place inside the chrysalis of her Lancia. Her frustration with language and her longing for Tunisia would dissipate, and by the time we arrived at our destination, a new creature—La Cardinale—wholly without the mortal trappings of fam-ily, bedhead, or bad moods, would emerge.

Paralleling this was my own metamorphosis. In my way, I was also trying to become Italian. Like Claudia, I wanted this place to accept me, to adopt me, and I'd put my whole being into the effort. I had my dresses made at the tailor and my shoes made at the cobbler, and as my wardrobe grew, so did my hair. I let it grow long, like that of the Italian girls I studied so closely.

Young women, especially foreigners, suffered dearly at the hands of *chachy*, testosterone-addled men, and the barrage of whistles and cat-calls could ruin a good mood and even a good day.

"*Ciao, bella!*"

"*Dammi un baccio!*"

"*Bel culetto!*"

Alone in my flat, I'd rehearse different expressions and different retorts, and I focused on mastering the body language, those Italian gesticulations that are sometimes whimsical and other times savage. When I could walk down the street unbothered, when I could silence a catcall with a withering look or a biting *idiota*, I felt like I was finally beginning to fit in. The Carolyns of Madison and of New York faded away as I even began to dream in Italian.

Just as Claudia began her day as one thing and ended it as another, I awoke in my flat each morning as a girl from North Carolina and while I drove out to meet Claudia, the transformation would take place in the chrysalis of my Fiat 600, and I'd walk up to her door not as Carolyn but as *Carolina*.

Settling ever deeper into this new identity, I began to recognize that the underlying structures of society were very different from those in New York. Unlike the corporations that powered Manhattan, what mattered in Rome was family. Families owned businesses and businesses defined families. In a grocery or a restaurant, grandparents, siblings, and children worked side by side. Loyalty, trust, and succession were strictly family affairs, and this utter reliance on blood relations made entrance into a family nearly impossible. But once you were accepted into a family, you belonged for life.

Ten

My first time working on a movie set was in Bordeaux, in the French countryside. The film was *The Lions Are Loose,* a comedy in which Claudia plays Albertine, a young woman who moves to Paris to experience the big city. I had no idea what to expect from a movie production, only that I would be away from Rome, away from Masolino, for three whole months.

The production was like a city, an entire civilization that had sprung up for the singular purpose of making this one movie. There were cars and trucks, cameras and lights, and seemingly everywhere, rivers of cables. Accompanying Claudia to her first scene, I was moved by the way an ordinary street corner, chosen specifically for this purpose, had turned into a "set," transformed, cathedral-like, into a sacred place.

Lights, tall like sunflowers, with oversized faces framed by angular metallic petals, formed a perimeter around the director and cinematographer as they examined the set's every detail. Then Claudia was summoned, and the director worked out the blocking with her, roughing out the contours of the action. Then, after a brief rehearsal, it was time to shoot. The camera started rolling, the director called for action, and all that mattered was what was in front of the camera: this person, this place, this moment.

The effect on me was immense. What happens in the body during times like this? What is it that was dormant and that comes to life? I'd seen a thousand movies, but it was in witnessing the making of one that I discovered what I wanted for my future.

We moved from Bordeaux to Paris, and production only intensified. Long, emotional days left me exhausted but exhilarated, and when the film wrapped, I felt like a different person. Masolino met me at the airport in Rome. He looked sharp in a jacket and white button-down, and it was wonderful to see his smile and to feel his arms around me. I liked the sensation of his hair between my fingertips, the taste of his lips on my mouth. But I was also aware of a space between us that hadn't been there before. He'd been immersed in his studies and I'd been immersed in production. We'd arrived at the present via different paths, and our connection, which always came easily, was elusive.

It worried me. I loved him and I loved Rome, but I also loved my time in France. Over the course of production, my French had improved, but more than a different language, French was a different reality. Instead of *signorina*, I'd been *mademoiselle*, and instead of Carolina, I'd been Caroline, which rhymes with *magazine* and *figurine*. Carolina was earthy and wholesome; in her was passion and fire. But Caroline was more refined and sophisticated, sleeker and more fashionable.

My experiences on set bonded me to Suso in new ways. Now when I sat with her, I had a better understanding of her as a storyteller, as someone who looked at the world through a lens of narrative. In every shop and café, she saw a location, in every lunch guest a character, in every conversation a scene. I also began to better understand her stature and the world she occupied. She seemed to know every Italian film-maker I could name: Roberto Rosellini and Mario Monicelli, Vittorio De Sica and Federico Fellini. And, of course, Luchino Visconti.

When I first met Visconti, I was again sitting with Suso in her living room. She'd mentioned he would be visiting and had invited me to stay to meet him. They were working on an adaptation of Giuseppe Tomasi di Lampedusa's *Il Gattopardo* (*The Leopard*), a divisive new novel about the 1861 unification of Italy, and they were meeting to discuss the screenplay.

Suso had explained to me that Italy's image abroad was a matter of obsessive national concern, and half the country considered *Il Gattopardo* a masterpiece while the other half thought it painted Italy in a negative light and was an irreparable embarrassment.

"To me, it works better to think of Italy as a kingdom," Suso said.

"What do you mean?" I asked.

"I mean, if Italy is a country, it's only just. Florence and Milan, Venice and Rome, Bologna and Naples. These are different civiliza-tions, different people, different dialects, different histories. And never mind Sardinia and Sicily."

She went on to explain that, a century earlier, during the *Risorgimento*, the feuding states were brought together under the rule of King Victor Emmanuel II. Sicily was annexed to the mainland, and with that, an era ended. Traditions dissolved, treaties fell away, and important people were relieved of their importance. The titular leopard in *Il Gattopardo* is one such person. A regal Sicilian prince, he is obliged to stand by as his beloved nephew, a soldier fighting against the aristocracy, eschews the prince's daughter and instead marries the daughter of the town's nouveau riche mayor. It is a melancholy story of masculinity humbled and of beauty exalted, and Suso had the task of helping to put Visconti's exacting vision into words.

The maid escorted Visconti into where we were sitting, and I had an impulse to bow out of respect. Imposing and impressive, he was immaculately dressed in a blue suit. Had I read *Il Gattopardo*, comparisons to Don Fabrizio—the regal Sicilian prince—would have been difficult to avoid. As he and Suso spoke, their conversation started broadly, with a focus on the major plot elements. It then zeroed in on the three main characters: Don Fabrizio; Tancredi, his rebellious nephew; and Angelica, the mayor's beautiful daughter. Several times I tried to find words worth saying aloud, words that were worthy of this conversation, but among those I knew, among the combinations I could assemble, none were sufficient.

When Visconti left, Suso laughed at me.

"I've never known you to be so silent, *cara* Carolina. Does Luchino intimidate you?"

"Intimidate, no. He terrifies me."

She waved this away.

"Don't mind what is on the outside. It's the world that shaped him like that."

"Shaped him how?"

Suso tried to explain about what it was to be a gay man in Italy at the time. With an aristocratic upbringing, Visconti lived at an intersection of intense societal pressures.

"That is why he stands so straight, why he makes sure nothing about him can be criticized." Here she shook her head. "Anyway, the outside of a person tells you what defenseless thing lives within." She said this like an afterthought and then continued. "He's different, you know, from De Sica."

Visconti, Suso explained, wanted *authenticity*. In contrast, De Sica wanted *reality*. She went on to recount the story of Cary Grant, then the most famous actor on Earth, lobbying aggressively for the lead role in *Bicycle Thieves* and of De Sica fighting tooth and nail to prevent this imposition. For De Sica, Suso explained, it was only in casting an unknown actor that the tale of a poor man humiliated in front of his son could convey reality.

But, Suso circled back to *The Leopard*, Visconti was theatrical, operatic, and it was her job to capture the *authenticity* he envisioned for *The Leopard*. If she had to scale back the production value for De Sica by thinking about unknown people and actual locations, she had to ratchet up the production value for Visconti, to bring opulence and grandeur to the aristocracy and context of the era.

After I met Luchino Visconti—who was, with the possible exception of Federico Fellini, widely considered Italy's most important filmmaker—my respect for Suso deepened. This, in turn, drew me closer to Masolino. But our relationship was evolving. The fever of our infatuation had broken. The symptoms that had once been dire—passion that clouded our thoughts, lust that confined us to bed—now eased. The temperature lowered, and we were able to sit without touching and cross Villa Borghese without collapsing together just out of sight. Where urgency had been there was now satisfaction, a sense of balance and health that would have put me at ease if the need to make money weren't so urgent.

Despite a full-time job, I struggled to make ends meet. In Claudia's contract with Cristaldi and Vides, his production company, she wasn't paid per project or even by the success of her films. Rather, like me, she was an employee who received a modest sum each month. Without any control over her own pay, Claudia had even less say in what I was paid. On top of that, in those days, it was unheard of for a young woman to live alone and to sustain herself financially. My agemates lived with their families, and if they worked at all, it was to support the household. Between the rent, the car, and the monumental pressure of doing my best to look presentable next to Claudia, who was always elegantly and expensively dressed, I had almost nothing left for food and other basics.

The holidays were approaching, and while I'd hoped to visit my parents in Madison, I simply couldn't afford the ticket. And even if my parents had offered to buy it for me, Claudia had a busy schedule, and there was no way I could take any leave to speak of this early in my time with her.

I stayed in Rome as winter set in and tried unsuccessfully to feel warmed by the Vatican's elaborate festivities. On Christmas Eve, I was feeling melancholy as the old elevator carried me up to the d'Amicos' flat. I missed my family. I thought of Edna and Big Bill, of my parents and my brother. How distant it all seemed. How foreign. And then my thoughts turned to the kindness and generosity that awaited me. Each of the d'Amicos would surely have bought a carefully considered gift for me. My skin burned with shame because I had nothing to give in return. Desperate not to show up empty-handed, I'd found some cardboard and other materials, and as my mother had taught me to when I'd worked with her in the flower shop, I'd fashioned a little manger scene. A single modest gift, a single modest gesture, for the whole family.

The exchange of presents began, and my humiliation became unbearable as, one after another, I received gifts from everyone in the family. A scarf from Lele. A broach from Suso. A bracelet from Masolino.

When it was my turn, tears welled in my eyes as I pulled the little crèche from its box.

"I'm sorry," I stammered.

The silence continued as I placed the crèche on the coffee table and settled back on my knees.

Finally, Lele spoke.

"Which of us brought a homemade gift? Which of us put this much love into a present?" Again there was silence. "Don't apologize, Carolina. Of everything given today, yours is the only one that echoes the true spirit of Christmas."

I lowered my head. Out of respect. Out of exhaustion. Out of gratitude. Among these people, I was a daughter and a sister. I was, without qualification, family.

Eleven

For *capodanno*—New Year's Eve—I accompanied the d'Amicos to the home of the director Vittorio De Sica. Emi, his daughter, was a close friend of Silvia, the older of Masolino's two sisters. I greatly admired the De Sicas. Emi was a friend; Titta Rissone, Vittorio's wife and Emi's mother, was a famous actress; and Vittorio was a handsome man, bursting with charm.

When I first met him, he kissed me on each cheek.

"Carolina, your face is beautiful," he said with a flirtatious smile. "Like a question mark."

The New Year's Eve party lifted my spirits. I danced with Silvia and Emi, and then with Masolino. Midnight approached and he pulled me close.

"Do you see where is De Sica?"

I looked around and, not seeing him, I shook my head.

"Where is he?" I asked.

"He left. He has another family somewhere in the city."

"Two families?" I was shocked. "Is it a secret? Does Titta know?"

"More like an understanding. Titta knows but she doesn't know."

"Will you be like that, amore? Will you want another wife?"

He paused for a second and then said, "Only if there were more of you."

We danced late into the night because I didn't want to leave. I didn't want the morning to come or the new year to come. I just wanted to stay as we were. Let Masolino's studies wait. Let the brilliant academic career pulling at him wait. And let Claudia and the movies and all of the travel wait. Because this, by itself, was enough.

The morning came and it brought with it a new year full of activities and demands. I welcomed all of it. Claudia had been invited to London to be presented to the queen, and I was elated. Queen Elizabeth, so young and so new to the crown, had captured the imagination of women everywhere. Beautiful and dignified, she was a steady presence and a unifying figure.

In addition to the queen, I was looking forward to seeing Penny. We communicated regularly and I was eager to spend time with her in person. But a few weeks before our departure from Rome, I received a devastating letter from her. She'd just received word from Brazil that Richard, her beloved boyfriend, had been killed while on his research trip to the Amazon. She didn't have details and knew only that an altercation with an indigenous people group had left Richard dead.

We touched down in Heathrow, and in the limousine on the way to the Dorchester Hotel, I lost myself in thoughts of death, of the brutal finality with which life is truncated. I tried to imagine the pain Penny must feel, the emptiness of wanting to hold someone who, only a moment before, was alive. Who can know what deep-water forces are at work at any moment? Why do some things last while others end? Why do we attribute *this* to chance and *that* to destiny?

I was staring out the window when Claudia pointed to a clothing shop.

"I like that place," she said absently.

For a few blocks, I drifted back to Penny, thinking nothing of Claudia's remark. But then I remembered that she had told me that this would be her first time in London.

"Have you been there?"

"Where?"

"To that shop? You said it as if . . ."

The unmistakable glimmer of recognition flashed across her face.

"I meant the colors," she said. "They remind me of La Goulette."

I found out later that she had been in London before. She'd been there as a teenager, pregnant and afraid. It would be a long time before she would be able to go public with her story. She'd gotten pregnant before the fateful beauty contest where she'd been discovered. I learned that she'd never even entered that contest and had only attended the event because it was something to do. But then a judge had pulled her onstage and declared her the most beautiful contestant. And so she'd won. But she had no wish to become famous, and even after offers of acting roles came in, she'd refused to be in the movies. She had no desire to be in the public spotlight and had agreed to sign Cristaldi's contract only when he convinced her that he could spare her and her family the public shame of being a pregnant teen by getting her out of Tunisia. He would send her to London to give birth, and instead of returning to Tunis with a son, she could go to Rome with a brother.

Driving through London, all of that was still unknown to me and, in fact, Claudia never breathed a word about it, not in all of our time together. She never broke character, and I give her full credit for it.

After the glittering thrill of dealing with the London press, of preparing Claudia, and of seeing her curtsy in her pink Nina Ricci gown before the queen of Britain's sprawling empire, I got into a black cab to meet Penny in Hyde Park.

There was deep sadness in Penny's eyes, and I hugged her for a long time.

"How's the queen?" she asked when she pulled away.

"She's a baby," I said, trying to bring levity.

"She was our age, you know, when she became queen."

"Can you imagine?"

As we walked, we talked about the passage of time, about getting older. I thought of Claudia, of what it was to be a movie star at such a young age, of what it must be like to shoulder the full weight of one's family. And I looked at Penny and thought of what it was to lose a young lover to death.

At the Albert Memorial—Queen Victoria's opulent monument to the memory of her husband—we sat on the steps and stared into the distance.

"Suppose I'll have to put up one of these dreadful monuments for Richard, huh?"

Even here, even now, Penny's humor was with her.

"I suppose so."

"He'd want a massive one too."

"We could build it over there, by the pond."

"Brilliant." She looked at me, sorrow filling her eyes. "Shouldn't take too long, should it?"

"We'll be done by supper."

"C'mon, then. Best get to work."

We stood up, and as we moved toward the pond, I slipped my arm into hers.

"Fancy a drink before we begin?" I asked.

Twelve

Even from my hotel window above the Boulevard de la Croisette in Cannes, I could tell that the bikini-clad figure below was Brigitte Bardot. Blonde and barefoot, she was floating lackadaisically down the beach, a swarm of paparazzi circling around her like planets orbiting a sun. How striking to observe her effect on them. And on me too. She'd risen to fame in movies like *Naughty Girl* and *The Bride Is Much Too Beautiful*, but with *And God Created Woman*, a film that scandalized America and led to the arrest of several theater managers who'd dared show it, Bardot had become synonymous with sex and sexuality.

What impressed me as I watched her sashay through the sand was how confidently she seemed to trust herself in this role. I'd witnessed a similar quality, though with less natural ease, in Sophia Loren and Gina Lollobrigida. They'd passed under my window earlier, each seated on the back of a slow-moving convertible, each waving to the throngs of fans lining the Croisette. Seeing this, I felt admiration but envy too;

not for fame but for the confidence it takes to trust oneself enough to be able to trust oneself to others.

It was my first time at Cannes, and Claudia and I were staying at the Carlton, the seaside hotel famously featured in Alfred Hitchcock's *To Catch a Thief*. At the heart of the Riviera, the Carlton's twin domes are rumored to have been modeled after the breasts of La Belle Otero, a notorious Spanish dancer and courtesan with whom much of Europe had once been enamored.

With not one but two films in competition, Claudia was the talk of the festival. It was not by chance that both films, *Girl with a Suitcase* and *La Viaccia*, feature Claudia as an unattainable object of beauty and desire. This typecasting was central to Cristaldi's star-making strategy. In *Girl with a Suitcase*, Claudia plays Aida, the innocent but alluring obsession of a teenage boy who is too young to be taken seriously and who must stand helplessly by as the world of men closes in around her. In *La Viaccia*, directed by Mauro Bolognini and filmed in stunning black and white, she plays Bianca, a prostitute who is out of reach—at least in the nonphysical ways that matter to her suitor, played by Jean-Paul Belmondo.

Having appeared in Godard's *Breathless* the year before, Belmondo was competing with the devilishly handsome Alain Delon to be France's biggest star. Unlike Delon, who was sleek and catlike, Belmondo had the lean body of a boxer. He was a muscular cherub that I, and Claudia, too, found attractive and disarming—though possibly this was amplified by the recent news that Claudia had again been cast opposite him, this time in *Cartouche*, to begin filming later in the year.

That Claudia had two films in competition at Cannes was an announcement that put Sophia Loren and Gina Lollobrigida, and especially Brigitte Bardot, on notice. Sophia would win best actress that year for her role in De Sica's *Two Women*, but the growing consensus was that for Claudia, the more accurate comparison, in terms of sensuality and international appeal, was with Bardot.

I accompanied Claudia on interviews and photo shoots that took us to the marina and the Croisette, all of which blurred together with the parties and the beach, the red-carpet screenings at the Palais and the late-night cocktails at the bars in the Carlton and Martinez. If it was all fun and games to me, it was only because I was too young to know any better. I would return to Cannes many times and with increasing responsibilities over the years, but at that first festival I didn't yet understand Cannes's significance, the gravity of the films or filmmakers present. I was too new and too naive to grasp how much it mattered, for example, that Yuliya Solntseva became the first woman to win the award for best director. Nor did I grasp the importance of Luis Buñuel's masterwork *Viridiana*, which won the Grand Prix—later renamed the Palme d'Or.

When the festival ended, there wasn't time to return to Rome or to see Masolino. Instead we flew to Trieste, the Italian city on the border of what was then Yugoslavia, where Claudia was cast as Angiolina, the lead in Mauro Bolognini's *Senilità*.

Here, again, Cristaldi had found a role for Claudia in which she would be enshrined on film and presented to the public as idealized femininity, as something always pursued yet never possessed. Adapted from the novel, the film is set in 1927 and is, in some ways, a simple story of unrequited love. But it is also a vigorous exploration of masculinity and of the treacherous intersection of male ego and male sexuality.

I like Claudia in this film. As a 1920s flapper, an ingenue who is aware but unconcerned with the agony endured by her suitor Emilio, she is, from one perspective, empowered and strong. From another perspective, she is callous and cruel. It was only my second film with Claudia, and I remember thinking how different it was to see an actor on set in comparison to her edited performance in a finished film. On set, without the camera's frame to direct one's attention or the soundtrack to help inform one's emotion, all you see is the actors going through

Claudia and Carolyn on the set of Senilità
(Carolyn Pfeiffer archive)

their scenes over and over again, building what will live as their final performances, adjustment after adjustment and take after take.

To me, a good actor is misunderstood and underappreciated, and I sometimes think the problem is with the word itself. Because the word *actor* connotes *acting* rather than *action*, it carries a suggestion of make-believe or pretend when, in fact, the actor's job is not to act *like* a character but to act *as* that character. Done well, the role becomes indistinguishable from reality. This is a careful deception that requires an immense amount of respect for the craft. Because just as an actor can fail to convincingly embody his character, he can also take it much too far and become lost within it. Which is what we witnessed on *Senilità* as Anthony Franciosa, who plays Emilio, assumed more and more of his character's obsessive personality. What was first impressive became increasingly uncomfortable as Bolognini, the director, tried to pull as much Emilio out of Franciosa as he could while also ensuring Franciosa's stability.

With this drama intensifying on set, Cristaldi sent word that Claudia had been cast in *The Leopard*, Visconti's sprawling epic about the aging Sicilian prince that Visconti and Suso had been working on. Claudia was to play Angelica, the young beauty around which the entire plot revolves. The film would shoot in and around Palermo and, even by Visconti's standards, would be a monumental undertaking. Aglow with pride, we could feel that something profound was happening in Claudia's career. By some twist of fate, she had been anointed. She had a destiny that now felt inevitable, and by some other twist of fate, I'd been drawn into the current pulling her toward it.

As news of Claudia's casting in *The Leopard* rippled through the set of *Senilità*, it seemed to enhance the unattainability of Claudia's Angiolina while driving Franciosa deeper into Emilio, his emasculated character. In a climactic scene, Emilio comes to Angiolina on a rocky beach. He begs her to choose him, to love him as he loves her. And when she rejects him, he pleads with her pathetically. And when this, too, fails, he begins to shake her violently. Instead of stopping the action, Bolognini let the cameras roll, capturing the scene in claustrophobic close-ups.

When Angiolina frees herself from Emilio's embrace, she begins to walk away. Except, in reality, it wasn't Angiolina freeing herself from Emilio but Claudia freeing herself from Franciosa. Unbelievably, as Claudia stumbled down the beach desperate to escape, Franciosa began picking up rocks and handfuls of pebbles and flinging them at her. This seemed to go on for an eternity until, finally, Bolognini ended it. He called out, "Stop, stop, stop," but it was no use. Franciosa hurled rock after rock, and it wasn't until he was physically subdued that he collapsed in emotion.

Senilità wrapped soon after and, following a few days in Rome, we were off again, this time to Paris to begin work on *Cartouche*, a swashbuckling adventure in the vein of *The Three Musketeers*. Jean-Paul

Belmondo plays a Robin Hood–like bandit who gains popularity with the peasantry and notoriety with the police. Full of physical comedy and elaborate stunts, it was a very different kind of movie from *Senilità*.

Philippe de Broca, the director, had worked with Claude Chabrol and François Truffaut. He'd even appeared in both *The 400 Blows* and *Breathless*—arguably the two films most responsible for the French New Wave, which was then the most influential cinema movement in the world—and was one of France's elite filmmakers. The ornate costumes and medieval sets added a fairy-tale dimension that blurred the lines between reality and fantasy. As Claudia's character, Vénus, spends much of the movie on horseback, de Broca enlisted me as her stunt double for certain scenes. To fill out my figure, I was padded up and sent off to tear about the French countryside on horseback alongside Jean-Paul Belmondo.

As Claudia, Jean-Paul, and I grew friendly, the on-set energy spilled into our personal lives. Sometimes, after work, Jean-Paul would challenge us to a race from the studio outside Paris to the Arc de Triomphe in the city center. With me driving Claudia's car, we'd taunt him through open windows, rev our engines at traffic lights, and drown in fits of laughter as our shortcuts sometimes edged us ahead and other times left us hopelessly lost. Eventually we'd meet at a café on the Champs-Élysées and end the day with an *apéritif.*

One evening, while Claudia was getting ready for a dinner, her patience was wearing thin. We were in her room and the problem of what she should wear was becoming acute. I was trying to be helpful, but her favorite outfits were boring, and the new ones were untested. It was a crisis in fabric form. Claudia was exasperated; her weight was the problem, now her silhouette, now her décolletage. Having been with her in these moments before, I sympathized. No anxiety is quite so pure as that produced by adding urgency to elegance. Besides, it is no small thing to have the responsibility of becoming La Cardinale, of being accountable to the public for La Cardinale's appearance and presentation.

It requires a special reserve of character to face the possibility of disappointing the public, and the last of that reserve was being called upon as I forced Claudia into a simple black dress. But, just then, we were interrupted by a knock on the door. Opening it, Cristaldi entered Napoleon-like, his shoulders pinned back by the news he bore: Claudia had just been cast in *8½*, Federico Fellini's new film. She was to play the muse of the protagonist, who was, as everyone knew, a stand-in for Fellini, the *maestro* himself.

Claudia was silent. In that moment, nothing mattered; not the dinner and not the problem of what to wear. Already cast in *The Leopard*, this was nothing short of a coronation, a victory so comprehensive that not even Cristaldi could have dreamed it. It wasn't simply that Claudia had been cast as idealized female beauty by two great directors—it was that the two great *Italian* directors had each cast her as the *Italian* ideal of female beauty.

The change in Claudia was instantaneous and profound. From inside her there surged a glow so strong that it washed her anxiety away. After a long silence, Claudia walked to the mirror and, with graceful nonchalance, twisted her hair into a simple bun. Nothing she could do and nothing she could wear would turn her into La Cardinale because the metamorphosis was now complete.

"I'm ready," she announced. "We can go."

On our way back to Rome, I reflected on the puzzle of roles and realities. Franciosa and Emilio. Claudia and La Cardinale. And what about me? Was Carolina a role or was it reality? Within me were Carolyn, Carolina, and Caroline. All of them different. All of them jealous. All of them vying for expression. But only Carolina could marry Masolino. Only Carolina could live in Rome. And only Carolina could dissolve herself into the role of wife to Masolino, mother to his children.

I learned somewhere that the word *context*—which refers to the circumstances surrounding a person, place, or thing—hadn't always been a noun. A compound comprising *com* (meaning "with" or "together") and *texere* (meaning "to weave"), the original Latin, *contexere*, was a verb that meant "to weave together." A poet uses words to *contexere* her poem, a priest uses scripture to *contexere* his sermon. Increasingly, it seemed that it would be with names and languages that I would *contexere* my identity.

The train moved south through the villages of Emilia-Romagna and the vineyards of Tuscany, and I could feel the way in which Italy's land and cinema were connected. There was something about the oldness of the terrain and of the deeply embedded traditions it sustained that was both safe and seductive, inviting and imprisoning. And I wondered if it wasn't these qualities that somehow provoked an obsession with the feminine archetypes—mother, virgin, whore. Why were these passions more entangled and more inflamed in the cinema of this country than in that of any other?

So much about patriarchy was assumed in those days. The maestro—full of ego and the desire to penetrate the unknown—was assumed to be male while the earth-deep power—the chaotic source of beauty, sensuality, and life—was assumed to be female. All of this was codified in myth—in religion, art, and story—and we were only then beginning to push back, to understand that the maestro can be embodied in a woman and that earth-deep power can be embodied in a man.

"We aren't ready for feminism," Suso had once said to me as I sat beside her on the sofa. "It can't work here. Not yet."

"*Ma perché?*" I protested. "What do you mean?"

"Can you imagine? Women earning more than men? Men staying in the home? No. It would pull apart the things that hold us together."

"But you're a feminist," I pleaded. "You lead, always, even with men."

"What I'm saying, *cara mia*, is that what is right is always right and what is human is always human. Anyway," she continued, her fingertips resting lightly on the keys of her Olivetti, "sometimes the word comes after. Isn't it true that you love before you know to call it love?"

I suppose that is true. I'd thought so much about love, but when Masolino met me at the station, I felt like I still didn't understand it at all. Masolino was beautiful, and I loved him so much. But intimacy is a construction of rhythms that devolves into chaos when it's disrupted. Just seeing him on the platform, I knew something in our chemistry wasn't right. Some crucial ingredient was either missing or else had soured. This terrible feeling was there in the way my smile responded to his; it was there in our greeting; and it was there in our embrace. Somehow, something in my body no longer recognized something in his.

At dinner, I was glad to see Suso and Lele, Silvia and Caterina. They asked me about Claudia, and they celebrated my past adventures as well as those forthcoming with *The Leopard* and *8½*. It was a warm reunion, but still there was something off between Masolino and me. I kept glancing at him, trying to figure it out. When Suso saw this, she watched me watching him. And, when I caught her eyes, I could see in them the caution she'd given me: *travel comes at a cost.*

Later, when Masolino suggested a *digestivo* on Via Veneto, I said that I preferred to go to my flat.

"I'll come with you," he insisted.

Why did I hesitate? I was unable to explain it to myself or to him, but I knew that whatever the problem, it wouldn't be solved by him coming with me.

"*Amore,*" I said, kissing him preemptively, "I'll see you tomorrow."

As I walked away, he said nothing, and I could feel his eyes on me. His silence was a plea for me to turn around, to draw him out, to smooth away all of the wrinkles, real and imaginary. But I didn't turn around. I knew what he wanted—for things to be as they were, for me to need him and to want him in the same way. But so much had happened since our engagement. I still needed him, and I still wanted him, but not as before.

Thirteen

U p until the digital revolution of the 1990s, little had changed in the basic principles of filmmaking. As a reel of film passes through a camera, images are captured at a rate of twenty-four frames per second. Once processed, the reel becomes a negative, the master from which a print is made. The print is then passed through a projector, which projects the images onto a screen, again at a rate of twenty-four frames per second. The result is a near perfect approximation of human vision, and there are many who will argue, even today, that no amount of digital sorcery comes close.

As magical as the invention of the movie camera was, there is one thing it could not do; it could not record sound. This limitation confounded filmmakers for decades while simultaneously driving innovation in cinema. During the silent era, dialogue appeared visually, on slides, while a live orchestra provided audio accompaniment. Then, by recording sound separately and marrying it to the film print, "talkies" were born. In 1927, *The Jazz Singer* was released, and "Wait a minute, wait a minute, you ain't heard nothing yet" became the first spoken line of movie dialogue. From then on, with both camera and sound recording at the same time, the clapboard—the universal symbol of film production—has been used to record an audio spike that corresponds with the visual of the clapboard snapping closed, thereby allowing an editor to sync sound and picture together.

But within the inconvenience of recording picture and sound separately is a universe of creativity and illusion. Because anything can be made to come from an actor's mouth: a different voice, a different accent, even a different language. Just as the mind is content to accept the rapid projection of still images as motion—a phenomenon known as *persistence of vision*—it is also willing to accept, within reason, any voice laid over an actor's moving lips as the actor's own.

Italy, perhaps uniquely, has long favored dubbing over subtitles. Even today, there is a popular preference for hearing, rather than reading, Italian words. I suspect there is no one reason for this. When Mussolini came to power in the 1930s, his fascist regime put a heavy tax on dubbed films with the intent of centering the Italian language as well as Italy's actors and cinema. Consequently, no one in Italy—neither Rossellini, Visconti, Antonioni, Fellini, nor any of the great directors of Italian neorealism—saw a single American film between 1938 and 1945. So when the war ended and the tax was lifted, dubbed movies again flooded Italy.

What a dubbed film lacks in authenticity, it arguably makes up for in casting and in creative control. The popularity of dubbed films allowed Italian producers to use non-Italian stars, which not only helped with financing but also allowed them to record non-Italian versions of the film for sale in the home countries of those actors. Economics aside, dubbing also allowed the filmmaker to find the right words to put into an actor's mouth after production rather than before it. If there is a purity to the visual storytelling of Italian films from this era, perhaps it is because dialogue was a supplement to a film's picture and not a primary narrative engine.

This was maybe especially true for Federico Fellini, a large and handsome man with short dark hair, a surprisingly high voice, and a wicked twinkle in his eye. He'd been a cartoonist, and even in his films, he liked to push and pull reality, drawing inspiration from paintings and dreams much more than from literature. Few films have been more celebrated or studied than *8½*, and so I'll just say that it is a profoundly visual work that uses a director's creative crisis as a way to reimagine time and narrative, and to suggest, perhaps, that each of us is the protagonist in the movie of our life.

When Claudia's character appears to Guido, played by Marcello Mastroianni, at the thermal baths in Montecatini, I was standing with Lina Wertmüller, Fellini's assistant (who would go on to become the first woman nominated for an Academy Award for Best Director for her film *Seven Beauties*). In this scene, Marcello is in line for a glass of healing water from the bath's hot spring when he suddenly stops. With his index finger, he lowers his sunglasses for a better look. And there, framed by Montecatini's marble pillars, is Claudia dressed all in white. She then glides over to him, offers him a glass of water, and is revealed to be a mirage, a figment of his imagination.

"What's this scene about?" I asked Lina.

"*Ma chissà?*" she said with an ironic shrug. "Who knows what any scene is about?"

On any other set, we wouldn't have dared to whisper during a take, much less speak in our regular voices, but our conversation was drowned out by the chatter and conversation all around us. And this was often the case; people were frequently talking and laughing as the camera rolled. For their part, since there wasn't a final script, the actors were free to say whatever they wanted: numbers, the alphabet, whatever. And since no audio, apart from a guide track, was being recorded, Fellini issued directives to both cast and crew during the take, played loud music, and generally did everything possible to create an energetic atmosphere that would somehow animate the acting and the action.

Fellini's creative chaos was a thrill to behold. There were few film-makers in Italy, indeed in the world, with more power. He was unde-niably brilliant, the kind of warm person who saw life through a lens of innocence and comic beauty. And *8½* was a much larger production than I'd experienced. The cast numbered in the hundreds, the costumes were elaborate, and massive sets were built on location as well as in Cinecittà, Rome's sprawling art deco studio campus that had hosted Hollywood epics like *Ben-Hur* and *Cleopatra*. All of this, combined with Fellini's careful cinematography and elaborate camera movements, created a galaxy in constant motion, a densely populated ecosystem unto itself.

Before the start of filming, Cristaldi had pulled me aside and told me that I was not, under any circumstances, to leave Claudia alone with the maestro. Fellini's appetite for shapely women was well known, and Cristaldi was certain that Claudia was precisely Fellini's type. This wasn't Cristaldi being jealous—or if it was, it wasn't only that. Claudia, also, did not want to be left alone with Fellini. It was her job to be available to him in emotionally vulnerable ways, and she wanted me to help reinforce her personal and professional boundaries.

"*Mi prometti*, Carolina?" Cristaldi asked. "Promise me you won't leave her alone."

"*Io prometto*," I responded.

I don't fault men their lust or their fantasies; the human being is a mystery, and even back then, I believed that what happens between consenting adults is their own business. But the difficult thing is power. Because with power, there is almost always someone who takes and there is almost always someone who is taken from. If Claudia was vul-nerable, it was because her role in the film depended on Fellini continu-ing to be enamored by her, and in a dynamic like that, a refusal of any kind can be consequential.

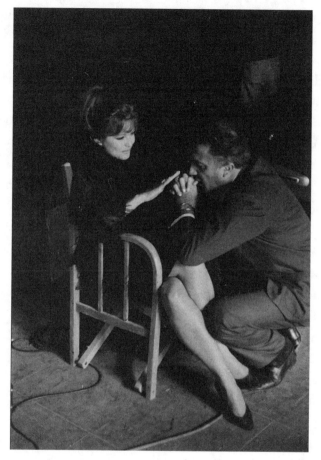

Claudia and Fellini on the set of 8½
(Photo by Gideon Bachmann, 1962 © Archivio Cinemazero Images, Pordenone - Italy)

At first Fellini's affections seemed both innocent and reciprocated. After all, he was a warm and affectionate person living in a warm and affectionate culture. There was always a lot of touching and physical contact, and the maestro was very up front about his process, the way he required high levels of intimacy and trust with his collaborators. With Claudia, it was no different. He hugged her, doted on her, and gave her nicknames: Claudina, Claudetta, things like that. But it was also apparent to me that he was engineering ways to be alone with her.

"I need to work with my muse," he said as he led her into his Studio 5 office at Cinecittà. "We don't want to bore you, Carolina. Why don't you wait for us on set?"

Claudia looked at me uncomfortably, and I didn't know what to do.

"Go," he said. "We'll be fine."

It may not sound like much, but it took everything in me not to do as he'd instructed.

"I'll wait here, by the door," I said. "I don't mind."

With that, I'd made it clear that I knew that he knew that I knew what he was doing. And, from that point on, even though he was the director and even though he had a million things to worry about that were much more important, it felt to me that we were at odds with each other.

The next day, however, he surprised me with a warm smile.

"You should be in the film," Fellini said happily. "You can be yourself as Claudia's secretary."

"You want me in the film?"

"*Ma si!* Claudia's character is Claudia, and it will be the same for you. Carolina in life; Carolina in the movie. *Va bene?*"

And so it was.

Mine is a small scene in which Guido, played by Marcello and universally understood to be an avatar for Fellini himself, is watching footage in a hushed theater. Seeing Claudia's character enter, he stands up to meet her, and my character alerts her that he is approaching. She then introduces me to Guido, who asks me to wait in the theater as he and his muse leave together.

"All right, I'll wait here," is my line just before they escape for an unchaperoned nighttime interlude, muse and maestro alone together at last.

Maybe it's nothing; I don't know. But, to me, it's something. To me, that was a line I was being given to memorize and to internalize, a line I was to say to Fellini the next time he suggested that I leave him alone with Claudia.

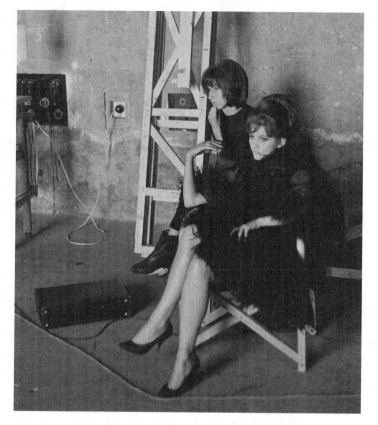

Carolyn and Claudia on the set of 8½.
(Photo by Gideon Bachmann, 1962 © Cinemazero Images, Pordenone - Italy)

Sure enough, a few days later, he again tried to peel me away from Claudia, and again I refused to be peeled away. I refused to say the line he'd given me to say: "All right, I'll wait here." From then on, this thing that to me was a silent battle between us, and that I have no doubt was to him even less than nothing, consumed me. It defined my experience on the film, and I came to resent it, to wish I could set it aside and participate in the reverie of creativity that everyone else seemed to be enjoying.

Then, as I walked by Fellini as he was speaking with Gianni Di Venanzo, the cinematographer, and Pasquelino De Santis, the camera operator—both of whom I liked and admired immensely—the maestro reached out and, with a laugh that to most people was charming, pinched my ass. He did this not only in front of Gianni and Pasquelino but in front of a dozen other people. And I think that was the point, for it to be seen and for me to know that he knew that I knew that this was his set and he could do as he pleased.

Federico Fellini is one of our great filmmakers and *8½* is one of our great films. But on that day, something in me turned against him. I wasn't angry or indignant, nor did I feel scandalized or somehow traumatized. No, it wasn't any of those things. I was just humiliated, plain and simple. I've thought about it, embarrassingly, for several decades now, and I always make a distinction between men who use sex publicly, as a way to assert power, and those who use power privately, as a way to demand sex.

I don't know if I told Claudia, nor do I remember if I told Masolino. Probably I wanted to but didn't. I know Masolino would have been upset. The problem was that, by then, our relationship had begun to stagnate, and we no longer shared as we once had. I was twenty-four years old, and I'd been engaged for two years. Yet the longer our engagement went on, the harder it became to talk about getting married. He was always studying and I was always with Claudia, and this divided life had now divided us. The result was that I no longer felt able to say the things I most wanted to say. *Are we too young? Isn't there still more for you out in the world? Because, for me, there is. And can't you see that there is more to me than Carolina, more to me than this one version that you have come to know?*

Filming of *8½* was ongoing when Claudia was summoned to Sicily, where *The Leopard* was getting underway. They had tried to prevent the productions from overlapping, but Fellini needed more time and Visconti couldn't wait any longer. Somehow, she would have to work on both films at the same time. We arrived in Palermo in the middle of summer, when the sun was blazing and the city, weightless and still, waited out the day's heat indoors. Nothing moved, and it was like entering an enchanting and delirious new world.

The production installed Claudia and me in a villa near the sea. It had an upstairs balcony that overlooked a cobblestoned street, and we kept the windows open to catch the breeze. Our first evening there, we walked to the beach and took our shoes off. The sun was low in the west and the wind, warm and soothing, moved lightly across the water.

"It has the feel of home," Claudia said as she looked into the setting sun.

The next day, we were invited to dinner at Visconti's villa in the hills above the city. Visconti greeted Claudia with a warm "Claudine!" They'd worked together before, and it should not have surprised me that he was fluent in French and that they communicated with each other in her native language. What touched me the most was not only that he remembered me from his visit to the d'Amicos', but that he'd also remembered my name.

"*Buonasera*, Carolina," he said with a smile.

"*Buonasera, maestro.*"

"*Chiamami* Luchino," he insisted. "*Per favore.*"

It's true that I was inclined toward Visconti because of my affection for Suso and because of Suso's affection for him, but even back then, when I was just an assistant, I could hear in his voice and see in his eyes that he was someone who took me seriously.

Visconti next introduced us to Burt Lancaster, who was commanding and statuesque. Seeing him in front of me, I was catapulted back to the theater in the center of Madison where I'd seen him in *From Here to Eternity* and *Gunfight at the O.K. Corral*. I was flooded with memories of staring up at the big screen and experiencing it as a window through which I could escape. And now Burt Lancaster himself, recent best actor Oscar winner for his role in *Elmer Gantry*, was shaking my hand.

"I'm Burt," he said politely, knowing all too well how unnecessary his introduction was.

What I didn't understand at the time was how fraught his relationship with Visconti had been. Visconti had been against casting Lancaster from the beginning, and when it came out that he had indeed been cast to play Prince Don Fabrizio Salina, the Italian press had had a field day mocking Visconti. Lancaster was seen as an American cowboy, lowbrow and unserious, and the role called for someone regal and grandiose. Visconti had wanted Nikolai Cherkasov, the Russian actor from *Ivan the Terrible* or, if it must be someone from the English-speaking world, Laurence Olivier. But Fox, the studio putting up the money, had issued a shortlist of only three acceptable names: Anthony Quinn, Spencer Tracy, and Burt Lancaster. Lancaster was the producers' first choice and Visconti's last choice. It wasn't until he watched Lancaster in *Judgement at Nuremberg* that Visconti very begrudgingly conceded.

That the casting of Burt Lancaster was so contentious made sense when seen from Visconti's perspective. Because in telling the story of a Sicilian prince whose aristocratic position is made obsolete in Italy's transition to democracy, Visconti was mining personal territory. He'd been born into aristocracy himself, so the prince's arc from relevance to irrelevance tracked with Visconti's own story about being caught between the past and the future, and about the struggle of resigning oneself to a new world. Just as Fellini, with *8½*, was dabbling in self-portraiture and had found an avatar in Marcello Mastroianni, Visconti was attempting something similar with *The Leopard*, and the role of muse mattered a great deal.

But, as it turned out, Burt's flaw was also his salvation. Because without a personal connection to the character and without an aristocratic model on whom he could base his Don Fabrizio, he used the closest thing he could find: Visconti himself. The efficiency with which this allowed Visconti to inject himself into the film—the dignity of his carriage, the specificity of his mannerisms, the excruciating internal struggle—not only helped the two men create the perfect character but also healed their relationship. For the rest of their lives, both would refer to this collaboration as one of the most meaningful in their respective careers.

After my brief conversation with Burt, Claudia introduced me to Alain Delon, who plays Tancredi, Don Fabrizio's handsome and mischievous nephew. Claudia had appeared with him in Visconti's *Rocco and His Brothers*, and they had a warm, sibling-like relationship. This was unusual because everyone—women and men alike—was attracted to him. He knew this, and it infused his movements with a pacing, feline quality that was restless and self-aware. But he was newly famous, and he had not yet gained control of the stallion-like energy that fame had unleashed into his life. In looking into his eyes, I could see something wild and distrusting looking back at me, and I hoped he could tell that whatever he saw in mine came to him in peace.

Visconti was warmer than I'd anticipated. Without losing any of his severity, he nonetheless had an accessibility about him. His background was in opera, and his commitment to the visual and to the authentic permeated everything about him. It was Visconti who introduced me to "primitive art" as he was then collecting Sicilian paintings of biblical scenes done on glass and framed in elaborate handcrafted wooden frames. "People's art," he called them, since there was no knowing who they'd been painted by. They weren't about the artist, Visconti explained, but rather were expressions of life, pure and simple. At my first opportunity, I bought three such paintings of my own.

As Claudia worked on her lines and settled into her character, we integrated ourselves into the massive production. Though we'd met with wardrobe people in Rome, it wasn't until Claudia's final fittings that the full extent of Visconti's vision became apparent. Costume designer Piero Tosi, with whom Claudia had recently worked on *Senilità*, was collaborating with a young costume maker named Umberto Tirelli (whose company would eventually work on everything from Fellini's *Amarcord* to contemporary films like *Braveheart, Pirates of the Caribbean,* and 2022's *Death on the Nile*) and had magically re-created an 1860s Sicily in which every detail was authentic. This included outfitting hundreds of soldiers, peasants, and aristocrats—a colossal effort best captured by the carefully embroidered handkerchief Claudia was to keep in her purse even though the purse would never be opened and the handkerchief would never be removed or seen.

With Claudia's arrival in Palermo, excitement was beginning to intensify. Everyone could now see the Angelica that Visconti had carried in his head for so long. While Piero and Umberto fussed over Claudia, I sifted through a bowl of ornate buttons, each one a hundred years old or more. Then, when Visconti came to consult with the hair and makeup team, I remember him taking a strand of Claudia's hair between his fingers and shaking his head.

"This, no," he said with a frown. "It can't be like this."

For her role in *8½*, Fellini had lightened her hair. Though that film is in black and white, it's clear that Claudia's hair is a light chestnut color. But Angelica was Sicilian, and Visconti needed her hair to be almost black.

"It must be changed," he said firmly.

But that wasn't possible. Claudia still had scenes to shoot with Fellini, and there was no way she could return to Rome with her hair a different color. What seemed like a minor detail soon ballooned into a genuine crisis. Wigs were ruled out. Repeated dying wasn't possible both because of continuity risks and because, in those days, dying processes were enormously destructive; the toll on Claudia's hair, and possibly her health, would be too much. The makeup people from both films got involved and then the cinematographers did too. Because while Fellini and Visconti were, ostensibly, united in wanting a solution, there was also a question of who would prevail and who would capitulate. It was just hair, yes, but it was also reputation, status, and a way to settle who, finally, was the more influential director.

The Solomonesque solution, arrived at after intense negotiations, was to divide Claudia's hair between them. From ear to ear, over the top of her head, a line was drawn, with the front half going to Visconti and the back half going to Fellini. A chestnut front piece was created to supplement Claudia's *8½* character and a black back piece was created for Angelica. It was an acceptable solution to both directors, though Claudia, who had no choice in the matter, was left feeling horribly self-conscious—albeit with a closet full of hats.

With Fellini ready to finish Claudia's scenes, we flew back to Rome. Upon arrival, we learned that additional scenes had been shot using a body double for Claudia and that, since I had been in Sicily, the role of Claudia's secretary had been given to a young German actress. This meant that the theater scene needed to be reshot and also that I would not appear in the final film.

"*Ma*, Carolina," Fellini said sympathetically, "you'll still be her voice, yes?"

I don't at all mind that I am cut out of the final film. My voice is there saying the thing Fellini wanted me to say. And maybe that is as it should be. Because, in the end, it's a film, a fantasy, an effort to make sense in art what doesn't make sense in life. We filmed the final scene—with the spaceship and the band and the entire cast—and it was glorious; it captured a joyful honesty to do with people and aspiration, with circularity and peace, and it is one of the privileges of my life to say that I, too, was there.

Meanwhile, Masolino and I grew further apart. Over sambuca one night, we tried to reconnect. He insisted I was the problem. He said that if only I were honest, I would admit that I wanted to break up with him. I told him he was wrong. I blamed travel and work, the never-ending, low-grade anxiety of being away from home. I promised him that things would be better once we had some calm and could find each other again. When we slipped into bed, he lay on his back and I lay on mine—and neither of us lifted a finger. Worse than the loneliness of aloneness is the loneliness of isolation because with it comes sadness and, worst of all, defeat.

As long as there is one small jar of love tucked away somewhere in the pantry of your heart, there is hope. Sometimes you think it is all gone, but you stumble upon a reserve about which you had forgotten. Then, maybe, your foot finds his under the covers. Or maybe you find the will to soften, to lean your head on his chest, to fit it between his jaw and clavicle. But sometimes it really is all gone. Maybe there was never as much as you thought. Or maybe too much of it was wasted—by you, by him, by the forces that pull this way and that. Whatever the case, I could barely breathe when I acknowledged to myself that, whatever I felt for Masolino, it was no longer love.

It was August when we arrived back in Palermo. The brutality of summer's heat had intensified so dramatically that filming was now possible only at night. Our days were spent dozing, sweating, praying for the slightest breeze to drift in from the Mediterranean. In the hazy exhaustion between long nights on set and sticky days lounging in bed, everything seemed to melt together.

We had only the ballroom scenes left to film. It's a decadent, mesmerizing sequence in which Don Fabrizio floats from room to room as he takes in a way of life fading into extinction right in front of him. Drawing from memories of lush balls held in his childhood home, Visconti stretches the sequence into almost a third of the film, which required almost a month to shoot. Each evening, a few hundred extras were outfitted in full period attire and countless candles throughout the villa were lit by hand. Lights, meticulously positioned by the camera department, evenly lit the entire set so that the three cameras could shoot anything from any angle.

And while all of this was going on, I would help Claudia into her magnificent white dress. The centerpiece of the accompanying undergarments was a champagne-colored whalebone corset from the 1800s. In my memory, Visconti's instruction was for her waist to be pulled in to fifty centimeters, under twenty inches. This meant Claudia was unable to sit down or use the restroom, and so a stand against which she could lean and rest was made for her. Even more physically taxing was that the corset cut so deeply into her flesh that, by the time it was taken off each morning, rivulets of blood encircled her abdomen.

Claudia, Burt, and Alain on the set of The Leopard
(Archive Photos/Moviepix © Getty Images)

As the ballroom sequence progresses, Don Fabrizio, growing ever paler, becomes the embodiment of Italy's aristocratic past as he comes face-to-face with irrelevance, old age, and, ultimately, with death. At one point, he leans against a granite mantelshelf and stares for a long time into a textured mirror. Tears fill his eyes and overwhelming melancholy obliges him to slip away to a quiet room where he can be alone.

Angelica and Tancredi find him there, alone, staring at a painting in which a dying patriarch is lying in bed surrounded by the youth and vitality of his children and family. It is difficult, with words, to describe how beautiful Claudia is as she goes to Don Fabrizio and takes his head in her hands. In a translucent white dress, she is youth and promise, the bright future of Italy. With Alain's Tancredi looking on, she kisses the old man gently and pleads with him to dance with her. He equivocates but then gives in to her, and what follows is, for me, one of cinema's great scenes. As they glide across the room, the crowd grows silent around them, and as the room falls under their spell, the film attains a kind of rapturous tragedy that conjures countless layers of opposites: old and new; innocence and age; past and future; optimism and resignation; life and death; endings and beginnings.

Is it a coincidence that notions of endings and beginnings also permeated my life away from set? At the regular gatherings at Visconti's villa, I'd begun a friendship with Alain, and he'd already promised me a job if I ever found myself living in Paris.

One evening, with Claudia and Visconti cheering us on, we almost died laughing as I taught him the Twist.

"*Comme ça*, Alain!" I instructed. "Heels forward!"

Claudia and Visconti look on as Carolyn teaches Alain Delon the Twist
(Carolyn Pfeiffer archive)

"*Mais*, Caroline, I'm doing my best. *Je fais de mon mieux!*"

Alas, these good times were in devastating contrast with the phone calls to Masolino, with their strained silences and the gathering clouds of what felt like an ending drifting nearer.

Lying beside Claudia on the beach late one afternoon, I was trying to find clarity. My relationship with Masolino was tangled up with my relationship with Suso. My relationship with Suso was tangled up with my relationship with the film industry. And my relationship with the film industry was tangled up with my relationship with Italy itself. To trouble my relationship with Maso was to risk the collapse of my whole life.

I was chasing these thoughts in an endless loop when a nearby group of men began to multiply. Fingers started pointing. Voices grew louder. Excitement crept through the lazy afternoon, and the only word we could make out was Claudia's name. Unnerved, we gathered our things and began walking toward the house. But the crowd followed us. We sped up—half-running and half-walking, half-entertained and half-afraid. The crowd grew bigger, louder, faster. And then it was avalanching toward us, closing the distance between us with terrifying speed. At this, we broke out running as fast as we could, hardly aware that we'd stopped talking altogether.

We slammed into the house, locked the door, and clambered upstairs to the balcony. The crowd pooled around the house, a chorus of explicit demands rising from it. Thinking I might somehow disperse it, I went to the railing and shouted for the men to go away. But chants of "Claudia! Claudia!" drowned me out. After a moment, I backed into the house, where Claudia had already called the police.

It wasn't a particularly consequential event, yet it unsettled me and deepened the malaise tightening its grip on me. Not long after, Suso arrived to see Visconti and to check on filming. With that Sunday off, Cristaldi chartered a boat to take a group of us—including Suso, Claudia, and Gioacchino di Lampedusa (nephew of the author of the novel from which *The Leopard* was adapted) and his wife—on a day trip out on the water. We left late in the morning and made our way north to Mondello, a remote seaside village where we tethered the boat beneath a rocky cliff and enjoyed a lazy lunch at a restaurant overlooking the sea.

It wasn't until three in the afternoon that we reboarded the boat, and as we moved into open water, the shoreline sank lower into the water. We were full and happy until, gradually at first, we noticed water gathering around our feet. At first, it was funny. Some in our group made dramatic gestures of finding buckets and bailing the water overboard. But it kept coming and coming, and as the humor quickly evaporated, we began exchanging anxious glances as no one wanted to be the first person to acknowledge that a gravely serious situation was beginning to unfold.

With the sun low in the sky, Cristaldi took off his Rolex, handed it to Suso, and dove under the boat. When he emerged, there was fear in his voice as he described a deep gash in the hull. The gash, he suspected, must have happened while we were eating lunch and while the boat was being battered against the rocks. As we absorbed the reality that we were miles from shore without any emergency equipment on board—no life vests, flares, or even a radio—the fear in Cristaldi began to infect us, one by one. Some people began taking off their clothes and madly waving them over their heads. Others continued bailing out water as fast as they could while still others began to pray. I'd never learned to swim, and as an animal fear entered me, I kept repeating to myself, *Don't panic, don't panic.*

Light drained from the sky, and any hope of rescue vanished. There was nothing to see and nothing to do, and a terrible stillness settled over us. The minutes ticked slowly by until, miraculously, a boat appeared on the horizon. How we shouted! With tears and with every bit of oxygen in our lungs, we screamed and waved our shirts and towels. And then we realized that none of it was making a difference. The boat hadn't seen us, and it soon disappeared from view. Our shouts died down, and in the silence that followed, no one spoke. The light was almost gone, and I think, at this point, each of us was forced to acknowledge the reality of death, the way it's always present, the way it can appear even when it is least expected.

Several agonizing minutes later, the same boat peeked back over the horizon. It made its way toward us, and we couldn't believe it. We waved towels and shirts, and there was laughter and shouting and even more tears. Except something wasn't right. The boat wasn't slowing down, nor was it turning to come alongside us. Instead it was barreling toward us with no intention of stopping. It broadsided us, and while I managed to hold on, several others were thrown into the sea. For a moment, there was total pandemonium until, finally, everyone was accounted for and hauled to safety.

Our rescuers turned out to be poachers fishing illegally. Not only were they inexperienced when it came to operating a boat, they also flatly refused to take us to Palermo out of fear of the law. There were bribes and arguments, and in the end, they dropped us off, shivering and exhausted, several miles outside of town.

The image of our boat taking on water took vicious hold of me. After lunch the following day, I felt off and told Claudia I needed to lie down. I found my way to our villa and collapsed into bed. When I awoke I was unable to move at all. My hands wouldn't close, and I couldn't even move to pull the sheet up over my shoulders.

Claudia was at a dinner at Visconti's, and as night pushed in through the window, I began to lose track of time and space. I was in that maze between awake and asleep, stumbling from one to the other, when voices penetrated the deadness. I opened my eyes to see Suso sitting beside me and a tall figure standing behind her. He stepped forward and I recognized the gentle eyes of Burt Lancaster, the leopard himself.

Suso purred softly, fussing over my complexion and my temperature.

"You're not well, *cara*," she said. "I'm sending you home."

Masolino met me at the station a few days later. We drove in silence but, parked in front of my flat, the silence became unbearable. If I had then laughed, if I had said, "Maso, I'm sorry. I've been so lost," he would have hugged me and all would have been forgiven.

When he spoke, I turned to him.

"My mother says you're not well," he said.

"My problem has to do with the heart."

For a long time, neither of us said anything.

"Masolino," I whispered at last, "what you want is something else."

"What do I want?"

"You want marriage. Family. A life here in Rome."

"I want those things with you."

"I know."

"Is it that you don't want them? Or is it that you don't want them with me?"

If only life could be like the movies. If only multiple takes were possible. If only you could try one thing, and if it doesn't work out, adjust and try it again. Over and over until you get it right. I wanted to say to Masolino that I did want those things. Of course, I did. That I wanted them with him. There would have been so much truth in those words if I were to say them.

But he wasn't asking for truth; he was asking for a decision.

Fourteen

s there a word for the period of time between the moment your relationship fails and the moment you realize it has failed? We had a future together, Masolino and I. This was true for a long time, but at some point, it stopped being true. It stopped being true even as I continued to believe it was true.

Conflicting emotions beset me as I boarded the night train to Paris. I'd hurt Masolino and I'd betrayed his family's investment in me as a sister and daughter. They'd been generous and supportive, and now I was leaving Rome and I was leaving Italy; I was leaving them. Had I been impulsive? Shortsighted? Had the decision to move to Paris been rash? The train lurched into motion, and I wondered if regret awaited me somewhere in the future.

After that night with Masolino outside my flat, I stopped going to lunches at the d'Amicos' and I buried myself in work. *The Leopard* wrapped and the spotlight on Claudia was bright. Hollywood had taken notice, and she'd already been cast in Blake Edwards's *The Pink*

Panther, which would shoot in Rome and in Cortina d'Ampezzo, in the Italian Alps.

With my attention deliberately focused away from Masolino and the d'Amicos, the next time I called home to Madison, I was surprised. After a brief exchange with my father, he handed the phone to my mother who said she'd received a letter from Suso. The connection wasn't good, and my mother's voice cut in and out. What I could make out was that, in her letter to my mother, Suso had asked her to speak with me. Suso wanted to know if my decision to leave Masolino was final or if it could still be undone.

That Suso was going through so much effort to keep me and Masolino together—and to keep me in their family—was difficult to hear because even though our engagement had ended, I wanted so badly to continue my relationship with Suso and the family.

"Did you write back?" I asked my mother. "What did you say?"

"I said the decision must be your own. And I told her that a broken engagement now is better than an unhappy marriage later."

Tears began to gather behind my eyes, petitioning for release.

"Mom . . ."

"Sugar, what is it?"

"I'm sad."

"Of course you are," she said. "But your way isn't easy. You know that by now."

She was wrong, though. I didn't have a way. All I had was a stubborn instinct, an inability to continue with something that wasn't right for me. And now I felt lost, unsure of the path forward. Because my Rome, the Rome I had come to know, was also the d'Amicos' Rome. For me, there was no difference between the two. I couldn't imagine a life there, even one with film and professional success, that didn't overlap with Masolino and his family.

When we traveled to Paris for Claudia to be fitted by Yves Saint Laurent for *The Pink Panther*, I couldn't help imagining what it would be like to live there. The energy was buoyant and young, and there was a feeling that important things were beginning to happen. If I moved, I could go by Caroline, live on the Left Bank, and maybe fashion a modest life for myself among the artists and students clustered around the Sorbonne.

Unlike Italy, which had been extensively damaged in the war, France—to its humiliation—had fallen to Germany early on, and Paris, City of Lights, had spent the war years in literal darkness, its lights switched off at night while its radios spouted Nazi propaganda. With the French government in exile, resistance to the occupation was most visible in the figure of Charles de Gaulle, a refugee in London, and in the defiant spirit of Paris's students.

Now that the war was over, France was undergoing a political reckoning. A monarchic president, de Gaulle was working to wrest away from the global superpowers, the United States and the Soviet Union, a corner of the world stage upon which France, and Europe, might stand once more. The problem was that, for many, national pride wasn't possible until the social and economic divisions that crisscrossed the country were addressed. In this, Paris's students were becoming radicalized; their numbers were growing, and they were developing a taste for revolution.

A similar defiant energy also possessed Blake Edwards, director of *The Pink Panther*, who was then high on the success of his last feature, *Breakfast at Tiffany's*. In that film, he'd cast the wholesome Audrey Hepburn as the quirky and fashionable escort Holly Golightly—who'd been something of a heroine to me and to countless other young women—and, in so doing, the film had slammed the door on the superficialities of the 1950s and had ushered in a more ambitious, more adventurous suggestion of where American cinema might go in the decade to come.

With some time off from Claudia's *Pink Panther* fittings, I made arrangements to see Alain Delon. It had been several months since our dinners at Visconti's villa above Palermo, but I hadn't forgotten his invitation to come and work for him if ever I were to find myself living in Paris. But even as I rang the bell and waited on the doorstep of his beautiful *hotel particulier* on Avenue de Messine, I was unsure exactly what I wanted or what I would say.

Alain greeted me warmly. Romy Schneider, the German star engaged to Alain, was there. I'd met her briefly on the set of *Boccaccio '70* and again when she visited the set of *The Leopard*. Visconti had taken a personal interest in her as he thought she had enormous unrealized potential as an actress. I could see why. She had a symmetrical face with perfectly arched brows. Beautiful, of course, but there was also something deeply vulnerable in her aqua green eyes, and I found, even in that short interaction, that I was immediately devoted to her.

When Romy excused herself, I looked into Alain's eyes and again saw that wild part of him pacing restlessly. But then he smiled, and I was reminded that to be alone with him was to know, without any doubt in your heart, that you are capable and you are unique.

Then, before I knew what I was saying, I began telling him that I was thinking of moving to Paris.

"You must, Caroline," he said with conviction. "Absolutely, you must. You will help me. We have a place for you here. We are going to make great films."

"*Vraiment?*"

"*Mais oui!*" he said emphatically.

One thing about Alain Delon was that, though he might have been mistrustful of those he didn't know, his loyalty to those he did know was immense.

"Come with me," he said, standing up and nodding toward the stairwell.

As I followed him downstairs to the offices on the ground floor, he moved decisively, as if we, he and I, were on a mission. In the office, he introduced me to Georges Beaume, his manager and partner, and the three of us began to discuss how I could join their team. After half an hour, it was decided that I would be Alain's director of development and that I would take the lead in looking for roles in English-language movies that might be right for him.

As I walked back to the hotel to join Claudia, I felt both exhilarated and exposed. Because to undo what had just been done, to change my mind and to stay in Rome, would be almost as consequential as the road that lay ahead.

Production of *The Pink Panther*, famously, was as prank-and-joke-filled as the film itself. It's often forgotten that *The Pink Panther* was intended as a movie about the gentleman thief Sir Charles Lytton, played by David Niven, and not a movie about the bumbling Inspector Jacques Clouseau, played by Peter Sellers. But so strong was the chemistry between Blake Edwards and Sellers—who'd been second choice for the role—that Sellers emerged as the film's star. To his credit, David Niven, who'd won the best actor Oscar a few years earlier, was unthreatened by the stolen spotlight.

Niven and I had become quite friendly. In fact, he'd once had a relationship with a woman from North Carolina, and something about that endeared me to him.

"If you ever get in trouble," he said to me one day as we watched Blake and Peter goof around, creating the character of Inspector Clouseau in front of our very eyes, "you call me. Okay? If you're ever pregnant or in jail, you can count on me. I mean that."

Niven was the one person that impressed my mother. They were of the same generation, and she'd always been a devoted fan. I'd tried hard to impress her with stories of the celebrities I'd met but, for her, there was only David Niven. When I showed him a gushing letter from my mother, he had me include a handwritten note in my response.

"Dear Frances," he wrote, "I love many girls from North Carolina but you I love the most."

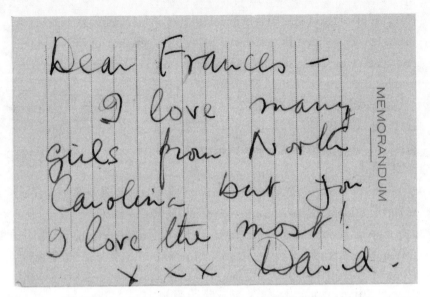

Dear Frances —
I love many
girls from North
Carolina but you
I love the most!
x x x David.

MEMORANDUM

David Niven's note to Frances Pfeiffer
(Pfeiffer family archive)

The Pink Panther is widely considered a comedy masterpiece, but it is also guilty of exploiting every possible stereotype. The least offensive of these, perhaps, is Claudia's role as an exotic princess. Though filming in Rome in Cinecittà, Claudia was terrified to be working with Hollywood stars. Not only was it her first American film but it was a comedy and her first English-speaking role. Once, while gathering herself in a quiet corner of the studio, her floor-length sari, which had been resting on an exposed electrical wire, caught fire. She shrieked, and if not for a quick-thinking set decorator who tackled her and extinguished the fire, she might have been seriously injured. It was a close call for Claudia and a reminder to all that a film set can be a dangerous place indeed.

As for Blake Edwards, he had short hair and big ears that were dwarfed by the thick, oversized dark glasses he frequently wore. And he was as dark as he was humorous, such was the spinning yin and yang that powered the engine of his comedy. In his hotel suite one night, he lit a joint. A small group of us had gathered for a nightcap, and the presence of marijuana was a novelty to me. I'd scarcely heard of it and certainly had never seen or smoked it.

When I said as much, Blake insisted I take a hit.

"What does it feel like?" I asked nervously as he held the smoldering cylinder out to me between his thumb and index finger.

He considered the question carefully for a long time.

Then, in a gravely serious voice, he said, "Like little leaves wrapped tightly in paper."

In her most challenging scene, Claudia is drunk and lounging sensually atop a tiger skin rug. Because it's in English and because the scene is a full six minutes long, she was worried about being able to pull off a convincing balance of comedy and inebriation. After rehearsing, Blake could feel her anxiety and, under the pretense of needing time to rearrange the lights, he sent her to lie down in a small room where he'd instructed assistants to light up their joints. Claudia, who was not with us in Blake's suite and had no experience of marijuana, did as she was told. When she emerged from the hotboxed room, her nerves were gone and, sure enough, her performance was pitch perfect.

As always happens, the end of production dispelled the heightened reality of bright lights and fancy sets. The intensity of camaraderie and collaborative focus was dispersed, and in comparison, the ordinariness of normal life felt drained of color. In the quiet of the recovery that followed, I went to Claudia and told her that I'd accepted a position with Alain and that I'd be moving to Paris.

I kissed her on each cheek and thanked her for the time we'd had together. When we first met, she'd been so full of potential, and now that potential had been realized. I was grateful to have traveled beside her on her remarkable ascent, and even if our paths now diverged, I knew we would remain connected by movies that would outlive us by generations.

Much more difficult was saying goodbye to the d'Amicos. With Masolino, our breakup was still raw. There was no anger, but neither was there reconciliation. That, I hoped, would change with time. But between his sisters and me, the emotional terrain was uncomplicated. We'd become family, and as we hugged goodbye, I knew that was one thing that would never change.

I found Suso watering plants on the upstairs terrace. Surrounded by the cascading terra-cotta tiles of Rome's rooftops, the terrace was a garden oasis. We sat together on a little bench shaded from the afternoon sun. We exchanged pleasantries and bits of industry gossip, and soon it was time for me to leave for the station.

"Do you have a place to stay?"

"I have a room."

"And money? Do you have enough?"

"I think so," I said.

She squeezed my hand, and as I responded in kind, I could feel that there was still a bond between us.

Turning to me, she said, "Paris is not like Rome, you know. There you can get lost. I mean, in the sense of the soul."

"I won't get lost," I said.

"Well, *cara* Carolina, we are here. We are still your family."

I would have been satisfied just to remain in relationship with Suso, just for this to not be the last time I saw her. And so her words touched me and have stayed with me, because it's true what they say: once accepted into an Italian family, it is forever.

Fifteen

Nights alone in a new place are pregnant with menace. I'd arrived in Paris without incident but also without notice. There'd been no one to meet me at the airport, no friend and no family. And now, alone in bed in my room in my run-down hotel on the neglected Left Bank, the decision to leave my life in Rome seemed hasty. I worried that my past would overshadow my future, that too much lay behind and too little lay ahead.

With a shared bathroom upstairs and a shared telephone downstairs, my dilapidated hotel—the Hôtel de la Tournelle—was occupied by an eclectic assortment of people with nothing in common except for a dream of one day living somewhere nicer. Still, I had a room of my own. It overlooked the Seine, which slid down the far side of the Quai de la Tournelle, and if I leaned out of the window far enough, I could see Notre Dame.

After settling in, I'd gone out to explore. Graffiti and litter seemed to be the defining characteristics of the neighborhood, but there were also shops and cafés. Crossing the Pont de la Tournelle, I'd looked up at the spire-like statue of Saint Genevieve, the city's patron saint, staring east to ward off invaders. Then, so that I wouldn't lose time looking for it on my first day of work, I found the Saint-Paul metro station, from which I would catch the train to Alain's *hotel particulier*.

Marianne Frey, who handled press for Claudia, met me at a nearby sidewalk café. Apart from Alain, she was the only friend I had in Paris, and I was grateful for her company. How different Paris was from Rome. Instead of cascading terra-cotta tiles, the city's rooftops were zinc, each a dark shade of gray. And the buildings, encircling city block after city block as if without end, were ivory and cream colored. Mostly, I paid attention to the women my age, who had an air of independence about them. Different from Rome, there was variety in their wardrobe and shoes, and there was something chic about the result, as if fashion was both a common interest and a collective responsibility.

Over the weeks that followed, I eased into Parisian life and into the always-fascinating world of Alain Delon. His parents had divorced when he was four, and he'd been placed in a foster home. This proved to be a primal wound from which he'd never recovered. Expelled from multiple boarding schools, he ran away at age fourteen, enlisted in the military at age seventeen, and, after three years—almost a year of it spent in military prison for unruly behavior—was dishonorably discharged. But then he was cast in *Send a Woman When the Devil Fails* and, shortly after, in *Purple Noon*, an adaptation of Patricia Highsmith's *The Talented Mr. Ripley*, which rocketed him to a dizzying level of fame.

Alain had then fallen in love with Romy but, at least for him, these two things, love and fame, were irreconcilable. He was nothing if not extreme, which meant that the fullest expression of fame prevented the fullest expression of love, and the fullest expression of love prevented the fullest expression of fame. Wanting to belong fully to all people as well as to only one person, his engagement with Romy had stretched into a three-year limbo that, even when I arrived in Paris, had no end in sight. They were known as "the eternal fiancés"—a charming enough moniker, but one that humiliated Romy.

I, meanwhile, was happy to not be in a relationship. Marianne had welcomed me into her circle of friends, a mix of journalists and photographers, artists and filmmakers, and we'd go to the Cinémathèque Française and to the cinemas on Champs-Élysées where films were played in their original language. After, we'd have animated, wine-fueled conversations about movies finally being made by and for our generation; movies that centered oppression and injustice, class and race; movies that pushed back against the era's preoccupation with violence and its puritanical aversion to sexuality.

At the center of this conversation was the French New Wave, a movement that rejected convention by reimagining cinema not as a product for mass consumption but as a vessel for personal expression. These filmmakers, many of them film critics who wrote for the magazine *Cahiers du Cinéma*, had been deprived of American films during the Nazi occupation of France. With the subsequent return of Hollywood films after the war, they (along with the Left Bank, a sister group of filmmakers headquartered across the Seine) grew increasingly discontent with French cinema. In comparison to the films of Alfred Hitchcock or Orson Welles, which they viewed as works authored by individuals with a singular vision, they saw French cinema as tepid and unimaginative, formulaic adaptations of classic literature.

François Truffaut, one of the movement's leaders, wrote a scathing critique of the Cannes Film Festival and was banned from attending it in 1958. He then made his first film, *The 400 Blows*, which would not only be invited to Cannes the very next year but would also win him the award for best director. This reversal from pariah to cause célèbre inspired a wave of new filmmakers and led to a bonanza of new films, among them *Breathless* and *Cleo from 5 to 7*. Intimate and documentary-like in their use of handheld camera shots, spontaneous cinematography, and experimental editing, these films represented a subversion of ideas, form, and content unlike anything cinema had yet experienced.

Every now and then, I'd see these filmmakers at parties or screenings: Agnes Varda with her dark bangs and her slim, Joan-of-Arc figure on the arm of her husband, director Jacques Demy. Or Jeanne Moreau, or Jean-Luc Godard, with his dark glasses and dimpled chin. They weren't celebrities in the way that Alain and Romy were celebrities, but they were charismatic and influential, fashionable both intellectually and artistically, and they, along with their films, informed the social circles in which I'd found myself.

The ice beneath Alain's engagement to Romy was growing thinner rather than thicker, and as Romy and I grew closer, I was reminded that Luchino Visconti, of all people, had played an important role in their relationship. Alain, Romy explained to me, had introduced her to Visconti. He'd developed tremendous affection for both of them, and in fact, Romy credited Visconti for much of her growth as an actor. After introducing her to Coco Chanel, the deity of French fashion, who attended to Romy's public image, Visconti cast her in his next play. It was over the course of his rigorous rehearsals that she'd transformed from a starlet into a confident and serious actor.

"Luchino says Alain and I both have Rembrandt's *V*," Romy said to me one day as we went through her Chanel wardrobe. She'd been cast in her first Hollywood film and was preparing for an extended stay in California.

"What is that?" I asked.

"Rembrandt's *V*? It's this, between the eyebrows," she said, tracing a line from one brow down to the bridge of her nose and then up to the other brow. "Luchino says Rembrandt used it in his paintings."

It was Romy's vulnerability that attracted me to her. She was someone who knew just how deeply she could be hurt and who was therefore standoffish with most people. Maybe that came from being a woman who'd been in the public spotlight since childhood. And maybe it was also why she seemed to like having me around. A counterpoint to public scrutiny, I was another woman in the house, one who wasn't a rival.

From time to time, I'd go with her to one of the fashion houses, Chanel or Dior, and she'd tell me about growing up in a family of actors. Her parents had owned a house in the Bavarian highlands with a view of Berghof, the estate belonging to Adolf Hitler where he'd dictated the second volume of *Mein Kampf.* As a girl, she'd watched him skulking about the property. After the war, she and her mother had appeared in German films together, but she soon outshone her mother and was cast in the *Sissi* trilogy, nostalgic movies about Empress Elisabeth of Austria. Those films endeared her to the industry and to the public, but she aspired to more ambitious roles and eventually came to bitterly resent being so aggressively typecast.

On the set of *Christine*, Romy met Alain and chose to leave Germany forever, publicly declaring that she no longer had any nationality. At this, the German press turned vicious. Because in choosing Paris, she was not only choosing Alain; she was choosing France. It was a betrayal that Germany would not soon forget.

Except that, now, Alain no longer seemed interested in marriage. Romy had bet everything on him and could do nothing but simmer in humiliation as the press endlessly speculated about Alain's relationship to the women and men with whom he was photographed.

Her fears were not unfounded. Soon after Romy left for Hollywood, Alain brought a new woman—Nathalie—to the office. I was offended on Romy's behalf. I couldn't believe Alain would do this. When Nathalie came down and sat beside me, I made a point of not looking up at her.

"What's she like?" Nathalie asked.

The innocence in her voice wrong-footed me, and I raised my eyes to hers. They were ferociously green eyes, and she had Alain's same marble-chiseled face, his same feline movements.

"What's who like?" I asked, trying to hold on to my anger.

"Romy. I know she's beautiful, but what is she like?"

There was nothing conniving in Nathalie's face, nothing territorial or mean spirited. It was as if she were asking as a fan, as if there was nothing at all untoward about the triangle she'd fashioned out of Romy and Alain's engagement.

In spite of myself, I became friends with Nathalie. From Casablanca, in Morocco, she'd always dreamed of making it big in Paris. But she'd wound up pregnant at seventeen and had been forced to marry the father, a well-to-do French officer who despised her ambitions and her outgoing nature. When Nathalie refused the role of obedient house-wife, he filed for divorce, took custody of their daughter, and had himself transferred to Germany.

"I feel for her," I said to Marianne. "I can't help it."

We were out at a party, and I was confiding in her that I suspected that the saga of Alain, Romy, and Nathalie had only just begun.

"What about Romy?" asked Marianne.

"I feel for her, too, of course."

"And Alain?"

"Yes, I also feel for him."

Marianne shook her head with a smile.

"*Viens avec moi*," she said, putting her arm in mine. "Come with me, I want to introduce you."

I followed Marianne across the room and was startled to find myself shaking the hand of François Truffaut and then of Louis Malle, a filmmaker who was not strictly associated with the French New Wave but who was nonetheless a leading figure in the new generation of filmmakers. François was short and attractive but, in contrast to Louis, who was handsome with a calm demeanor, he seemed skittish and uncomfortable.

Marianne explained that I'd recently moved from Rome where I'd been working in the Italian film industry. At this, both filmmakers grew animated. Though shy, when it came to film, François could talk anyone into the ground. He recounted how he'd apprenticed with Roberto Rossellini and underscored in detail the considerable influence the Italian director had had on him. Malle joined in and they explained that much of the French New Wave was grounded in Italian neorealism.

"Without one, the other doesn't happen," said Truffaut.

As the evening went on, the conversation shifted from Fellini and Visconti to Hollywood. Expecting them to criticize American films for their bloated budgets and picture-ready stars, I was surprised to learn that they were big fans of directors like Howard Hawks and Alfred Hitchcock, and that their knowledge of early Hollywood was encyclopedic.

Afterward, as Marianne and I walked to the metro, I was in a good mood, high on the way that cinema broke down borders and turned strangers into friends.

"Interesting things are happening in Paris," Marianne said with a smile. "You'll be happy here, Caroline."

Sixteen

B ut the Paris of the French New Wave was not the Paris of Alain Delon. Stylish and charismatic, Alain's life was filled with fast cars and enigmatic characters. In fact, it isn't an exaggeration to say that his life very nearly resembled an Alain Delon film. *Le Samouraï* maybe, or *Le Cercle Rouge*. Fascinated by nightlife and by society's underbelly, he befriended gangsters from Corsica and Yugoslavia, assembled an entourage of intimidating bodyguards, and had a genuine love of the alcohol-fueled late-night hours. But he was also smart, with a sense of humor, and he took art as seriously as anyone I have known.

The result was a layer of gloss, a sense that Alain was at the center of something in the culture. An attitude maybe, or an aesthetic. This Alain was different from the fun-loving Alain I'd met on *The Leopard*, the one to whom I'd taught the Twist. Here in Paris, he was *Delon*, famous and aloof. But, ambivalent about the larger-than-life image projected onto him, he was locked in an antagonistic relationship with the public.

Ivan, one of Alain's bodyguards, thought it amusing to hang around the office and pester me for a date. With a thick neck and big hands, he was rugby-player large and always wore the same black leather jacket and the same silver chain. I'd declined Ivan's proposals so many times that, so as to rob him of the ability to pester me into the future, I finally capitulated.

"If I go," I said with an edge, "it's as a friend, *d'accord*?"

"Yes, of course," he said in an accent from somewhere in Eastern Europe. "That is all I ask."

I don't know why Alain kept Ivan around, but there was a lot about Alain I didn't know. I'd learned some things about celebrity. The way there is a space between the person and the persona. The way it took effort and sometimes courage for one to embody the other. Because of this, the excesses and eccentricities that so often accompany celebrity have never bothered me. It isn't my place to judge, and I don't envy the job of maintaining a relationship with the public. Fans have only to lose interest and the relationship is off. So, at least in my view, it's the fans who create the star as much as the star who creates the fans. They give and withhold their attention, and the star quickly learns what is expected.

And what the public expected of Alain, Alain was happy to deliver. To be the bad boy, the breaker of rules and the defier of convention. It was a quality that came as naturally to Nathalie as to Alain. Sometimes, if Alain was traveling, Nathalie would take me along to Castel or to Chez Régine, which was owned by "Queen of the Night" Régine Zylberberg and which was the de facto capital of Parisian, and maybe European, nightlife.

Other times, I'd go with Alain and Nathalie to Tancrou, to the country house where Alain kept his cars, guns, and dogs, all of which he adored in equal measure. And there, away from everything, the old Alain, the Alain from *The Leopard*, would emerge. He'd tell stories and play practical jokes, and his eyes would be a little brighter, his smile a little more vulnerable.

It happened once that he and I were driving back from Tancrou alone in his convertible. Alain alone is a special thing. He wants to know you and he wants to solve your problems. Night was falling and he was asking me about Uncle Goat, my family, and race relations in North Carolina. In my upbringing, he saw adventure, and I knew he was imagining how he would fare with a life of horses and Southern norms. Suddenly, the traffic began to slow. Ahead of us, a police checkpoint was stopping and searching cars. There was an immediate change in Alain's energy. I kept talking, but some silences are not like others, and I realized he was no longer listening.

Then, from under his seat, he pulled out a pistol and thrust it into my open bag.

"You don't mind, do you?" he asked rhetorically. "They won't search you."

Indeed, we were waved through the checkpoint. When we were out of sight of the police, I took the pistol out and held it in my open palm. Through the corner of my eye, I saw him steal a glance at me. As a memory, it isn't much. But I remember the weight of the gun, the texture of the grip. And I remember wondering why Alain kept a gun in his car. I never knew. Still, for me, it was a moment of intense intimacy.

But just as Alain appeared to have lost interest in marriage, it felt like he'd also lost interest in the work I'd come to Paris to do. The thing with Nathalie was exciting and new, and Romy would soon be returning from America. As it was, his unsettled personal life seemed to take priority over the English-speaking roles I flagged for him. Which was fine. But I needed more; I needed work to which I could apply my full self.

In a decision that sealed the fate of his engagement, Alain took Nathalie with him to Spain for production of *The Black Tulip*. When pictures of them together began to appear in the press, it became evident that he'd chosen Nathalie over Romy. A wild spirit from the provinces over a princess of the silver screen.

Romy returned while they were away. To my surprise, she was calm, a vision of serenity. Calling me up to the apartment, she showed me what Alain had left for her: a dozen yellow roses and a note breaking off their engagement.

She looked at me for a long time, tears wetting her eyes.

"There's nothing to hold on to, is there?" she said.

I could only think of clichés—family, art, love—but they all felt like stale platitudes. I hugged her and she rested her head on my shoulder for a moment. When she stepped away, she held her gaze high, and the moisture was gone from her eyes. Before Alain returned, she had packed her things and moved out.

Little changed when Alain returned. I continued to feel underchallenged. The stallion of Alain's celebrity continued to gallop him around this way and that. The gloss faded from his relationship with Nathalie and they were soon fighting. With everything going on, my role in the company was getting lost. I loved Paris, its beauty and its energy. Marianne had become a close friend, as had Louis Malle and his brother Vincent. There were also weekends in Normandy with journalist friends from *Paris Match* and *Jours de France*, but none of it took away the fact that something was missing.

On top of this, there was Ivan. After I'd begrudgingly agreed to a date, I met him at a restaurant near the office and tried to make the best of it. Conversation was uninteresting but, in the name of civility, I admitted to an interest in art. This was true. Since buying the three Sicilian glass paintings in Palermo, I'd resolved that, resources permitting, I would do what I could to add to my little collection.

"Are you an artist?" Ivan asked.

"Me? No," I said, laughing. "But I like art very much."

"What kind of art do you like?"

"Art that results from life," I said. "What people call 'primitive art.'"

I told him about the pieces I'd bought in Palermo, about how meaningful it had been to purchase and own them.

"I understand this," Ivan said thoughtfully, adding, "My mother made art."

"Really?"

He nodded.

"She only worked in the home and never showed anyone. At night she sat at the table with pencil and paper. She's dead now, but I kept her drawings."

"I'm sorry to hear that."

"It was a long time ago. It's okay."

The check came and I insisted on paying my share, but he overruled me.

"Can I show you?" he asked.

"Show me what?"

"My mother's drawings. I want to know if you think they are good. Maybe you keep one."

"I should go home," I said.

"No, Caroline, it's still early," he pleaded. "Please. It will mean so much."

He was sweeter than I'd anticipated, and the fact was that I didn't have anything else to do. Reluctantly, I agreed. At his flat, he dug in his pocket for his key and opened the door. Out of some instinct, I hesitated. But then I entered, and Ivan followed behind me. Then I remember turning, and I remember wondering why he was locking the door. And I knew, then, that he wasn't locking people out but rather was locking me in.

"What?" he said, laughing as he took my wrist in his enormous hand.

"Ivan—"

He pulled me to him and wrapped both of his arms around me. I shouted for him to let go of me, but he pushed me onto the couch so that I was pinned beneath him. I kept shouting, begging for him to stop, to get off me. I pounded at him with my fists but there was no air in my lungs. Panic overwhelmed me, and I could not believe that what was happening was happening. One fist gripped my hair and the other my wrists as he forced himself into me. No amount of protest or struggle mattered. His breathing intensified and his sweat dripped onto me, and when he was finished, he rolled off me.

He stood up and said something that was supposed to sound friendly, but my ears were ringing, and my head was spinning. Stunned, I lay on the couch a moment longer, and then I stood, arranged my underwear and my skirt, and left.

When I walked onto the street, gone from the world was the quality of *more*. The dam that separated life and art had returned. The streets were not steeped in history or in art. They were just streets, wholly indifferent. To meaning. To beauty. To anything at all.

Seventeen

Trauma to the body is a scalpel that slices open the cadaver of human nature. It cleaves the sternum of thought, cracks apart the thoracic cage of values, and disembowels the contents within. Out come civility, intelligence, and love. They are removed without ceremony and tossed onto the garbage heap of human concepts: history, identity, morality.

In a trance, I walked quickly from Ivan's flat. In the people I passed, I didn't see people. Rather I saw nothing, only shapes and colors and sizes. To separate out anything, to apply thought to any of it, would be to create distinction, to assign identity. The whole world was like this—a collage of shapes, colors, and sizes. All of it connected, nothing in it separate. If I could only maintain this state, if only I could preserve the valuelessness of the universe, if only I could keep myself from deploying thought—then the thing would be kept at bay.

In the shower, the trance shattered, and what happened in Ivan's flat rushed at me. What I hated most of all was the connection rape suggested between Ivan and me, the line it drew from him to me. Because I didn't want Ivan to be *my* anything. Not my friend. Not my enemy. Not my tormentor. And I would rather die than be *his* anything. His friend. His acquaintance. His—the thought of the word turned my blood cold—victim. No. It wasn't possible. I would never be that. Not for Ivan and not for anyone.

But unmistakable in the revolting aftertaste of rape is the overpowering flavor of guilt. Were Ivan summarily executed in front of me, I would still have felt that the fault was mine, that the whole thing would never have happened if only I'd dressed differently or behaved differently. I chose not to tell Alain, and I didn't feel like I could tell anyone else without it being pointed out to me, either by a friend or by a police officer, that I really should not have gone out with a thug like Ivan, and I really should not have gone home with him. Didn't I know any better?

I became curt, even with my friends. Or, more accurately, especially with my friends. I remember standing with Louis Malle a week later, looking at the *Lawrence of Arabia* poster outside the Champs-Élysées theater. On the poster, Peter O'Toole brandishes a saber as he races across the sand dunes of the Sahara atop a noble-looking camel. Behind him, explosions litter the desert landscape, a biplane hovers menacingly in the distance, and hundreds of armed horseback riders, all of them pursuing, or perhaps following, O'Toole's Lawrence, fan out in the background.

What an absurdly masculine fantasy, I thought.

"Are there no women in it?" I asked.

"None," said Louis.

"None, like only a few?"

"No, none meaning none at all. *Pas de femmes.*"

"But it has a cast of hundreds."

"If not thousands. It's a lot of men."

Louis was then finishing up *Le Feu Follet*, a devastating portrait of an alcoholic and suicidal writer that, though not usually included among his major works—films like *Au Revoir Les Enfants, Pretty Baby,* and *Atlantic City*—is a remarkable accomplishment. I hadn't seen it at the time, but I knew from his earlier work that women and feminine arche-types were a central focus of his films. His second feature, *The Lovers,* about a young mother who, after a night of passion, absconds with a man she just met, had been an international sensation. Banned in several states, it was at the center of the landmark US Supreme Court case in which the definition of obscenity was furiously debated and in which Justice Potter Stewart had famously concluded, "I know it when I see it."

As we walked, Louis talked about the actresses he was excited about: Jeanne Moreau, Brigitte Bardot, Anna Karina. His sentiment was that movies needed more women in them. It was a reasonable enough thing to say, but I wasn't charmed by the thought of women in the hands of men, even in the case of male directors.

"For what?" I snapped. "To look at? To see them groped?"

"I mean," he said, struggling to defend a sentiment that so obviously didn't need defending, "I mean that man defines woman and woman defines man. Back and forth like that."

"You think woman is the opposite of man," I said tersely. "That's the problem."

I walked a few steps ahead only to feel Louis slip his hand into my arm.

"*Mais* Caroline, *qu'est-ce qu'il y a?* What's wrong?"

We found something to eat, and I apologized. He asked me why I was on edge, and I told him that I was feeling stuck professionally, which was true.

"You're unhappy?" he asked.

"Not unhappy," I said with a shrug. "I'm just . . ."

"In need of change?" he offered.

"*Oui,*" I said. "In need of change."

A few days later, Marianne told me that she'd learned of an actor who was looking for a secretary.

"Is he French?"

She shook her head.

"English?"

She shook her head again.

"Marianne, I can't go back to Italy right now."

"He's not Italian."

"Who is it?" I begged.

"Omar Sharif."

"Who?"

"Sheik Ali," Marianne said. "From *Lawrence of Arabia*."

How unexpected. My first reaction was positive. Omar's appearance in the film—as a silhouetted figure on horseback who appears on the horizon and who gradually draws nearer and nearer until he is towering over a bedraggled Peter O'Toole—was being lauded as one of cinema's great character introductions. But I also had reservations. Omar was popular across the Arab world, but there was no way of knowing if a career awaited him in cinema beyond that region. If it came to it, was I willing to leave Paris? Leave Europe? Could I see myself living in Cairo?

Marianne was confident it would be a good fit, and she set up an interview. I was to meet him in the Egyptian Room in the Louvre where he was being photographed by *Life* magazine.

On my lunch break, I went to the Louvre, but when I arrived at the Egyptian Room, it was empty. Unsure what to do, I wandered among the sphinxes and sarcophagi for twenty minutes before concluding that there'd been a mistake. Maybe he'd been held up or maybe I'd gotten the time wrong. Either way, I needed to get back to the office, and so I left.

Then, as I walked down the Louvre's long hallway, I saw an entourage of people—including Milton Greene, the famous photographer, and Nadine Puissesseau, *Life*'s Paris editor—surrounding Omar. With short, dark hair and enormous, brown eyes, he wore a loose-knit ivory sweater that complemented his skin and framed his brilliant smile. He was impossibly attractive. Unprepared for the sheer force of his charisma, I put my head down and hurried past them to the exit.

Out on the street, Marianne was getting out of her car.

"How did it go?" she asked. "Did you like him?"

"I can't do it, Marianne."

"What do you mean?"

"I can't work for him."

"Of course you can, Caroline. What are you saying?"

"I can't," I said with total sincerity. "He's too good-looking. There's no way I can work for him."

Marianne laughed and marched me back into the museum where I shook Omar's hand. Milton and Nadine soon left, and Omar, Marianne, and I went out for lunch. A connection came easily, and by the end of the meal, he'd offered me a job at triple my current salary—more than I thought possible, or even decent.

The only catch was that Omar would be out of the country for a few months on personal business. I was eager to be away from Ivan, though, and rather than wait for Omar to return, I resigned from my position with Alain. It was a friendly departure. Both Alain and Georges offered to rehire me if it didn't work out with Omar, and I knew that I'd continue to be in touch with both of them and, of course, with Nathalie.

Through Marianne, I took a job as the unit publicist on *The Train*, a sprawling coproduction starring Burt Lancaster and directed by Arthur Penn—director of *The Miracle Worker* and, later, of *Bonnie and Clyde*—about French railroad workers who save a collection of art during the Nazi occupation. Because of my work with Claudia, I was comfortable handling the media and found that publicity work came to me easily.

But that was before Burt Lancaster, unhappy with Penn's contemplative approach to the material, insisted that he be replaced. Persuaded by Burt, the producers of *The Train* hired John Frankenheimer, director of *Birdman of Alcatraz* and *The Manchurian Candidate,* without telling Penn he'd been replaced. This was in violation of the rules of the Directors Guild of America, which stated that a director cannot be hired until their predecessor is fired. Confusion broke out in the press and on set, and the production was ultimately shut down, the script rewritten, and the budget increased. The film is remembered by many as the last big action movie shot in black and white and, to me, as my very first job as a publicist.

In November of 1963, Omar, who still hadn't returned to Paris, asked me to go to London to work with his childhood friend, who was developing a script about Mustafa Atatürk, founder of modern Turkey. I was happy for an excuse to see Penny and eager to meet her new husband, Michael Wigram. But, while there, President Kennedy was assassinated. The whole world was shaken to its core. That the president of the United States of America—a country that, after the chaos and brutality of World War II, had emerged as a stabilizing global power—had been assassinated reopened fresh wounds and resurrected memories of the turmoil that accompanies political uncertainty.

In London and across Europe, there was crying in the streets. Entertainment houses closed, massive vigils were held, and thousands of people attended special church services. When I called home, my mother described the outpouring of grief throughout Madison. But to my chagrin, Telstar-England's broadcasts included reports of parties and celebrations in the South. Football games were canceled everywhere, but not in parts of the South. Even though everyone I knew expressed their condolences to me as if Kennedy's death had been a personal loss, this filled me with shame.

The endless news broadcasts and the chilling, oversized headlines— KENNEDY ASSASSINATED—seemed to promise that the decade's violence and volatility were just beginning. I was happy to receive word, then, that Omar was back in Paris and that I could begin my work with him. Some structure and routine, I thought, would restore a sense of order. I went to meet him at his Avenue Foch apartment early one morning. Falling back on my Southern manners, I stopped at a *marché* for a bouquet of daffodils.

I then knocked on the door and waited. When there was still no response, I knocked again. At long last the door opened. There, in front of me, was a beautiful dark-haired woman in a bathrobe. I assumed this was Omar's wife, Faten Hamama, the famous Egyptian actor, and I greeted her politely and presented the daffodils.

Taking them from me, she tossed them on a nearby chair.

"Hi. I'm Sue Barton," she announced in perfect California English. "Come in, Carolyn."

Eighteen

Only some dreamers have dreams. For the rest of us, dreams are headlights that blind and paralyze. What we have, instead, is dreaming itself. As a girl, summers gifted me big empty days, vast expanses of time that I wiled away by turning the tobacco fields around Madison into jungles and moonscapes, the horses I rode into dolphins and dragons. None of it was directional; none of it built up to some greater objective or purpose. That was never my way of dreaming.

For me, to dream was to blur the possible and the impossible, the real and the surreal. Childhood lends itself to this abstraction, but it isn't long before the sharp knives of adolescence and education slice the world into smaller and smaller pieces: land and sea, plant and animal, male and female, Black and white—on and on until the individual, in all her minute specificity, is separated out from the cosmos.

But, every now and then, all of this comes undone. Once, while crossing the Atlantic, I ventured up onto the ship's deck late at night.

Without wind or the moon or any human-made light, there was no distinction between the darkness of the water and the darkness of the sky; each blended into the other. I knew in my mind that below was water and above was sky, but in my body, there was no difference. I'd experienced this oneness at other times too—with Masolino, with Claudia—but now, as my work with Omar got underway in earnest, I encountered it more frequently.

Our first film together was Fred Zinnemann's *Behold a Pale Horse*, set during the brutal civil war in Spain that had installed Francisco Franco as the country's fascist dictator. Having directed films like *High Noon*, *From Here to Eternity*, and the adaptation of Robert Bolt's era-defining play *A Man for All Seasons*, Zinnemann, an Austrian-born filmmaker and a forefather of so-called Cinema of Resistance, was one of MGM's leading directors. He was also an enduring critic of the rise of fascism across Europe and so, prevented from filming *Behold a Pale Horse* on location in Spain, the film instead shot across the border in France.

But the surreal thing, for me, was that I found myself in the company of the film's stars, Gregory Peck and Anthony Quinn. Quinn had been in countless films, including Fellini's *La Strada*, and Peck had just won the best actor Oscar for his role as Atticus Finch in *To Kill a Mockingbird*. Both actors were household names, and I'd grown up watching them at our theater in Madison. Back then, I'd half believed I could escape through the screen. And now I'd done it; I'd made it to the other side.

How disorienting to sit with Anthony Quinn at lunch or share a joke with Gregory Peck between takes. But it was different for Omar, as these were his coworkers, flawed and human. Amusingly, he couldn't stand Anthony Quinn. They'd met on the set of *Lawrence* when David Lean, the director, had sent Omar to meet Quinn at the airport. Quinn was to play an Arab sheik, and Lean wanted him to spend as much time as he could with Omar in order to learn about Arab life and mannerisms. But when Omar brought a bouquet of flowers with him to the airport and presented them to Quinn, Quinn was scandalized. Ferociously macho, he was undone by the idea of receiving flowers from another man.

Their relationship only worsened. One possibility is that Quinn was threatened by Omar's rising celebrity and, naturally imposing but purposefully so on *Lawrence*, insisted on pushing Omar around in their shared scenes. Omar put up with this bullying for as long as he could, but when Lean failed to intervene, Omar placed a large rock on his mark and stepped onto it.

"Mr. Quinn," he said sharply, "you may be an international movie star, but I have starred in many Egyptian films, and one thing I know about is *upstaging*."

Omar was then under a contract to producer Sam Spiegel not unlike the one Claudia was under to Cristaldi. Like her, Omar had no say over the roles he took. When production on *Behold a Pale Horse* wrapped, Spiegel sent us to London, where Omar was to appear in *The Yellow Rolls-Royce*. On that film, I met Rex Harrison and Ingrid Bergman, who rather awkwardly had a terrible time remembering her lines.

As much as I could, I spent my time with Penny. We'd both turned twenty-five that year, but our lives were beginning to go in very different directions. Where I'd ended my engagement in favor of independence, Penny had gotten married and given birth to a son, Lionel. He was already two, and not long before my arrival in London, she'd had a daughter, Sophie. Seeing Penny with two children was one of my first brushes with motherhood—not as a daughter but as a nonmother, as a woman who had not, or had not yet, chosen motherhood.

Upon returning home to Paris, I received word that Visconti was in town and wanted to meet with me and Omar. Naturally, we assumed Visconti was considering Omar for an upcoming role, and Omar was eager to make a good impression. But after a pleasant dinner, nothing seemed to come of it until I later received a letter from Suso explaining the real reason for Visconti's visit. She'd asked Visconti to invite us to dinner because she wanted his opinion of Omar. She was worried about me and wanted to make sure it was a good and safe environment. Though disappointing to Omar, it was a touching gesture to me and I made it a priority to maintain my relationship with Suso and the d'Amicos.

When Frances, my own mother, flew over to visit, I was elated. I'd written every week without fail, splurged on long-distance calls on special occasions, and had even returned home for short visits when finances allowed. Still, it was a treat to have my mom with me in Paris, and I was proud to show her around just as I'd done in New York and Rome.

She'd loved *Lawrence of Arabia,* and when I arranged for Omar to take us to dinner, he took her hand and ceremoniously kissed it.

"Mrs. Pfeiffer," he said, "how do you feel about your daughter working for an Arab?"

If Omar and I were a unique match, we nonetheless suited each other well. And, as the 1960s grew ever more volatile, the bond between us intensified. We were both foreigners and had only each other. Playing the Hollywood game wasn't as easy for him as it was for other actors, but I was proud of him and he was proud of me. When I told people that I worked for Omar Sharif, he'd correct me by saying that "I'm the actor Carolyn Pfeiffer works for."

Even though we had little in common, our lives overlapped completely. The least important details of Omar's job trumped the most important details of my life. And I loved it. I loved my discontinued romances and my ever-changing plans. I loved the extended stays in obscure places and the greetings I'd learned in a dozen languages. Most of all, I loved that Omar was loved everywhere and that I had a hand in satiating that hunger.

Soon sets, locations, festivals, and hotels began to merge into each other. Bellhops would meet our black limousine and would fuss over our luggage. Flashes of excitement would slip through the barricade of professional silence that had mobilized to greet us. As we entered the lobby, heads would turn. Mouths would whisper into ears. I'd walk confidently, pushing dark sunglasses onto my head and lowering my designer handbag onto the reception desk. I'd breeze through paperwork, get room keys, and go to the casino, where I'd find Omar looking over the gaming tables, planning his night.

In the elevator, his presence would halt conversations, but he was oblivious to this and would talk casually about an upcoming film or bridge tournament. Next we'd walk down carpeted hallways with overhead lights illuminating circles of drab floral carpet. His attention would be on the newspaper in his hand, and I'd talk about his scheduled appearances and press appointments. In his room, I'd tip the bellhop for our stay (Omar tipped both on arrival and on departure) and make sure he had everything he needed. Then I'd leave, and he'd nod absently, still studying his paper.

"Come to the tables with me, darling," he said at a festival in Sanremo on the Italian riviera.

"Not tonight, Omar."

"But I don't have anyone to talk to, and you always bring me luck."

Ten minutes later I was standing behind him at the baccarat table. The hours passed, but I'd failed in my role as talisman. He was tens of thousands of lira down. He bet aggressively and lost again. At that, I excused myself and left him to his negotiations with the gods of probability.

When I went down for breakfast the next morning, I was immediately aware of the hotel staff. They were buzzing with excitement, and I soon learned that Omar had had a tremendous night. He'd won hundreds of thousands, maybe millions—nobody was quite sure. I brought coffee to his suite and found him smiling, eager to send me down to collect his winnings. I'd never thought of money as something that takes up space, but millions of Italian lira was different. A brown paper bag was found, and I hurried across the lobby, an armful of cash in my arms.

Faten, Omar's wife, was a famous actor in Egypt, and she sometimes visited him in Paris. They had a son, and despite Omar's long absences, they seemed to make the marriage work. That said, Omar slept with more women than I could keep track of. Fans and waitresses, hotel maids and famous actresses. It didn't matter. His lovers would sometimes wake me in the dead of night, desperate to reach him. They'd sob and beg me to take up their cause. He tells a story of a woman ordering him to make love to her at gunpoint. Maybe that story is true; maybe it isn't. Personally, I believe it. On one occasion, an actress arrived at my door, her wrists cut open.

"You treat women so badly," I chided him one night at Chez Régine. "They're disposable to you."

"But they pursue me, Caroline," he insisted with a shake of his head. "What do you expect me to do?"

"It's not true that it's never you who makes the move."

"It is true," he argued. "Look. Do you see her?" He nodded at a young woman out with her date. "She made it clear thirty minutes ago that she wants me."

I watched the woman for several minutes but couldn't detect any sign of interest.

"You're wrong," I said. "She's on a date."

"Want to bet?"

"You know I don't bet."

"It's a good thing," he said. "Watch."

He then excused himself and went to the men's room. Sure enough, a moment later the woman left her date and slipped into the bathroom after him.

Omar's star was becoming one of the brightest in the cinematic sky, and the laws that govern ordinary people were losing their grip on him. Between womanizing and gambling, he was slaloming in and out of behavior that might be defined as addictive. What I can say is that he tried. He tried to find a center, a grounding weight substantial enough to offset the temptation. But the problem was that neither he nor I were tethered to any one place. We lived in hotels, and hotels, in their commitment to consistency, are also efficient dispensaries of predictability and loneliness. So what began as Omar's cultured and measured way to disrupt this monotony—a nice dinner and an hour at the tables—spiraled into increasingly ambitious excursions into hedonism.

If any of this should have diluted my affection for him, it didn't. Even when his promiscuity was at its most inconvenient, when his lovers threw themselves at my mercy and I was forced into the role of the sympathetic friend in the wee hours of the morning, I did so without judgment. And when his gambling left him broke, I was eager to lend him all I had. Because he was all I had. His life was my life and so were his debts and his dalliances. Anyway, we had the wind at our backs. With his next film, *Genghis Khan*, to shoot in Yugoslavia, Hollywood had finally cast him in a lead role, and I knew that great things were headed our way.

Nineteen

The countryside surrounding Belgrade is gentle. The hills are covered with a tangle of forest interrupted here and there by crystalline lakes and picturesque villages. And, of course, by the majestic Danube, which begins in Germany and flows through ten countries before emptying into the Black Sea. It's joined by the Sava River in Belgrade, a proud city brought to its knees by World War II and its aftermath. Josip Broz Tito, the president of Yugoslavia, was systematically consolidating power, and an immense weight was being lowered onto the population. The people seemed hardened to the point of defeat, overcome by a resignation that, in comparison to Paris's uplifting energy, left me despondent.

Since dictatorships don't share democracy's stubborn preoccupation with consensus, resources can be mobilized quickly, decisions can be made efficiently, and warring factions can be obliged to work together productively. These qualities, combined with Yugoslavia's beautiful and diverse terrain and its inexpensive labor pool, meant that *Genghis Khan* was exactly the sort of movie that Hollywood could funnel through this production paradise.

Omar was extremely serious about his craft, and with *Genghis Khan,* sprawling in ambition and scope, he recognized the opportunity to ascend Hollywood's list of leading men. Yes, he'd once again been cast as an ethnic other, but with a cast including James Mason, Telly Savalas, and Françoise Dorléac, the film was a big investment for Columbia Pictures, and believing it had the potential to propel him more fully into the mainstream, Omar brought all of himself to the part. And because leading roles are unlike smaller supporting roles in the amount of time they require, all of Omar's time was taken up by Henry Levin, the film's director, and by the department heads—all of whom depended on him to carry the film.

This created a void in my life. Once production was underway, Omar didn't need me in the same way as he had on other sets. I'd been pin-balling from place to place, jumping from rock to rock, and the sudden lack of movement was jarring. Without social engagements to speak of or travel to organize or press to manage, there was less for me to do. I communicated with Omar's agent and business manager, managed his fan mail, got his clothes to the cleaner, and made sure he had everything he needed in the morning and on set, but the demand on his time by so many others meant that I had more time to myself.

I became friends with Françoise Dorléac, a blonde beauty with red lips and a delightful smile. A French Carole Lombard, perhaps. She was Catherine Deneuve's older sister, and she reminded me of a combination of Penny and Nathalie, humorous and kind but also impulsive and free-spirited. At the time, she was dating Jean-Pierre Cassel, but he'd stayed in Paris to be with his two-year-old son, Vincent (who would grow up to be an international star). It was nice to have a girlfriend on location, but she, too, had a demanding role that kept her busy.

Just when I'd resigned myself to months on end of dreary and lonely routine, I began to take notice of Ciga, a striking Serbian who worked in the production office. Tall and forlorn, he had eyes of bottomless sorrow, and they were the only things in all of Yugoslavia that captivated me. The first time I'd met him, he was distributing the call sheet for the following day. He'd handed me Omar's copy, and I took it from him without thinking and without looking. But he'd held onto it tightly so that it slipped from my grip. It could have been a mistake, but maybe he saw that I was rushing, that I was taking the call sheet from him without looking at him. Maybe he knew that if he gripped the paper tightly enough then I would have to look up at him. And maybe he knew that if I looked up at him then I would have to look into his eyes. And maybe he also knew that if I looked into his eyes then I would fall in love with him.

Receiving the call sheet from Ciga became the highlight of my day. He would hold it out to me, and I would look into his eyes to see how difficult he was going to make it for me to remove it from his grip. What I discovered was that if I smiled, he also smiled. And when that happened, the embers buried within his sorrow-filled eyes would glow with life. The more I smiled at him, the more he also smiled. And the more he smiled, the brighter the embers in his eyes became.

For a long time, there was only the battle for the call sheet. There were no words and no touching, and I knew his name only because it was on the call sheet and because the production coordinator sometimes shouted at him to do this and to do that.

One day, after leaving Ciga, Françoise pulled me into her room.

"Caroline, you can't tell anyone," she said, panic in her voice.

"Tell anyone what?"

"Do you promise?"

"Of course, I promise," I said, now worried about her. "What? What is it?"

"I think I'm pregnant."

Françoise was the lead actress, and her boyfriend, who had not visited set, was at home in Paris. If we didn't find a solution as soon as possible, the personal and professional consequences would be dire. She didn't want anyone to know, and so I found my way into the good graces of Lidija, a woman who washed dishes in the hotel's cafeteria. What we needed, Lidija explained, was mustard powder. A good soak in a mustard powder bath was guaranteed to induce a miscarriage.

Without a better idea, I set out by myself to find mustard powder. I went to a dozen different shops and markets but was only able to find mustard balls, ground mustard seeds mixed with horseradish and dried into a ball for preservation. Lidija assured me that this would work. Mustard balls were the next best thing and would have the same effect as mustard powder.

I drew a boiling hot bath and poured in two shopping bags full of mustard balls, breaking them apart and stirring them into the water.

"In you go," I said, sitting on the side of the tub.

"Okay, but you have to wait in the other room."

Françoise was extraordinarily shy but I didn't feel good about leaving her alone.

"Then you have to sing," I said.

"Why?"

"So I know you're okay. So I know you don't have a reaction."

She complied, and I sat with my back against the door as she sang French lullabies for twenty minutes. Alas, it turned out to be a false alarm and we never found out if mustard balls are an effective remedy.

But the next day, Ciga was anxious.

"You mustn't go around by yourself," he said. "*Please.*"

When he said this, two things occurred to me. The first was that Ciga genuinely cared about my safety. The second—on which I spent much more time imagining the possibilities—was that he'd missed me and had gone out of his way to find out where I'd been.

That Sunday, Ciga offered to show me around Belgrade. He'd borrowed a car, a white Yugo that was identical to the countless other white Yugos that filled the streets, and we drove past the Temple of Saint Sava and the glorious Cathedral of Saint Mark. At Belgrade Fortress, where the Sava and the Danube meet, we walked along the ancient walls to where we could overlook the city. As we stood there, he took my hand in his. How many people had stood where we were standing? Had seen what we were seeing? Had felt what we were feeling?

Ciga loved his city and he loved his country. He did his best to explain Yugoslavia to me. The six republics. Their history with the Germans, Austrians, and Hungarians. He told me about Nikola Tesla and about how the assassination of Archduke Franz Ferdinand in Sarajevo had ignited the First World War. He told me about how World War I had turned into World War II and about how, in the Cold War that followed, Tito had come to be president for life.

"He holds it together now, but everyone knows."

"Knows what?" I asked.

"That war is coming."

"You don't like Tito?"

"I don't like oppression. It builds and builds. And eventually . . ."—he opened a closed fist—a quiet explosion.

The sun was setting as we sped through the city's streets. The affections between us came easy. I let my hand touch his arm and slowly move up to the back of his neck. I rested my head on his shoulder, and it felt like a natural thing to do. When we stopped, we just stayed like that, my head on his shoulder.

His friends met us for dinner at a cafeteria-style restaurant, a sprawling space overrun by drunks. When I excused myself to go to the restroom, Ciga sent one of his friends with me. This, I realized, was to defend against the hopelessly intoxicated men. There were so many of them, and none of them seemed happy. Masculine energy, aggressive and lascivious, coursed through the room. To experience it was to experience something of the raw, male appetite, and I was grateful for a bodyguard.

Ciga's friends, all of them dissidents, came with us to his apartment. Through a tiny kitchen, we entered a tiny living room. On the couch, I sat next to Ciga and pulled his arm around me. There was beer and *šljivovica*, made from fermented plums, and very little English. I didn't mind. Ciga explained that, as a child, his father had been a ranking officer in the military before Tito came to power and that his family had owned the entire building. Then the communists had confiscated everything and had divided the building into tenements so small that nothing of value remained.

Ciga was a leader among his friends. He had that presence that some men have: it was to him that conversation was addressed, and it was his word that was final. I liked the weight of Ciga's arm around me. And I liked the male bonding, the sexual power of giving Ciga stature in the eyes of his peers.

When his friends left, I stayed. We stood opposite each other in his bedroom, and I let him undress me. My scarf. My jacket. My jeans. It was a feeling of being treasured, of being something that, to the other, is revered. I helped remove his clothes, and he lifted me against the wall. Sex is sometimes external, a focus on the other. But it can also be internal, to do with yourself, with trusting that you are desired and accepting that you are enough.

The next day, along with the call sheet, Ciga brought me flowers.

"You don't like them?" he asked.

"Of course I like them."

"If I knew you better, what would I give you if not flowers?"

"A memory," I said, smiling up at him.

It has always interested me the way that attraction manifests differently in different cultures. What I could do for Tony, back in New York, was model, engage the sense he had of himself as an artist. What I could do for Masolino was to be a student, to admire him and appreciate the legacy that had produced him. What I could do for Ciga was to try my hand at compassion, to be a soft landing in a cold and uncaring world.

We stole away from set whenever we could. We walked along the Danube, explored Knez Mihailova—Belgrade's answer to Via Veneto in

Rome—and visited Gardoš Tower, north of the city. Then, with a break in shooting, we left Belgrade and headed south. The sloping landscape around the city became increasingly striking until, an hour later, we were surrounded by the grandeur of towering blue hills and lush forest.

Ciga turned off the engine, and I followed him until we came to an overlook. Below us was a series of serpentine oxbows in the Uvac River so astonishing that they looked like a series of M's and W's written in nature's own cursive. We sat silently in the grass beside each other, and I found myself telling him about New York and Rome, about Paris and London.

He grew quiet and said, "I don't understand so much travel."

"What do you mean?"

"I mean—if you watch a leaf in a river, you learn a lot about the river, but you learn nothing about the leaf."

"I don't know," I said with a shrug. "I've always cared more about people than about places."

"But you are where you come from. It defines everything about you."

"Does it? To me, what matters is where you're going and how far you've come."

"Is one place any better than another?"

"I guess not," I said, "but if you're given the whole world, why settle for one small piece of it?"

"Because how else will you ever know who you are?"

"People," I said. "What if instead of one leaf in the river, there are two?"

He pulled me to him so we were facing each other, his legs under mine, our foreheads touching. We stayed like that, talking in quiet voices and feeling a current of energy flow between us.

I liked how a part of Belgrade Ciga was, how perfectly he belonged to it. Not that it was easy for him. Because of his politics, he was constantly harassed and beat up by the police and secret police and by opposing political groups. In this there was something scrappy about him, something deeply invested in the city and the country. And because I was so different in my orientation to the world, it created an intriguing tension between us. He endured the hostility and oppression of the society around him, and to be with him was to feel protected, insulated, safe. Life with Omar, life on the road, the moving, the jumping, was endless; as much as I loved it, I also loved the way Ciga was rooted. To flow with the current is one kind of pleasure. But to be so anchored and unflinching that the current must flow around you is quite another.

Over the weeks that followed, we drew closer still as we found an overlapping interest in art. If you knew where to look, and Ciga did, Belgrade produced art in abundance. There was art intended to sell—harmless cityscapes and the like—and art intended to speak. Of the latter, there were many shades: from the controversial and the subversive to the outright banned. Belgrade's Academy of Fine Arts, from which the artist Marina Abramović would soon graduate, was churning out a crop of politically engaged voices. Among this group was Radomir Damnjan, a painter who'd once pulled an unconscious Abramović from her own burning art installation, which she had designed as a metaphor for the smoke created by the older generation that the younger generation is forced to inhale.

Damnjan, who worked out of a tucked-away studio, was an acquaintance of Ciga. He would later become serious about performance art, and then minimalism and more abstract work. Today he is quite prominent, but back then he was still unformed, just beginning to push the boundaries of realism by using pale tones and oversimplified faces that, to me, captured a sense of hauntedness or frozenness. His work seemed to suggest a present that need not have been, a future that need not be. I purchased my two favorite paintings, which continue, even now, to shine their brightest when political tensions are at their darkest.

After work late one night, we walked to Ciga's flat. Belgrade at night is quiet. In daylight it is loud and it works hard, but then the darkness dissolves the buildings and nothing is left. The movie had almost wrapped, and the question of our future hung heavily over us. As we walked, I put my hand in his back pocket and he put his arm around my shoulder. When we arrived at his flat, we slipped into bed and fell asleep on our sides, stomach to stomach, his arm under my head.

When I awoke, we hadn't moved. He was still there, asleep, his stomach still touching mine, his arm still resting under my head. And I imagined us like this in the future, in Paris, in New York, anywhere at all. I wanted us to be like actors in a stage play where, between acts, one backdrop replaces another. Or like two leaves in a river that go wherever the current leads.

"Carolyn," he whispered.

"Yes," I said.

"Will you marry me?"

What no one knew on the final day of shooting, as Ciga handed me the call sheet for the very last time, was that I'd said yes. He'd asked me to stay with him, to be with him always, and I'd said yes. He had an uncle who worked as the night watchman at Napoleon's tomb in Paris. Through him, Ciga would find work. We would rent a little apartment on the Left Bank, and we would scrape together a life for ourselves. Like so many who begin their lives together with nothing but the love in their hearts, we would make it work. Somehow and somewhere, a future awaited us.

I had to tell Omar, but something in me didn't want to. Maybe I knew that the seductive illusions of life on set had gotten the better of me. Maybe I knew that I'd gone too far down a road and that my decisions would not make sense to anyone who had not accompanied me down that road. I don't know. I wanted Omar, with all of his infidelity and indiscriminate love, to care without caring, to be unquestioningly happy for me. After all, who was Omar to have an opinion about my personal life?

I waited until the last minute, until we were walking to the set for the last of his scenes, and then I said it casually, purposefully downplaying the gravity of the thing.

"No," snapped Omar. "You're not marrying him."

"Omar . . ."

"Where is he?"

Omar spun around and beelined for the production office. I ran after him and arrived just as he caught sight of Ciga. Though Ciga outweighed him by fifty pounds, Omar had no trouble barking Ciga into a corner.

"You won't marry her," said Omar viciously. "You can't."

Ciga looked at me, but I didn't know what to do or say.

"How will you provide for her?" he continued. "Tell me, my friend. How?"

Ciga gathered himself.

"I have language skills. I write well."

"You're going to teach Serbian in Paris, is that it? My friend, do you think there are people in Paris waiting for you to teach them Serbian?"

"I can report on what is taking place in this country. The West will want to know."

This was a dangerous thing to say in public, and as a crowd was gathering, even Omar knew he couldn't push the matter any further. I pulled Omar away and walked with him out of the office. Looking over my shoulder, I saw that Ciga's head was lowered, his confidence and certainty shattered.

Soon after this, Omar got a phone call that changed his life forever and, in ways I could never imagine, mine too. It was from David Lean, director of *Lawrence of Arabia,* who had, since *Lawrence,* worked to assemble an even grander film. Tapped to direct by Carlo Ponti, the Italian producer who'd discovered and then married Sophia Loren, the film was to be colossal in ambition and scope, an all-star production with no expenses spared that was meticulously tailored to sweep the

Academy Awards. The title: *Doctor Zhivago*. It was to be one of the biggest films ever made, and David Lean's first call had been to Omar to offer him the title role.

It was a turbo boost leveling Omar up from movie star to superstar. There would be no more typecasting, no more exoticism, no more othering. He would never again have to play a barbarian or a sheik or someone of ambiguous ancestry. He, Omar Sharif, had been handed the most coveted role in Hollywood, the most coveted role in the whole wide world.

Excitedly, Omar told me he wanted us to go to Cairo to visit his family before we settled in Spain, where *Zhivago* was to shoot. I was elated. But as I thought about it, something sober occurred to me. I'd fly to Paris. Then from Paris to Cairo. From Cairo to Spain. And, from Spain, where? I realized it would always be like this: me traveling while Ciga stayed behind. I would be asking him to give up everything for me, and I would be unable to give him the one thing he wanted out of our relationship: my presence.

Ciga and I ate dinner that night at a restaurant close to his flat. As I told him about *Zhivago* and about Egypt, I tried to paint a picture in which we were together and happy.

"It's a big movie, Ciga. Bigger by far than *Genghis Khan*."

"Where will it shoot? Russia?"

"In Spain. The Soviets banned the book."

"How long will it take?"

"I think a long time. Maybe a year."

He was quiet and I touched his foot with mine under the table.

"More travel," he sighed.

"Yes, but together," I said. "I'll ask Omar to make sure they hire you."

"And after that?"

"What do you mean?"

"After that, what?"

"Ciga, what do you mean? After that there will be something else."

"We'll go where you go, and I'll work on the movies you work on."

"Soon you'll have your own friends, your own job, your own everything."

"And then you'll go, and I'll stay."

We were both quiet. As the silence grew longer, I became aware of clinking cutlery, of chatter, of traffic, and of the world closing in around us, cocooning us within a problem of culture, of geography, and of the unfavorable odds that hound those who would cross boundaries and endeavor to span worlds. That night, our lovemaking lacked direction. We both knew it was no use and so we abandoned the effort. Me because I couldn't figure out if someone who truly loved me would pull back so forcefully. And him because he couldn't figure out if someone who truly loved him would pull forward so forcefully. We were together in loneliness, together in futility, but in the world that mattered, we were a galaxy apart.

The next morning, we sat side by side on the bed. We were out of time. I didn't look at him because I couldn't face the abrupt capitulation of our grand ambitions, and I couldn't face the reality that, sometimes, not even love is enough.

"Did we make a mistake, Ciga?"

He lowered his gaze.

Every relationship is surrounded by a border so raw and so fragile that it is rarely approached. Whatever happens, there is always the security of that border. But sometimes you take a wrong turn, or you say the wrong thing, and you find yourselves there. And you both realize that a relationship is nothing at all; it's an orientation, a shared idea, and nothing more. How fragile. How tenuous. And so you stand there together electrified, looking at each other, each of you wondering what the other will do.

The silence went on, and it was confirmation that the right thing, the correct thing, was for him to stay and for me to go, for him to live his life and for me to live mine. It was, in its truest sense, what we both wanted. We had only to resist the temptation to assign blame, to exact on each other the vengeance of our disappointment. His shoulder leaned into mine ever so slightly. I responded in kind, and it was enough. The danger passed as we lifted each other out of the relationship we'd created. How foolish we felt for imagining a future together, for talking the big talk of marriage, for taking ourselves and each other so seriously. Because it was with our sincerity that we'd betrayed each other. He could never have left Belgrade, and it was something I should never have expected of him.

I left him with a hug, bitter and full of affection. And then we kissed, and what was there at the beginning was still there. But we pulled away just the same, separate and together. And, with that, our relationship was no more, and there was no longer a border around us. In fact, there was no us at all anymore; we were just two people with different places to be.

In my room, I let myself cry. I wanted to indulge in guilt and hurt, to dredge up memories of Masolino, but I kept those doors closed and instead cheered myself with thoughts of *Zhivago* and with visiting Egypt.

Soon after returning to Paris, Omar and I were on a plane to Cairo. As we began our descent, I stared out the window. The landscape looked alien, an endless expanse of desert punctuated with canyons and rock formations. And as we made our final approach into Cairo, not only could I see the flat sprawl of the city, but I could also see the river Nile and the unmistakable triangular protrusions of two pyramids in the distance. A thrill shot through me, as if we were flying into the history books of my childhood.

Setting foot on the tarmac, I was enveloped in unfamiliar sounds and smells. The desert air was dry and unmoving. The main thoroughfares, lined with towering palm trees, were orderly, with freshly painted traffic lines. Red and white trams kept pace beside us. But as we drove into smaller streets, they became congested. Beside women with traditional long dresses and covered heads were others who were smartly dressed in blouses and fitted, knee-length skirts. Uniform concrete buildings pushed in around us. The smell of street food and charcoal fires filled the car. Kiosks selling everything from spices and fruit to rugs and live animals were everywhere.

That night, Omar and Faten took me to a party beneath the Great Pyramid. With dark hair and innocent, almond-shaped eyes, Faten was beautiful and modest, decisive and soft spoken. In her dignified presence, my short skirt and knee-length blond pony coat felt obscene. But I had nothing else to wear, and neither she nor Omar said anything. We arrived to find pickup trucks, motorcycles, and many Mercedes parked side by side in the desert sand. Music emanated from a cluster of tents offering food and places to relax. Men in business suits sat drinking beer and smoking hookahs.

But what caught my attention were the horses corralled nearby.

I mounted a desert pony with a group of riders. The sky was dark and luminous, countless shades of sapphire and indigo, and the stars, those not buried beneath white moonlight, had been dug up and scattered carelessly along the horizon. I rode alongside the group as we entered the cold shadow of the pyramid. The air changed, and the sound of the open desert was interrupted. Then I nudged the sides of my horse and we moved ahead. In the horse, I could feel North Carolina. In the wind, my voyage across the Atlantic. I nudged the horse harder. We were approaching full gallop now and I let go of everything. Of the people and the places. Of Ciga and of Yugoslavia. Finally, I let go of myself.

I urged the horse onward, and now it was running ragged, holding nothing back. We rocketed out of the shadow of the Great Pyramid, and there were shouts from the crowd. But I didn't care. I let go completely.

And, in that moment, I was free.

Twenty

octor Zhivago is a movie that uses sweeping historical events as a backdrop for the intimate human drama playing out in the foreground. The making of the movie—one of the largest productions and highest-grossing of all time—took a full nine months and stands as a sweeping historical event in its own right. For me, those months in Spain tell the story of a small-town girl from North Carolina who comes into her own, who reckons mightily with romantic ideas about life and love, and who, in the conclusion, finds the courage to set out on a life of her own.

Doctor Zhivago follows Yuri Zhivago, a poet doctor who, caught in the Russian Revolution, must fight against the state's overpowering emphasis on the collective in order to retain his individuality. With a budget nearly quadruple that of *The Leopard*'s, MGM went all in on the notoriety of Boris Pasternak's novel, its increasing relevance vis-à-vis the escalating Cold War, and the unparalleled star power that director David Lean was able to assemble.

Unable to shoot in the Soviet Union, it was decided that the film would shoot in Spain and Finland, and that the Russian capital would be constructed from scratch, as a set. Moscow, as erected in the Madrid suburb of Canillas, was a colossal undertaking and took almost eight hundred workers more than six months to build. It covered ten acres and was complete with buildings, boulevards, monuments, and bridges. Meanwhile, a squadron of costume designers was tasked with outfitting armies and peasants, Orthodox priests and Soviet socialites. The cumulative effect was a spectacular re-creation of Russia in the early part of the last century.

But one thing no studio, no matter how much it spends, and no director, no matter their accolades, can control, is the weather. As luck would have it, the production had selected Spain's warmest winter in fifty years to make a movie that depended on vast countrysides and towering cityscapes buried deep in snow.

We waited and we waited. North of Canillas, around Candilichera, high on the Soria Plateau, more sets had been built, including the dazzling "ice palace" that, even in the current age of digital wizardry, stands as an astonishing feat of imagination. The production had a base in Candilichera, and because it was assumed that snow would first fall at the higher altitude, the cast and crew had gathered in anticipation.

But still we waited.

To keep morale up, David Lean hosted a dinner for the film's cast, which included Julie Christie, Geraldine Chaplin, Alec Guinness, Tom Courtenay, and Omar. It was an impressive meeting of talent, and grateful to be included, I was seated beside the film's screenwriter, Robert Bolt. Hunched over professor-like, as if from the countless hours he no doubt spent writing at a desk, he seemed to always have a pipe in his hand. In a tweed coat, he had a mop of brown hair and a serious but pleasant face, broad forehead, and inquisitive, piercing blue eyes.

As we talked, I recognized in him an old soul with an intimidating intellect. As in all of his work, *Zhivago* included, Bolt's central obsession was the individual who, at odds with the society around him and under maximum pressure, refuses to abandon his principles. He'd been nominated for an Academy Award for the *Lawrence of Arabia* screenplay and was about to begin working with director Fred Zinnemann on the film adaptation of his own play, *A Man for All Seasons*, about Sir Thomas More's opposition to Henry VIII. He would later write other screenplays, including for *The Mission*, starring Robert De Niro and Jeremy Irons, about a Jesuit missionary in colonial South America.

"Have you read *Zhivago*?" Bolt asked me.

"Your screenplay?" I asked. "Of course."

"No, Pasternak. The novel."

I confessed that I'd been so focused on the film that I hadn't gotten to the novel.

"You might read it," he said. "I'd quite like to discuss it with you."

His voice had a warm, academic quality, but I thought I could also detect a spark of interest.

"Next Saturday, then?" I offered.

"I'm sorry?"

"Can we discuss it next Saturday? I'll read it this week."

"Very good," he said. "It's a date."

The production housed Omar in a large apartment on what was then Calle General Sanjurjo, with room enough for a live-in cook, a butler, and me. My first assignment was to go to Cairo to collect Omar's son, Tarek, as he was to play Yuri Zhivago as a boy. Faten, Omar's wife, was filming outside of Cairo and unable to bring him herself. Over time, she and I had developed a careful alliance. I admired her and would have liked for her to trust me. Alas I am sure she assumed that I was one of the many women with an unseemly interest in her husband; or, if not, that I was somehow complicit in Omar's infidelity.

When at last snow began to fall, filming began. But the situation, instead of improving, worsened. Lean had taken a chance in hiring Nicolas Roeg, the youngest cinematographer then working in England

Director David Lean and cast on the set of Doctor Zhivago
(Bettmann © Getty Images)

(and who, with films like *Walkabout* and *Don't Look Now*, would go on to be an enormously influential director), but Lean was unhappy with the early dailies and promptly fired Roeg. The stakes were too high, and so Freddie Young, Lean's frequent collaborator, was brought in to take over.

By this time, Robert Bolt and I had already spent a night together. Between us there was such tenderness. His wife, the mother of their three children, had recently left him. She'd run off with the carpenter, and it was a body blow from which he hadn't recovered. And I had a tattered idea of what I thought about sex and relationships and love. Everyone begins with an assumption of marriage, as if marriage were the only possible culmination of attraction. That was what it was with Maso and that's what it was with Ciga. But with Bolt it was different; without the possessiveness or the focus on creating a "we," it more closely resembled friendship.

Where Ciga and I had bonded over art, Robert and I bonded over literature. I have always loved books and had always been a reader, but my reading had never been systematic, and my knowledge of literature was nothing compared to Robert's. Much of our time together was spent remedying this. He'd suggest a book, I'd read it, and together we'd talk about it. After Pasternak's *Doctor Zhivago*, he suggested *College of One*, by Sheilah Graham, which tells the story of her education in literature by her lover, F. Scott Fitzgerald. Robert knew what he was doing, in other words. It was a titillating game of role-play, an esoteric way to engage mind and body. He, the experienced writer, I, the innocent ingenue. It was a lovely, passing affair that, when he soon returned to London, transitioned into a friendship that would last for the rest of his life. On the day he left for London, he gave me his draft of the *Zhivago* script, its margins overrun with his handwritten notes.

Carolyn and Omar on the set of Doctor Zhivago
(Carolyn Pfeiffer archive)

When Tarek's scenes were finished, Faten came to collect him. She stayed for a full week, which was long enough for my nervousness around her to ease and for me to think my affection for her was being reciprocated. I liked watching her with Omar and Tarek. They were a beautiful family, and whatever she knew about Omar's philandering, there was something admirable in how she carried herself.

When she returned to Cairo with Tarek, our housekeeper came to me with a pair of lacy underwear.

"Mrs. Sharif forgot them," she said bashfully.

The housekeeper was uncomfortable discussing this with Omar, and so I promised to return them to Faten when I saw her next.

Meanwhile, *Zhivago* was churning into an ever-greater juggernaut. The scale of production was so ambitious that we couldn't help but believe that we were making the greatest film of all time. MGM believed it, too, and they opened up a press office in Madrid that was dedicated to this single film. Then, realizing that MGM needed a younger person to handle the film's younger talent, the studio asked Omar if it could pay half my salary and have me handle PR for Geraldine Chaplin, the eldest daughter of Charlie Chaplin, and Julie Christie, who was then Hollywood's reigning it-girl.

This meant that all press requests from Hollywood and around the world involving either Omar, Geraldine, or Julie went through me. I'd briefly been a publicist on *The Train* and had plenty of contact with the press over the years, but it had mostly been confined to Europe. This was Hollywood proper, the biggest of the big leagues.

Julie Christie was having the best year of her life. Also cast in John Schlesinger's *Darling*, her *Zhivago* scenes had been front-loaded so she could get to London to work on *Darling*. Born in India and raised by her mother in rural Wales, Julie was a fellow traveler among the cultural elite and would sometimes pull me aside for advice on how to navigate this or that etiquette-related challenge. But she also had a reserved quality that prevented a true friendship from forming. This was in contrast to Geraldine Chaplin, who soon became one of my closest friends. Few people were as famous as her father, yet Geraldine didn't have an ounce of pretension in her. It's true that she was still young, only twenty at the time, and still distrustful of the spotlight, but she was also sincere and curious. She had long brown hair, delicate features, and a uniquely enigmatic look.

As spring arrived and the snow began to melt, the art department was called upon to produce miracle after miracle in an effort to sustain the illusion of a white winter. Tons upon tons of white marble were crushed to produce the effect of snow, and this was supplemented by endless bags of salt. Rollers were put on the blades of the horse-drawn sleds so they could "slide" through the "snow." As the sweltering summer months arrived, my heart went out to the actors who, bundled up in coats designed to withstand subzero temperatures, were forced to perform in eighty-degree weather.

When Faten returned for a visit, I greeted her warmly. Then, remembering the underwear she'd forgotten on her last visit, I brought them to her. Instead of taking them from me, she looked up at me. In her eyes, whatever warmth existed between us was gone.

"These are not mine," she said.

"I'm sorry, I thought—"

"Carolyn," she said acerbically, "if you had done this a few years ago, I would have had you fired. But you know what? I have learned *tolerance*."

What she meant was that she'd learned to tolerate people who, intentionally or not, brought attention to her husband's infidelity. I'd never dreamed of crossing Faten, and it hadn't occurred to me that a misunderstanding could put my job at risk. The exchange left me feeling guilty and defensive, though I suppose I can understand how painful it must be to have one's personal betrayal thrust so plainly into view.

Whispers of a best picture Oscar soon crept onto set. The only catch was that in order to qualify for the Academy Awards, the film needed to be finished and released in theaters before the end of the year. It was already summer, and with months of production remaining, the chances of accomplishing this feat were remote. Still, David Lean did all he could to spur the effort forward. There is a scene in the film in which a train is passing through a decimated village. In it, a woman is desperate for her infant to be taken to a better life, and she chases after the train with the baby in her arms. With the train in motion, Omar holds out his hand and manages to take the baby from her. The woman then continues running, frantically reaching out to Omar as she tries to join her child on the train.

As it happened, I'd fallen in with some mischievous stuntmen, and they convinced Lean to cast me in the role of the desperate mother. I was excited about getting into costume and about having a little stunt cameo in such a historic film. Indeed, this would have happened if Omar hadn't insisted that it was too dangerous. Had it been more important to me, I might have overruled him, but he was coming from a place of genuine concern, and I let it go.

Because of the moving train, the scene was carefully choreographed and the pressure to get the shot in a single take was enormous. The role had gone to a Hungarian actress, and when Lean called for action and the train rumbled into motion, she began running alongside it. Everything seemed to be going well. The woman, in a blind sprint, caught up to Omar and successfully handed the prop baby to him through the train's open door. But as she struggled to pull herself up, she slipped and was dragged beneath the train. We were sure she'd been killed, sliced into pieces by the metal wheels. The train slammed on its brakes, and as cast and crew converged on the place where she'd disappeared, a cry went up. By some miracle, she was alive.

I felt fragile afterward, unsettled by what might have happened if I'd done the stunt. I might have lost an arm or a leg, maybe even my life. But it's a treacherous word, *if.* With two letters, it switches the train of reality from one track onto another, sending it through histories that might have been, into futures that might yet be.

One *if* that I carry with me to this day is what might have happened if Geraldine hadn't asked me, after filming one day, to go with her for a drink in Madrid's *centro*.

Omar Sharif, Penny Wigram, Dominick Elwes, Tessa Elwes, Robert Bolt,
Geraldine Chaplin, Carolyn Pfeiffer, Silvia Pinal & Janine Limberg
(Carolyn Pfeiffer archive)

We were joined by others from *Zhivago* and, at a tavern with brick walls and heavy wooden tables, we found ourselves among other film people from other productions. The lighting was dim, and the room was crowded and noisy. As a result, one had to lean forward to hear anything. I was doing my best to listen to Geraldine's remarkable story about her stint tending elephants while working for a French circus when I brushed against the back of the man sitting on my other side.

Turning to apologize, he beat me to it.

"I'm sorry," he shouted.

"It's okay," I shouted back.

He looked at me, confused.

"Croquet?" he shouted.

"Not croquet," I said, laughing. "Okay! I said it's okay!"

"I don't like croquet," he shouted, his English accent now evident. "Thank you, anyway. I hope you have fun."

He had a comic book smile, big and perfect, and a face that was playful and smart.

I leaned close to his ear.

"You aren't funny," I shouted.

"What's that about?" asked Geraldine when I turned back around. "Him?"

"No, you," she said. "The smile on your face."

Later, as I emerged from the restroom, the Englishman was waiting for me. He smiled at me and took my hand. Leading me around a corner, we were suddenly by ourselves. He then kissed me, and though it was unexpected, it wasn't unwelcome. He then proceeded to inform me of two discordant realities that he'd already reconciled. The first was that he had a wife and children waiting for him in London. The second was that he intended to pursue me until I instructed him otherwise.

"It's messy," he conceded, "but that's how it is."

In the days that followed, the Englishman engineered encounters between us and seemed to be always ready with a suspiciously perfect compliment. Did he think I didn't know the encounters were planned? Or that the compliments were prepared? Seeing him go just beyond the overt, I tried to stop just shy of it. I'd hold the gaze of his hazel eyes for a moment too long, or I'd let a little sway into my hips when I knew he was watching me walk away.

On a film set, where nothing is as it seems and where everyone is working together to fabricate reality, it sometimes isn't easy to remember why a thing is right or wrong. We fell deeply, and even dangerously, into something that felt like love. We allowed ourselves the fantasy of *if*. What *if* we followed our feelings? What *if* we wandered for a while down this other reality? Now the long hours of production passed quickly, and when my work for Omar was done, time would slow way down. And in those evening hours, we had all of Madrid to ourselves, the stone bridges and the church towers, the cobblestoned streets and the red wine.

It was an unruly romance, one that took everything and asked nothing. After one *corrida* at the Las Ventas bullring, we spent the night in a small hotel in the city center. We made love with such uncomplicated ease. Between us there was no hurt from the past and there was no hope for the future. We didn't share space, or finances, or children. With every caress and whisper, the affection between us intensified until, finally, there was nothing else.

After, as we lay intertwined and unable to move, I said what was in my heart.

"I love you," I whispered.

There was a long silence, which I didn't mind. I wasn't saying those words because it was what I wanted to hear in return. I was saying them because it was how I felt and because I wanted him to know.

Twenty-One

The battles of *Zhivago* raged on as summer turned to autumn. When August arrived and we were able to glimpse the end of production, I was overcome by a feeling of dread. Because soon there would be no more publicity, no more juggling multiple clients, no more being the point of contact for industry press. How could I go back to the way things used to be? There would also be no more Englishman. The fantasy of *if* would end, and the liminal dream of film production would give way to real life.

Here I realized that the life I wanted was not the life I'd had before. I no longer wanted to be a secretary, someone whose life fit neatly into another's. And I no longer wanted to be unrooted and untethered. In acknowledging this, I realized that I needed to start imagining a life beyond my life with Omar.

My goodbye to the Englishman was a careful display of restraint. There was no talk of love and no mention of the future. Our affair had happened in the present, and our goodbye could be no different. We had the job of turning the *if* of our fantasy back into the *is* of reality, of switching the train back onto its original tracks.

Hugging me, he whispered in my ear, "You take care, okay?"

I pulled away and smiled wanly.

"I don't even like croquet," I said.

Omar and I flew to London for his additional voice recording. After Tito's Yugoslavia and Franco's Spain, London was inspiring. Newly colorful and newly vibrant, it was almost unrecognizable from the city I'd first encountered six years earlier.

"I'll be thirty years old soon," I lamented to Penny. "It's right around the corner."

We were in her house, in the playroom on the fourth floor. Lionel and Sophie, no longer the toddlers they'd been, were climbing on us happily.

"You know what they say," said Penny. "Time flies when you live on movie sets and work eighteen-hour days."

I chuckled and said, "I just need a change."

"You think *you* need a change," she said, squeezing Sophie in her arms.

Penny had been at home with her children for several years, and I was surprised to hear that she was thinking of again finding work outside the home. The more we talked about it, the more serendipitous it seemed that we were both thinking about a major change.

"We could start a publicity company," I said, only half in jest.

"We *should* start a publicity company," she replied. "I'm serious. Think of it. I'm a journalist, you know talent, and we both know the press."

Just like that, a seed was planted.

Doctor Zhivago was released in theaters mere days before the new year. David Lean had slept in the editing room and had managed to complete the film in time to qualify for the Academy Awards. It was a smash hit at the box office and all but swept the Golden Globes. Going into the Academy Awards with ten nominations, tied with *The Sound of Music*, it walked away with five Oscars, including best adapted screenplay for Robert Bolt.

But there was no way not to feel disappointed. Nine months is a long time to spend on anything, and when time is all you have to give, sometimes no exchange feels adequate. We had all put so much life into the film that it startled me to discover that *Doctor Zhivago* was just a movie; somehow, I'd forgotten that detail entirely.

Omar's next role was as a Nazi intelligence officer in *The Night of the Generals,* another ambitious Sam Spiegel production, starring Tom Courtenay and a young Christopher Plummer, and that reunited Omar with *Lawrence of Arabia*'s Peter O'Toole. About the murder of a Polish prostitute and a plot to assassinate Hitler, the film was to begin shooting in Paris and then move to Warsaw.

I'd become friendly with Tom Courtenay on *Zhivago*. He was an English actor, based in London, and didn't want the hassle of navigating Paris alone. To make things simple, he moved in with Omar and me in the Avenue Foch apartment provided by the production. With angular features and a conventionally English look, Tom was young, sensitive, and an avid supporter of Hull City football club. While shooting in Paris, he would dart back to England whenever he could to see them play. Once, upon returning to Paris, he discovered assorted pubic hairs in his bedsheets—telltale evidence that one of Omar's sleepovers had made use of his room. Tom was enraged. He confronted Omar, and their relationship almost didn't survive. Never in all my life have I seen someone so angry.

Soon after, *The Night of the Generals* moved to Warsaw. We arrived at night and were met with an eerie sensation. This unease deepened as we drove through the old city and ghetto. I remembered my Uncle Frank's stories about the war, but the devastation endured by Poland was beyond anything I could have imagined. In late 1944, with the war already lost, the Nazis had carried out a vindictive campaign to raze all of Warsaw. There was no military purpose to it, and yet the Nazis destroyed nearly 90 percent of the city. This included more than ten thousand buildings, among them libraries, churches, schools, hospitals, and museums. What had been rebuilt since the war had been done using debris from the ruins, and it felt like we were now driving through a haunted place, through a smothering sense of unhealed history. Sorrow so deep and loss so unfathomable still filled the night.

There was something perverse about the weeks that followed. With Peter O'Toole, Tom Courtenay, and Omar dressed in Nazi uniforms and replaying violent invasion scenes from the German occupation, it felt wrong, as if the film's good intentions did not sufficiently outweigh the trauma of returning swastikas and tanks to the streets of Warsaw.

Omar and I next flew to Naples, where he'd been cast opposite Sophia Loren in *C'era Una Volta*. Predictably, returning to Italy brought up complicated emotions: nostalgia and melancholy but also joy and happiness. Taking the train to Rome, it felt like a homecoming. The d'Amicos had invited me to lunch, and as usual, it was attended by artists and intellectuals, each more impressive than the next.

Afterward, I sat with Suso on the upstairs terrace just as I'd done three years earlier. Then, I'd come for her blessing; now I'd come for her counsel. I explained to her about all that had happened over the course of *Zhivago* and how Penny and I were talking about starting a PR company in London.

"A company like that would suit you well, no?"

"I don't know," I said. "What I really want is to make movies."

"But making movies is making relationships and finding stories. The time will come."

"I'm not sure I can start a company."

"Carolina"—there was a sternness in her voice—"do you know why I wanted it to work with Masolino, why I involved myself like that?"

"You've always been so kind to me. More than I deserve."

"It wasn't kindness, *cara*. I wanted you to stay with Masolino because you had the courage to cross an ocean by yourself." She paused and then said, "Look at me."

I did as she instructed.

"You can do anything, Carolina. That I have never doubted."

Later, I found Masolino and asked him to walk with me. We bought gelato and went up to Villa Borghese, to the Medici Villa that overlooks all of Rome. Below us were the Spanish Steps and across the city was the dome of Saint Peter's Basilica. We talked about inconsequential things, about work and cinema. But we didn't talk about our engagement, about the relationship that so long ago had been so full of potential. That we let be; it had become a part of Rome, a layer of its history forever buried.

Encouraged by my conversation with Suso, the impossible notion of moving to London was beginning to feel possible. We could do it, Penny and I. We could launch a PR company and we could make it work. Goose bumps spread across my skin as, once again, the possible started to feel inevitable. It could happen. It *would* happen. All that was left was for me to find the courage to speak with Omar.

C'era Una Volta, sometimes titled *More Than a Miracle* in English, is a fairy tale set in medieval Italy. Filming took place in and around a sprawling convent, which also housed some of the cast and crew. I spent my free time writing to Penny and to my family and wandering the convent's endless maze of nooks and passageways, its hidden rooms and secret courtyards. But as the weeks wore on, I realized that I was procrastinating, looking for reasons to prolong the security of the present while forestalling the uncertainty awaiting me.

Finally, I did it. I found Omar and I told him that I needed to set out on my own.

"I need to live my own life," I said. "And I can do this. I can start a company. I know I can. I'll find a replacement, of course. I wouldn't just leave—"

"Carolyn," he said evenly.

"Are you disappointed?"

But his face lit up and he smiled his brilliant smile.

"You can leave," he said, "on the condition that you take me on as your first client."

Twenty-Two

I f World War II was the earthquake that triggered the tsunami of generational conflict and if the ensuing twenty years were the ocean across which it gathered momentum, then London was the shore onto which it crashed. Wave upon wave of youthful energy swept the city. The working class, forever reined in, was unleashed. The sons and daughters of bartenders and police officers became artists, musicians, fashion designers, photographers, and filmmakers; and the social order of the day was subverted. The upper classes were finding their richest experiences not at high tea but in West End clubs and in London streets on which their parents and grandparents never stepped foot. Yet, for all the churn and power, no one knew quite what was happening, only that everything, inside and out, was changing.

It was into this divine chaos that my public relations firm, Carolyn Pfeiffer, Ltd., was born. At the printer, Penny and I stared down at our newly printed letterhead. Above our names, in handsome typeface, was the word *directors*. Working out of my tenth-floor flat at

Bare Essentials, *London, 1969*
(Photo by Frank Habicht)

Porchester Place, an angular midcentury apartment tower north of
Hyde Park, we were just west of Mayfair and Soho. The flat was
small, but we didn't need much. Having worked in marketing and as
a journalist, Penny would handle most of the writing. With my background and talent relationships, I'd take the lead on clients. Of those,
we had only three—all from *Zhivago*: Omar Sharif, Tom Courtenay,
and Geraldine Chaplin.

And so, we got to work. We reestablished contact with *Paris Match*
and got to know London's Fleet Street editors and journalists. I wrote

letters to everyone I'd met since moving to Europe—the d'Amicos, Claudia, Visconti, Alain, Romy, Nathalie, François Truffaut, Marianne Frey, Louis Malle, Robert Bolt—to let them know that we were open for business and that, if they ever needed anything in London—a movie opened, an interview scheduled, anything at all—then we would do it better than it had ever been done before.

To be viable, we needed more clients, but we also needed to do right by Omar, Tom, and Geraldine. Omar was frequently in London on business, and I was his default dinner date, his sidekick at the White City dog races that he loved so much, and at times his guest at the various evening engagements to which he was invited. After *C'era Una Volta*, he was being considered for the lead role in the film adaptation of *Funny Girl*, the successful Broadway play, and needed to go to Hollywood for meetings with executives. He asked me to go with him, and I readily agreed. I'd been to LA with him before—on one trip, though without Omar, I'd attended Frank Sinatra's fiftieth birthday party at the Beverly Wilshire Hotel—but always as his secretary. This was an opportunity to introduce my company and to deepen relationships with studios and publicists who might subcontract publicity work to us.

Penny and Carolyn
(Photograph by Terry O'Neill)

After a week of meetings in Hollywood, during which I reconnected with Lee Solters, a legendary publicist known for his flamboyant handling of stars like Mae West and Cary Grant, I found myself out to dinner as the date of a screenwriter named Ted Allan. The dinner, a celebration of the film *Hombre*, was at Lucy's El Adobe Cafe, on Melrose Avenue. In a cute, knee-length green dress and shawl draped over my shoulders, I was excited to meet Paul Newman, Diane Cilento, and some of the others involved with the film. Newman was there with Joanne Woodward, his wife; Diane, who would receive an Academy Award nomination for her role in the film, was with her husband, Sean Connery.

I was seated between Sean and Diane—between husband and wife. Sean had just wrapped the new Bond film, *You Only Live Twice*, and Paul's new film, *Cool Hand Luke*, had just been released. I thought myself lucky indeed to be in the company of such handsome and famous men. Conversation was pleasant, and Diane shared some anecdotes about getting into character as a pioneer woman and riding on a stagecoach through the Arizona desert.

It was while Diane was speaking that I felt Sean's hand on my thigh. Taken aback, I swiped it away and tried to focus on his wife's story. But moments later, he pulled the hem of my dress up, forcing his hand between my thighs. I instinctively crossed my left leg over my right, but this did nothing to deter him. He kept insisting, forcing his hand higher. Shocked and unsure what to do, I excused myself and went to the front of the restaurant to gather my composure. When I came back, I told Ted that the light was in my eyes and asked if he'd mind switching places with me.

After dinner, I told Ted what happened.

"Yeah," he said with a laugh, "Sean does that sometimes."

On my return to London, I stopped in North Carolina for a brief visit with my family and then flew to Madrid to spend some time with Geraldine Chaplin. Not only was Geraldine's father Charlie Chaplin, but her maternal grandfather was Eugene O'Neill, the Nobel- and Pulitzer Prize–winning playwright whose work *Long Day's Journey into Night* ranks as one of the twentieth century's greatest plays. Geraldine had inherited an astonishing concentration of cultural significance and, as a child, remembers sitting with her brother Michael at the gate of the family villa and announcing to passersby that they were the children of Charlie Chaplin. They had no idea why, but they would invariably be met with reactions of awe, as if there was something magical about their last name.

Geraldine Chaplin with Boris, her French Bulldog
(Reporters Associes/Gamma-Rapho © Getty Images)

Yet underneath the grandiosity of her heritage was a quiet creature still uncertain of her own powers and of the effect on the world that she herself might produce. She'd grown up immersed in the arts but was cautioned away from an artistic career by her father. Stubbornly, she'd aspired to be a ballerina, but it was a dream she came to in her later teens and was therefore not to be. So, after that stint caring for elephants at the Cirque d'Hiver in Paris, she turned to modeling, and it was her photograph in an airplane magazine that landed in the hands of David Lean, who was then casting *Doctor Zhivago*.

Geraldine had met the Spanish filmmaker Carlos Saura while we were in Spain shooting *Zhivago*, and they were soon both romantically and artistically inseparable. Saura, like Luis Buñuel, his friend and mentor, was a political filmmaker. With Spain still under Franco's authoritarian rule, Saura was establishing himself as a deft navigator of the regime's censors. He'd found international success with *La Caza*, a story about three veterans of the Spanish Civil War, and he'd cast Geraldine as the lead in his follow-up, *Peppermint Frappé*. For Geraldine, it was a marriage of art and politics that suited her well. Her father had been famously blacklisted by the FBI when he'd taken the family to Europe on a vacation only to discover that he was not allowed to reenter the United States. It made sense, then, that Geraldine was now ensconced in the creation of political cinema, an existence that connected her to an international network of political activists.

Through her and Saura, I met Guillermo Cabrera Infante, a celebrated Cuban writer whose parents had founded Cuba's Communist Party. Guillermo had recently published *Three Sad Tigers*, a literary masterpiece that had drawn comparisons to James Joyce's *Ulysses*. Under the anglicized pseudonym G. Caín, he'd also written the script for *Wonderwall*, a film that had become an improbable vehicle for some of London's rising talent, including Jane Birkin and George Harrison, the Beatle, who was composing the score.

As the world of leftist politics opened up to me, so, too, did that of theater. This was primarily through Tom Courtenay, a reluctant celebrity who, even though he was a popular film actor, had a strong preference for theater. We had a shared love of animals, and when he was cast in Manchester opposite Helen Mirren in *Charley's Aunt*—a role that would keep him away from London for several months—he gave me his cat, Roger, a female who spent her days reclining, centerfold-like, on my living room windowsill.

For someone so unassuming, Tom's fame was remarkable. I remember receiving a call from Buckingham Palace, and the voice on the other line introducing himself as the master of the household.

"May I help you?" I asked.

"Yes," the master of the household replied. "I should like to know whether Mr. Courtenay *would* be available *if* Her Majesty, the Queen, were to invite him to a luncheon."

What I didn't understand was that the request was worded so that the queen wouldn't be refused. If the master of the household had instead said, "Her Majesty, the Queen, *has* invited Mr. Courtenay to lunch," then Tom would have been given the power to decline the invitation. And one must never refuse the queen.

With *Charley's Aunt* opening in Manchester, Penny and I decided we would both attend as it was one of our first big events. The day before we were to leave, an American journalist named Jon Bradshaw called. He was doing a profile on Tom Courtenay for *The Telegraph Magazine* and wanted to arrange an interview. It would be a big story, and therefore a big deal for our company, and so I suggested that Bradshaw join us on the train to Manchester.

With Bradshaw seated across from us on the train, he peppered us with questions about getting our company off the ground. When banking came up, he frowned.

"Don't you need a husband?" he asked.

"Excuse me?" I said, puzzled.

"Oh," Bradshaw said, laughing. "You thought—No, sorry. I mean legally. It's bullshit, but isn't it illegal for a woman to open a bank account in England?"

"Good save, Jon Bradshaw," I said with a smile.

He wasn't wrong. It was 1967 and it was still perfectly legal for banks to deny accounts and credit cards to unmarried women and to require married women to have their husbands cosign with them. To get a credit card at Selfridges, a popular department store, I was successful only after fighting with the clerk and then having it out with her manager. As for a bank account, that was easier since Penny was married to a banker who was happy to help.

I had never met anyone like Jon Bradshaw. With a warm and wonderful smile, he had the confidence of someone who is accustomed to supplying a room with its gravity. And though I wished I could pretend otherwise, he was also talented, well informed, and, if all that weren't enough, seductive. A journalist to his core, he was cut from Hemingway cloth, had traveled the world, and had a great deal on which to report. Recently back from covering Rhodesia's (now Zimbabwe) independence from Britain, he was deeply enamored of the tragic, the infamous, and the dangerous—and with people like Tom Courtenay, who were able to harness the collective imagination.

Tom was reliably impressive in *Charley's Aunt*, and the cast was given a standing ovation. We made our way backstage with flowers and congratulations, and Bradshaw arranged to meet with Tom for breakfast in the morning.

It was at this point in the evening that Bradshaw revealed that he had neglected to book a hotel room for himself.

"Did you have no plan at all?" Penny asked in disbelief.

"That is a very valid question," said Bradshaw.

We were feeling celebratory and so we went for a drink in the room Penny and I were sharing. But what began as one drink turned into a conversation that continued until dawn. Bradshaw told us about his adventures in South Africa and Vietnam, in the Caribbean and South America. He believed, truly believed, that an individual could change the world, and he was just as interested in those who would do so by darkening or destroying it as he was in those who would do so by remaking or renewing it.

By four in the morning, Penny was sound asleep, and Bradshaw and I were wading into the deep waters of dreams and personal callings.

"But what is PR, really?" he asked earnestly.

"I suppose it's about relationships. It's being someone who connects different kinds of people for the benefit of them both."

"Is it fulfilling?"

I couldn't tell if there was subtext to his question.

"It's a living," I said defensively. "Anyway, what is writing, really? Is *it* fulfilling?"

"Good God, no! It's absolute torture. I can't stand it. But it's the only thing I've ever been good at. So I don't really have a choice. But, from time to time, it takes me to interesting places."

"Like where?"

"Like here. With you."

My defensiveness melted.

"Anyway, you'd have loved South Africa," he said, smiling. "Up in a Cessna out over the veldt. Wildebeest and elephants scattering every which way. Camping out on the savanna. Acacia and baobab trees. Lions and hyenas at night. Everything as deadly as it is beautiful."

By sunrise, Bradshaw was shirtless, showing off the scar on his back where he'd been stabbed in a bar in Rhodesia. An ornery Afrikaner hadn't taken kindly to his suggestion that white rule would someday end, and a fight had broken out.

When Penny began to stir, he said, "Courtenay will be at breakfast waiting for me."

"And after breakfast?" I asked.

"Heathrow. I leave for Trinidad tonight."

"Well," I said, wishing we'd had more time together. "Good luck, Jon Bradshaw."

That afternoon, as Penny and I arrived home, I thought of Bradshaw flying off to Trinidad, and London felt quiet.

Soon after, Françoise Dorléac was scheduled to arrive from France. Françoise was the beautiful French actress for whom I'd found mustard balls in Yugoslavia during *Genghis Khan*. Since then, both her career as well as that of her sister's, Catherine Deneuve, had continued to climb steadily higher. She'd recently wrapped *The Young Girls of Rochefort* opposite *Singin' in the Rain*'s Gene Kelly, and I'd set up a press day for her in London. I was looking forward to seeing her and also to being rejuvenated just by seeing an old friend. Buoyant and full of love, she was one of the most magical people I knew, and I couldn't wait for her to call from Heathrow to let me know she'd arrived.

But she never called. When my phone finally did ring, it was my good friend the photographer Terry O'Neill on the other line. He was to photograph Françoise and had just received word that there had been an accident. Françoise had been late for her flight and had lost control of her car as she raced to the Nice airport. Her car had flipped over multiple times and burst into flames, trapping her inside. Bystanders reported seeing her struggling to open the car door. But it was jammed, and she died in the fire. She was twenty-five years old.

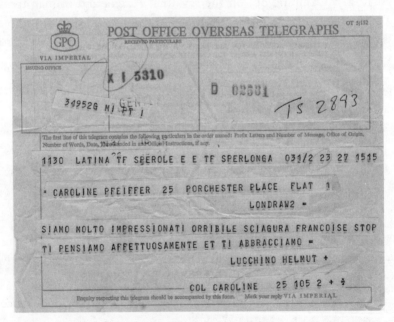

Death of Françoise Dorléac telegram from Luchino Visconti and Helmut Berger
(Carolyn Pfeiffer archive)

It was the first time that a friend and agemate had died. *She was too young*, I thought. *Too good. Too kind.* Her death unmoored me and contributed to a feeling of fragility and unpredictability that was making its way around the globe. The news was always terrible and everyone seemed to be losing hope. There were gruesome reports of massacres in Vietnam. In Paris, tensions were rising between the authorities and the students. There were protests and skirmishes, and it was obvious that the worst was still to come. In the United States, racial tensions were beginning to boil over. Malcolm X had been assassinated and Martin Luther King Jr. had become a lightning rod for the vitality of the Civil Rights Movement as well as for the ugly fight against it.

In the gathering uncertainty, I felt a desire for connection, and so I kept Nathalie on the line when she next called me. Her ex-husband, the French officer, still prevented her from seeing her daughter, but a lot had happened since I'd left my job with Alain. She and Alain had married, and she'd given birth to a son, Anthony, whom she adored. She was also trying to jump-start an acting career and was attached to a film that hoped to shoot in England. We talked about how I might help if the film's financing came together, and then, with business out of the way, I asked her about Anthony and about Alain.

"He asks about you," she said. "Alain does."

"Send him my love," I said, smiling.

"I will when he comes back," she said and then inhaled deeply. "I just now chased him from the house."

I knew their marriage had soured, but Nathalie now said that divorce was inevitable.

"He's a wild animal, Caroline. He has instincts and no brains. He hurts people without knowing he causes pain—like a cat who tortures a mouse just because it is his nature."

"Nat, I'm sorry."

"No, it's okay. I went to bed with a prince and woke up with a husband. What can be done? But the reason it's bad is because there is still love between us. And because we have Anthony, who we love more than life itself. But, in the end, it will be better for us if we aren't together."

I could hear in her voice the way marriage and motherhood were jealous of her, the way each wanted all of her even as she wanted more than both of them.

"Caroline," Nathalie went on, "you come from a small town, yes?"

"Yes."

"When you left, did you run away? Or did you chase after something?"

I took a moment to reflect.

"I left to chase after something. I always thought there was something important for me out in the world."

The line cracked with static and then evened out.

"And you?" I asked.

"Me? For me, it's the opposite. I ran."

"From what?"

"From a prison. From a life I couldn't live. I didn't want the life of my mother, a life of suffering. When I got pregnant and we were forced to marry, everything changed. Our daughter was born, and my husband became my oppressor. For the sake of my daughter, I tried hard to be what he wanted . . ."

She rarely spoke of her daughter and her voice trailed off.

"I'm sure it wasn't easy," I offered.

"Every day was another death," she said. "Every day, I disappeared even more from my own life. Finally, I found the courage to ask for a divorce, and I came here, to Paris, to get away. That's when I met Alain. And with him it was more than love. It was destiny, something beyond my control. You were there; you remember how it was. I thought I could bring my daughter here, but Alain was famous, and it humiliated my husband. Imagine, there was his wife, the mother of his baby girl, in all the newspapers with the famous Alain Delon. It poisoned him. In the courts, he made me look unfit. He wanted blood. He wanted to destroy me. He wanted me to know what it is to lose a child."

I could hear the pain in her voice and wished I could do more than just listen.

"In this, he was successful," she went on. "I lost custody of my daughter and now he prevents me from seeing her. If I call, he hangs up. If I send letters, he burns them. All I have left of my daughter is her name."

"What is it, her name?"

"Nathalie."

"She's named after you?"

"No. My name is Francine. You didn't know?"

"I had no idea," I said.

"I only started using Nathalie here in Paris because it gives me a connection to my daughter." Here her voice grew strained. "I was so young, Caroline. I never imagined that leaving a bad marriage would also mean losing my daughter."

Nathalie was so fearless, so untamable, and I wasn't ready for her sadness.

"It makes me blind with madness," she continued. "To be helpless. To carry the weight of emptiness."

"But you can't lose hope, Nat. She'll remember you. And she'll grow up. One day she'll want to know the truth. You have to believe that."

"That's why we'll never be done with each other, Alain and I. I'll never allow Anthony to be taken from me. Never. I'll die before I'm separated from him. And for Alain, it's the same. His parents divorced and they put him with a foster family. He blames everything on that. So he won't allow himself to be separated from his son. Even if we divorce, we will be together; it will never be over. We didn't have love when we were young, so now we will kill each other to make sure Anthony has enough."

"Everyone says marriage is hard."

"It's not marriage that's hard. It's being a woman that's hard. And if Alain thinks I'm one of these *worthy* women, he's mistaken."

"What do you mean, 'worthy'?"

"The idea that it's a woman's role to be *worthy* of a man. I despise that mentality of submission. Let no one ever call me *worthy*."

It isn't easy to convey just how oriented toward marriage and dependence a woman's life was obliged to be in those days. It was just a few decades ago, but so much of the public and professional spheres was off limits, not just culturally or socially but legally. A possible consequence of this is that fashion, and the question of what one did with one's body, was not only personal but also political. To rage against oppressive clothing was to rage against gendered oppression, full stop. Through fashion, one could express oneself, yes, but one could also protest society's expectations for women.

Twiggy, for example—her hair short and boyish, her look androgynous—was the newly anointed icon of fashion, and while she represented a new expression of femininity, her cropped hair and her short shorts were also an indictment of society's treatment of women. Likewise, the designer Mary Quant, who was methodically slicing away at the hem of women's skirts, hiking them up ever higher, was trafficking not only in provocation but in a very real kind of power. As a groundswell of styles and colors flooded London, boutiques sprouted up throughout the city, clustering in Soho, in Mayfair, and down on King's Road in Chelsea. And as fashion turned into a fever, it felt unmistakably consequential, as if far more than fabric were at stake.

While walking down Carnaby Street one day, I noticed a small crowd gathered around the psychedelic mural on the side of Lord John, a popular men's store. I was on my way to have lunch with Robert Bolt, the *Zhivago* screenwriter. Since our brief affair, he'd married Sarah Miles, a young actress on her way to being famous, and he'd invited me to meet her. But I was early and so paused to see what had attracted the crowd. As I'd suspected, it was a photo shoot, and I thought I recognized the photographer at the crowd's center. Sure enough, during a lull in the activity, I found myself shaking his hand. It was Terence Donovan.

Like everyone, I knew him from his photography. I loved his photograph of Twiggy in front of the Union Jack. It's a powerful image, not only because of its composition and staging but because it so perfectly captures a generation yearning for change.

Twiggy, wearing an ensemble by Mary Quant, June 1966
(Photograph by Terence Donovan © Terence Donovan Archive)

Along with David Bailey and Brian Duffy, Donovan was a part of the so-called Black Trinity—the trio of celebrity photographers who were central in the creation and branding of Swinging London. With their iconic images of David Bowie and the Beatles, of Mick Jagger and Jean Shrimpton, they were the collective inspiration for the protagonist in Michelangelo Antonioni's *Blow-Up*, which was nominated for two Academy Awards and won the Palme d'Or at Cannes. Unlike their predecessors, these photographers eschewed meticulously art-directed shoots in favor of a dynamic and improvised approach. They sought out the influencers of the day and photographed them in provocative poses either in their studios or in the streets.

They were so important that Julie Christie credited her career to a single photograph taken of her by Terence Donovan. John Schlesinger—an Academy Award–winning director—had seen Donovan's portrait of her on the cover of *Town* magazine and had given her her first role in film. A year later, Julie was cast in *Zhivago*, and a year after that she received the Academy Award for Best Actress in Schlesinger's *Darling*.

When Terry asked for my phone number, it wasn't clear if I would be hearing from him for personal or for professional reasons. I left Lord John with a smile and hurried to Soho where I was meeting Robert Bolt and Sarah Miles. Despite my romance with Robert, I was eager to meet Sarah even if I didn't envy her the task of meeting me, one of her husband's former girlfriends.

But she was more than equal to it. When I reached my hand out to greet her, she brushed it aside and hugged me tightly.

"Robert's told me about you."

"We were—"

"Lovers, I know," she said mischievously. "I make him tell me everything. Literally, everything."

Robert blushed in his professorial way.

Sarah, who had enormous round eyes and a fearless sense of adventure, smiled brightly. "You can't marry a writer if you don't like stories, can you?"

We ate and Robert talked about the recent premiere of *Vivat! Vivat Regina!*, his play about Mary, Queen of Scots and her cousin Queen

Elizabeth I of England. Having completed its summer-long run in the Chichester Festival over the summer, *Vivat! Vivat Regina!* is a duel of wits between the two women: Mary, played by Sarah, who is willing to exchange power for love, and Elizabeth, played by Eileen Atkins, who has chosen power over love. While the two women never meet in person, Mary eventually becomes the prisoner of Elizabeth and is ultimately beheaded for treason.

"Robert's in love with his Elizabeth," said Sarah.

Robert looked down bashfully and pulled out his pipe.

"How could I be?" he said. "I wrote Elizabeth as a witty, intelligent man."

"And Mary?" I asked. "How did you write her?"

"As the very heart of womanhood."

"She's bloody unplayable," said Sarah. "That's what she is."

Robert laughed.

"I'll do better with *Ryan's Daughter.*"

Ryan's Daughter, to be directed by David Lean, was Bolt's current project. It was an adaptation of *Madame Bovary* to be set against Ireland's political turmoil, and he was writing the central role specifically for Sarah. She kissed him on the cheek and put her hand high up on his thigh.

"Another benefit of marrying a writer."

He smiled and looked over at me.

"And how is your nomadic soul? Will it be London that finally pins you down?"

"The courtship has only just begun," I said, laughing.

"You must visit us at Mill House," said Sarah, referring to their home in the country. "And Robert will make sure you do our PR."

Robert nodded. "Yes, anything we can do to better the chances of our little island."

After lunch I noticed a pet store adjacent to the restaurant, and I stopped to admire two sand dollar–sized turtles paddling about in a window aquarium. Robert offered to get them for me, and when Sarah insisted that he do so, I had no choice.

Back on the street, I held the little aquarium in my hands and looked at Robert.

"Will you name them?" I asked.

Robert thought for a minute and reached out an index finger.

"Let's have that one be Updike," he said. "The shy one can be Salinger."

When I returned to my flat, Penny looked at the aquarium suspiciously.

"Are you carrying turtles?"

"I am."

"What, on purpose?"

I found a place for Salinger and Updike on a bookcase by the window, just out of Roger's reach. Then I made tea for us, and I told Penny about lunch and about meeting Terence Donovan before that.

"I don't see you wanting to be with a photographer," Penny offered.

"He might call about work and he might not call at all."

"He'll call."

"Why do you say that?"

"Because I can see a photographer wanting to be with you."

I waved her flattery away.

"Can I ask you something? Would you call me nomadic?"

"Nomadic? Why do you ask?"

"Robert called me nomadic at lunch. He was asking if I planned to stay in London, and I thought it was curious."

"It wouldn't occur to a nomad to call herself nomadic, would it?" said Penny, laughing.

"It's complacency that I can't stand, not stillness."

"We complement each other well; it's aimlessness that I can't stand, not change."

"Don't you ever dream of something radically different, though?"

She took a sip of tea.

"Yes, sometimes. With all this talk of women's lib, I've half a mind to get a postgraduate degree. For someone like me, that'd be rather subversive, don't you think?"

Terence Donovan called the next day, and Penny was right: it had nothing to do with business. He'd invested in a restaurant, the Trencherman, on lower Kings Road, a new partnership with one of London's best chefs. We met there, and were soon talking comfortably.

"It's fashion that started everything, you see. When fashion started changing, photography changed with it. First, pop art came along and made everything geometric. But it was the miniskirt that really got things going. They tried it in France first, you know, in the couture houses, but it really caught on here in London. Now the whole world's dying to see the latest fashion trend, and that's where photography and the magazines come in. All of a sudden *Vogue* can't print enough copies."

"Why England?" I asked. "Why did the miniskirt become so popular here?"

"My opinion? The working class has always molded ourselves to fit the world, and for the first time, I think we're figuring out how to mold the world to fit us."

"Are you saying that you're molding the world?" I asked with a laugh.

"In a way, I think so. Look, if you give a camera to a rich lad and one to a poor lad, they'll photograph the world differently, you see. The rich lad's thinking how things *ought* to be. But the poor lad's imagining how they *could* be. I was born dirt poor, so I've spent my life creating images of the way that things could be."

I'd always loved visual media and was fascinated to hear his philosophy on photography.

"Do you never photograph things or people as they actually are?" I asked.

"One lesson I've learned is there's nothing honest about photography. There's this illusion that the camera doesn't lie, but in fact the whole skill is making it tell the right lie. There's the responsibility, you see. Maintaining integrity in the process."

He went on to explain his fascination with the word *image*, with the way it carries opposing definitions. On the one hand, it suggests objectivity, a captured likeness. On the other hand, it suggests a manufactured representation.

"That's called a *contranym*, you see," he explained.

We began spending our evenings together, and then our nights. I went on the pill, which was newly legalized and which was having an impact that was nothing short of revolutionary as millions of people acclimated to a reality in which the possibility of pregnancy was largely neutralized.

"Is it safe?" I'd asked Penny.

"Men swear by it," she'd said.

Indeed, "the pill"—its eponymous title uncontested by all other pills—was a radical short-circuiting of the social and sexual equilibrium. Sex without pregnancy was a separation of cause and effect unlike anything in human history. More than the Vietnam War or the mushrooming use of drugs or the race to land on the moon, it was with the pill that a new era dawned on a new generation.

As the year ended, a current of rebellious, rising energy was palpable. Penny and I had done well. Our company had not only survived; it had grown. So much so that my flat on Porchester Place was overflowing with paperwork. In need of more space, I moved into a flat on Connaught Place, a handsome building overlooking Marble Arch.

On my first night in the new flat, Terry brought me dinner from his restaurant. We liked each other, but I couldn't yet tell how serious it was. We sat on moving boxes and ate, and when he left, I took Roger to the window and looked out at Hyde Park.

Nineteen sixty-seven was winding down, and my thirtieth birthday was around the corner in the new year. As I stood there, I felt alone but not lonely, at peace with myself but also restless, eager to keep going. I also felt a sense of place root inside me, and I remember thinking, perhaps for the first time in my life, that I might never move again.

Twenty-Three

There hung over everything a sense that *something* was about to happen. It was a steady state of agitation that affected us in both good and bad ways. The newspaper headlines seemed to forecast global catastrophe, while on the street, a youthful optimism was bubbling up all around London. This energy fueled Penny and me, and we could already see that our relentless grinding was paying off. We'd willed the dream of our company into existence, and now our names were getting out there, our work was being recognized, and good things were starting to happen.

When the phone rang one morning, I answered, and after a brief conversation, put the receiver back down.

"Who was that?" asked Penny.

"That was Peter Brown."

Peter Brown was the assistant to Brian Epstein, and Brian Epstein was the manager of the Beatles.

"Well," said Penny excitedly, "out with it!"

"He said 'the boys'—that's what he called them; he said the boys want to meet with us."

"About what?"

The Beatles were then at the height of their power and popularity. They'd just released *Sgt. Pepper's Lonely Hearts Club Band*, a momentous album credited with catalyzing that year's Summer of Love in San Francisco, and though retired from touring, the Beatles were beginning to experiment with other entrepreneurial efforts. To do this, they were in the process of forming a new company, Apple Corps. And one of Apple Corps' first undertakings would be the Apple Boutique, a clothing store, and they wanted Penny and me to do PR for the opening and the shop.

Like so many others, I loved the Beatles. Beneath their upbeat melodies and their deceptively simple sing-along lyrics, there was an understated depth of emotion and experience that elevated their music from trendy to timeless. Paul and John had been in their teens when their mothers had tragically died and it was out of the resulting hurt and hope that arose one of the most formidable musical partnerships in history. But the shiny exterior of the Beatles' happy-go-lucky image had worn thin and deep divisions and unsolvable conflicts had already metastasized within the group.

Penny and I met them at their Savile Row offices in Mayfair. Peter Brown opened the door for us, and we walked in on an arresting *tableau vivant*. Paul, seated at the upright piano in the corner, was working out a song. Ringo, parked in a chair by the window, gazed out of it contentedly. George, who might have been the leader of any other band, looked on from one end of a couch. Sitting on the other end of it was John, rather dourly flipping through the pages of a magazine.

Peter invited us to sit and proceeded to explain about taking the Beatles' groovy philosophy of peace and love for a spin around the landscape of English capitalism. The Apple Boutique, to open on Baker Street, was, in Paul's words, to be "a beautiful place where beautiful

Closing day at the Apple Boutique
(Wesley/Hulton Archive © Getty Images)

people can buy beautiful things." We were soon joined by the Fool, the merry band of eccentric Dutch designers charged with designing the shop and the merchandise, and we went about discussing details.

We got along well with the boys, and though the Fool seemed to operate in a world of its own, in all it seemed to be a productive relationship. But then, only a few weeks after being hired, we learned that Brian Epstein had died. Considered the fifth Beatle by many, Epstein had been plagued by depression, by pills, and by the fact that there was no legal expression for his sexuality. His death created a catastrophic absence of leadership that not only fomented existing divisions within the band but also exposed the dire state of their finances.

Despite this tragic news, the opening of the Apple Boutique just before the holidays was a rapturous, psychedelic affair with half of London showing up to celebrate. Inspired by the mural at Lord John on Carnaby Street, the Fool had a richer, denser mural painted on their storefront (an extravagance for which they neglected to get the necessary approvals and would eventually have to paint over in plain white). With crowds, music, and an abundance of media coverage, the opening of the boutique was a major victory for Carolyn Pfeiffer, Ltd.

invites you to the preview of
their shop at 94 Baker Street,
London, W.1
on December fifth at
seven forty-six o'clock sharp

Apple Juice and Champagne
Fashion show by the Fool 8.16 o'clock

R.S.V.P.
Penny Knowles and Carolyn Pfeiffer
Flat 2, 10 Connaught Place, W.2
PAD 6215

Invitation to the Apple Boutique opening
(Carolyn Pfeiffer archive)

With the new year—1968—the dark clouds over international politics grew more menacing still. Instead of announcing their headlines, the newspapers now screamed them. The Tet Offensive was escalating the war in Vietnam; the Prague Spring was exacerbating tensions between the Soviet Union and Czechoslovakia; and the assassination of Martin Luther King Jr. had brought a deeply divided America to the brink of chaos.

Against the backdrop of this spreading turmoil, we soldiered on with our publicity efforts. Having worked well with the Beatles, we continued to handle the Apple Boutique. We also came on to do PR for *Wonderwall,* for which George was composing the score. During the production of that film, I became friends with Jane Birkin, who was only twenty-two and whose husband, the composer John Barry, had recently left her.

She'd taken the divorce badly, and, between setups, I'd do what I could to console her as she continued to work through her heartache.

When *Wonderwall* was invited to premiere at the 1968 Cannes Film Festival, George planned to support the film by asking Ringo to join him at the festival. This meant Penny and I would have them both as clients. If this weren't enough, Geraldine called soon after. Her new film, *Peppermint Frappé,* had also been invited to compete in competition, and she and Saura would be attending. And, of course, Omar would also be there. He'd recently wrapped production on *Funny Girl,* and while it wouldn't open until the fall, the industry gossip was that his chemistry with Barbra Streisand was remarkable and that Columbia had a huge hit on its hands. Maintaining a public profile was therefore not only in Omar's best interest but also was studio orders.

It was an impressive client list for any publicist, but for us—two young women unaffiliated with a larger firm—it felt like a coup. Almost from nothing, we suddenly had a star-studded roster to take to the biggest film festival in the world. We'd been legitimized. In just over one year, we'd gone from upstart outsiders to recognized players.

When Penny came into the office the next day, she was aglow. Assuming it was because of our good news, I thought nothing of it. Despite her misgivings, she'd grown fond of my turtles, Updike and Salinger, and would feed and dote on them as we talked through our deadlines and clients. But this morning she was almost unrecognizable as she picked up Salinger and stroked his head with the pad of her index finger.

"What is it, Penny? What's going on?"

She looked at me innocently but could not suppress a smile. "I really shouldn't say anything."

But the harder she tried not to smile, the more her smile grew. Her hands went to her stomach. "I'm pregnant," she said.

She and Michael had hoped for a third child, and I was elated.

"When it's your turn," she beamed, "I pray you're spared the morning sickness."

"Who says I'm going to have a turn?" I said, laughing.

I couldn't imagine the stability required for motherhood. Even now, at thirty, I could barely imagine motherhood at all. Even though I was just starting out with Terry, our relationship didn't seem to be on that trajectory. For some reason, the bond between us wasn't cementing. Not that it couldn't, but somehow, it hadn't. He was moodier than I first realized, more prone to bouts of depression. There was something about him that I'd yet to figure out.

Penny's pregnancy came at a hectic time. In addition to preparing for Cannes, Penny's onetime roommate, Grace Coddington (the model with fiery red hair I'd first met at a dinner party years earlier), had started as an editor at British *Vogue*. She'd also married the restaurateur Michael Chow, and through them Penny and I were brought on to oversee the opening of the first Mr. Chow restaurant in Knightsbridge, a restaurant that would become known for its refined atmosphere and expensive but delicious Chinese food. The opening was a magical evening. A painter by training, Michael was a reluctant entrepreneur and stayed within artistic circles. This contributed to the restaurant's instant success that would attract everyone from the Beatles and the Rolling Stones to Mae West and Federico Fellini.

Then, on the heels of the opening of Mr. Chow's, Franco Zeffirelli, the Italian director with whom I'd grown quite close, had Paramount Pictures hire us to handle publicity for the premiere of his new film, *Romeo and Juliet*. It was the first Shakespeare adaptation to use actors close to the characters' ages and, as a consequence, was wildly popular with audiences young and old. Winner of multiple Academy Awards— and nominated for best picture and best director—the film still stands as the most commercially successful Shakespeare adaptation to date. Managing press for the two leads, Olivia Hussey and Leonard Whiting, fell to us. Both were mere children who, in a matter of days, were transformed into international celebrities.

May arrived and preparations for Cannes got underway in earnest. In the days leading up to our departure, excitement between Penny and me had never been higher. But, a few days before we were to leave, Penny confided that this pregnancy had not been like her others, that something wasn't right with her body.

"I'm fine, really, but I'm to reduce my activities. Doctor's orders," she said. She looked at me with a hint of concern. "It means I'm not to travel."

I took a moment to absorb this.

"You're strong, Penny. Rest. I'll be okay."

"Are you sure?"

Thankfully, the logistics were already in place. George was bringing his girlfriend, Patti, and Ringo was bringing his wife, Maureen, who was then pregnant. The four of them were going to fly from London, and Geraldine and Saura were going to fly from Madrid. Meantime, I was going to meet Omar in Paris and we'd take a train the rest of the way.

When I arrived in Paris, Omar met me at the station, and we made our way to our platform. People recognized him and stepped aside, their eyes darting from him to me and back again. When we were seated, a waitress brought our drinks, whiskey for Omar, water for me.

A group of nuns on the platform recognized him through the window and huddled together whispering. I pointed them out and Omar waved, sending a ripple of excitement through them.

"Does it get old, all the attention?"

He laughed. "People have a relationship with the characters I've played, but no relationship with me. That I'll never get used to."

As the train left Paris behind, he turned to me.

"It's why you and I work so well."

"Why's that?"

"Because you see who I am. Not as a character but as a person."

Our drinks came and Omar tipped the waitress. Then he smiled and raised his glass.

"To Cannes!"

The gentle splendor of southern France is a special kind of beauty. As the train snaked through rolling hills and along glassy rivers, past villages and small towns, the terrain grew increasingly Mediterranean. When we arrived in Cannes, I got Omar to his hotel and then caught a taxi to Antibes, where the Beatle contingent was settling into a private villa at the Hotel du Cap-Eden-Roc.

Entering the suite where they'd gathered, I smiled when I saw Maureen, Ringo's wife, on her hands and knees ironing her gown. There were armies of people at her beck and call, but she was a working-class girl from Liverpool, and the notion of tasking someone else with something she could do herself had never occurred to her. Then George appeared. They all distrusted French cooking, and he'd gone to bring back a simple dinner of fish and chips.

Ringo's birthday was approaching, and George, Paul, and John wanted to surprise him with an original Picasso. So while George and Ringo ate, Peter Brown pulled me aside and asked if I could get to Picasso.

"Even if I could get to Picasso," I said in disbelief, "what would I say?"

"Just ask him."

"You want me to ask Picasso for a painting?"

"Yes."

"Well," I said, "let's see. How much do they want to spend?"

"Spend? No, they just want a doodle, a squiggle on a napkin or something. You know, as a favor to the boys."

After a toast to *Wonderwall* and to the French mastery of fish and chips, I excused myself and headed back to Cannes to meet Geraldine. She wanted to introduce me to Truman Capote, who was staying at the Carlton. As we walked there, we came across Louis Malle and François

Truffaut. They were visibly irritated about something and, with a cluster of other directors, were talking earnestly among themselves.

"Do you know what's going on?" I asked Geraldine. "Is it the protests?"

Geraldine nodded.

"They're starting to spread," she said.

We found Truman in his room overlooking the Croisette. Short and feisty, he had a ferocious energy about him.

"Bloody Mary?" he asked as soon as introductions were out of the way.

As he mixed our drinks—the best Bloody Mary I've ever had—he recounted his recent heartache of being jilted by his boyfriend, his air-conditioning repairman who'd gone back to his wife. Then, drinks in hand, we sat by the window and looked out over the Mediterranean. The sun was shining, the Riviera was crowded, and the mighty Cannes Film Festival was underway.

The next day I arranged for Peter Brown and me to meet with Gustav Kahnweiler, Picasso's art dealer. We met at Le Blue Bar, a fashionable Cannes bar-café, and I laid out the request.

"It's a favor," I said with an uneasy smile. "You know, for the boys."

Kahnweiler looked at me sternly and then shook his head.

"No. *Ce n'est pas possible.*"

He then added that if *the boys* were to purchase an existing work, he could possibly get Picasso to add his signature, but that under no circumstances would the maestro agree to a freebie.

That would have been the end of the matter except that the next day my phone began to ring, and it would continue to ring for weeks afterward, as gallery owners and art dealers across the world, having caught wind of my meeting with Kahnweiler, concluded that I was the Beatles' art buyer and that the Beatles were in the market for something on the scale of a Picasso.

By now, reports of student protests were accompanied by whispers that de Gaulle was on the verge of deploying the military. This deepening crisis shone a spotlight on the French filmmakers at the festival because the government had removed Henri Langlois, a godlike figure in French cinema, from his post at the Cinémathèque Française. In response, Truffaut and Godard had formed the Cinémathèque Defence Committee, whose protests led to Langlois's reinstatement. But the episode was still fresh, and the filmmakers felt themselves to be at odds with the government. In light of the spreading student and worker protests, they felt an obligation to disrupt the opulence of yacht parties and red-carpet premieres.

In some ways, what was going on in France was isolated, but at the same time, there was no denying that a spirit of revolution was sweeping the globe. In Poland and East Germany, students protested their authoritarian governments. There were also student movements in Mexico City and around the United States where people were taking to the streets and demanding change. To me it felt like the entire planet was convulsing with riots and upheaval and that Cannes, instead of a film festival, had become a volatile political convention.

The screenings proceeded cautiously. *Wonderwall* screened out of competition, a psychedelic supplement to the gravity of the official lineup. The celebrity of George and Ringo attracted other celebrities, and the event, while crowded, was fun and glamorous.

But then, at the screening of *Peppermint Frappé,* the situation came to a head. Just before the film began, Godard and Truffaut took to the stage.

Truffaut spoke first.

"The country is under siege," he shouted. He was painfully shy, and this made his agitation even more dramatic. "The radio announces by the hour that factories are occupied or closed. The trains have stopped, and the metro and buses will be next. So for the Cannes Film Festival to continue is ridiculous."

"We're talking about solidarity with students and workers," added Godard. "You're talking about dolly shots and close-ups."

François Truffaut and other directors shut down the 1968 Cannes Film Festival
(Photograph by Jack Garofalo/Paris Match Archive © Getty Images)

They were then joined onstage by Louis Malle, Claude Lelouch, Roman Polanski, Carlos Saura, Geraldine Chaplin, and a group of other filmmakers who all called for the shutdown of the festival in solidarity with the protesters.

It was a standoff between them and the festival's director, Robert Favre Le Bret, who signaled for the curtains to be lifted and for the film to begin. But the filmmakers stood their ground, and as the velvet curtains rose, they grabbed onto them in a collective effort to keep them down. Le Bret escalated the confrontation even more by commanding the projectionist to start the film. And now the opening credit sequence of *Peppermint Frappé* was being projected onto Geraldine, the directors, and the half-drawn curtains.

It is an image forever seared into my memory.

The audience came to life, some shouting at the filmmakers but most shouting at Le Bret and his underlings. The two factions then turned on each other and, as mayhem broke out around me, there arose a sudden concern for safety.

The festival was promptly canceled. No one knew what was going on, only that a countrywide strike was imminent. If that happened, the entire country would shut down—no trains and no planes—and there was a possibility that civil war would erupt, that de Gaulle would be overthrown, or that the government itself would collapse.

It was a mad dash to get my people out of France. I found Geraldine, who along with Saura wanted to stay to witness what would happen. I desperately contacted travel agents, hotel concierges, and airlines. A combination of dogged persistence and multilingual negotiation peppered with splashes of good fortune proved just sufficient enough to extricate us all before an eleven million worker strike brought the country to a complete standstill, while de Gaulle secretly fled to Germany.

I arrived back in London and fell into a deep sleep. When I awoke in the morning, the intensity of Cannes was still so present that I had to work to remember the details of my life. I had a company. I had a cat and two turtles. And, in Terry, I had a relationship. Sort of. Penny came over and I was still a mess and not at all myself. I offered her coffee and then remembered that she was off caffeine because of the baby. Feeling foolish, I looked at her, seeing her for the first time since she'd arrived. Her blonde hair fell to her chin and her eyes were red, not with tears but with sorrow.

"Oh, Penny, what is it? Is everything all right?"

She started to say something, but her voice quivered and she fell silent. And then I realized that she'd had her hand on her stomach the entire time. My eyes moved downward, and I could see in the way that she gripped her sweater in her fist that it was pushing against the source of her pain.

"I lost it, Carolyn. The baby's gone."

She'd been so healthy. She'd done all of the research, gone to the best doctors, done everything she could. And still she'd miscarried. I hugged her and would have held her longer, but she pulled away, drawing her shoulders back, clenching her jaw, clearing her voice.

"I'm fine. Really. I'm just . . . sad."

"Take some time, Penny."

She nodded and we agreed that she'd take the time she needed. She left and I felt disoriented, like the *something* we were expecting was now happening. The world had gone mad, and the innocence had gone away.

That evening, Terry took me to dinner. We went to a new restaurant, and his excitement for it created a mismatch in our moods that helped me see the mismatch in our relationship. I could see now that the part of him that was out of reach to me would always remain so. The inequities in France didn't interest him. He'd overcome difficult beginnings and had little sympathy for those unable to do likewise. But I was still stunned by Cannes, still working through the fact that the festival had been shut down by people who believed in solidarity and in humankind, by filmmakers who believed that, even if it could be used to lie, the best use of a camera was to expose truth.

After dinner, I pleaded exhaustion. It was an excuse, a line, and I knew he knew that, for me, the thing had run its course. And, with that, I also knew that he had his pride and that I would no longer hear from him.

Whatever our attraction to each other, it wasn't enough. It was comfortable and caring but without love or anything more. I had no way of knowing then, of course, that he would be unable to escape the depression that plagued him and that he would eventually take his own life. But I did know that he was one of his generation's great photographers and that our relationship, however brief, had had a formative effect on me.

As I approached my flat, I stopped at Marble Arch. I tried to see it for the first time, to be present, to allow myself to experience the majesty that was always there. I was feeling melancholy, separated from something vital. I longed for connection—tactile, one being to another. I wanted urgency. And I knew where I could find it. So I allowed what had been on the periphery of my mind since the day I set foot in London to come front and center.

Twenty-Four

—————

The knocking on my door was in unison with the beating of my heart. In calling the Englishman, I was acting against my better judgment. But purposeful actions are attended by a motorcade of justifications. Once the notion of calling him occurred to me, it was just a matter of time.

I hadn't seen or heard from him since *Zhivago*, and I'd never told a soul about him, not even Penny. He was a phantom, real but known only to me. If I never saw him again, he'd have become a memory—less than a memory, someone who never existed at all. But I wanted to see him again. I wanted to conjure him like the ghost that he was. Because he was right there, close enough for a morning coffee or a lunch or a dinner or a nightcap.

As I walked nervously to the door, I knew I wasn't going to only see him one time. I was going to be present; I was going to let the thing go where it wanted. I opened the door and we stood across from each other, neither of us moving for a full minute. The thrill of recognition started in my eyes. And then it spread around my face, turning the corners of my mouth ever so slightly upward and pulling the skin of my forehead taut. A wave of warmth washed down my body and activated my senses, bringing each to desperate attention. My tongue adjusted in anticipation. My breath too. And my ears strained for the softest sound.

It was the sexiest silence in all my life.

He came toward me, slipped his arms around me, and walked me backward through the entrance, down the hall, and into the bedroom. Our eyes found each other, and there rushed between us a current of longing, of desire, and of the most pleasurable thing of all: anticipation.

Even after it was over, neither of us had spoken. We were flush, out of breath, smiling big smiles until, finally, I said, "Hi."

We drank wine at my kitchen table, my shirt unbuttoned, his lost to the bedroom. We luxuriated in those affections that come effortlessly to lovers who can never love each other fully because they are unencumbered by all that is mundane and ordinary. The room was dark, save for an overhead light that framed us as if in a chiaroscuro painting. The look in his eyes changed, and I saw that he was not looking at me but rather was seeing me within something else, within something beautiful.

If Terry's passion was food, for my Englishman, it was light. It fascinated him, and I loved the relationship he had with it. Light spoke to him, moved him, directed him. Most of all, I loved when I found myself encased, as I was now, in lighting that captivated him.

When he was leaving, I held the door open. He put a palm on my cheek, his fingers wrapping around the nape of my neck, and he kissed me.

"Come again," I said.

He smiled, and when I realized that I was already thinking about the next time, I knew that the bottled-up affection between us would be released. There was no reversing it. I didn't know what would happen, but I did know one thing for certain: that, one day, it would have to end.

Twenty-Five

After he'd gone, I brushed my teeth and looked into the bathroom mirror. In my reflection, I searched for the girl I used to be. Was she in my lips? My cheekbones? My eyes? As a girl, I'd done the same thing: I'd searched in my reflection for the woman I would one day become. So much of girlhood is spent waiting. You see the women around you—faces beautiful, hips and breasts pronounced—and you understand yourself to be what the flower bud is to the bloom. You wonder what will happen, when it will happen, and what the result will be.

And now I knew. My body was like that of the women I'd observed as a girl. I knew something of its capability, its appeal and power. I'd had lovers and I'd been engaged. I'd traveled the world and lived in some of the world's great cities. I'd also started and was running a successful business. Though there was so much I still wanted to do in my professional life, I was challenged and fulfilled. But my personal life was more complicated. I was thirty years old, living alone, and teetering on the brink of a relationship with a married man.

This inner turmoil was mirrored in the intensifying volatility of the outside world. Andy Warhol was shot that June. Two days later, Robert Kennedy was assassinated. Race relations were reaching a breaking point, and it was obvious to everyone that the war in Vietnam had become an unmitigated disaster. Patience was running out, and in everything there seemed to be a hunger for endings. An end to the injustice, an end to the violence, an end to the decade.

In a melancholy parallel, the Beatles, as good a proxy as any for the 1960s, were themselves negotiating more with endings than with beginnings. Their gospel of generosity and integrity had not rooted well in the arid soil of Baker Street. The Apple Boutique had bled money, and eight months after overseeing its opening, Penny and I oversaw publicity for its closing. To triage the fiasco, we turned the event into a party that was guaranteed to overwhelm London's police force. For as long as supplies lasted, everyone who showed up was welcome to one piece of merchandise free of charge. On the night before the closing, the Beatle wives and girlfriends came and took what they wanted from the shelves. It was a significant dent in the inventory but not enough to dissuade the mob that overran the store the next day.

Indeed, the Beatles were launching into their crescendo. The divisions were already deep, the damage already done. With "Hey Jude," a moody anthem fully seven minutes long, the beginning of the end was underway. Paul McCartney's ode to John Lennon's son in the midst of John's divorce from Cynthia, it is a song onto which everyone can project something. Everyone has a Jude. Everyone has something they want someone to not take badly. Everyone knows of a burden unjustly borne on the shoulders of someone they love. And, in the na-na-nas of the song's coda, there is an ecstatic togetherness that elicits smiles and hugs and tears.

I bought the single, and because I couldn't get enough of it, I took it with me to Saint-Tropez, where Romy Schneider had been cast opposite Alain in Jacques Deray's *La Piscine*. After the humiliation of their broken engagement, Romy was worried that Alain would be unfair to her in the press even though he'd requested her for the part. She'd asked me to be on hand just in case.

La Piscine is a film that could not have been made even a year earlier. Not only was it intimate and explicit but it was a foray into uncharted sexual territory. Among the most provocative scenes is one in which Alain's character strips and then proceeds to whip Romy's character before they fall into each other's arms.

Romy and Alain on the set of La Piscine
(Photograph by Jean-Pierre Bonnotte/Gamma Legends © Getty Images)

The layers of metaphor were many. Considering Alain's betrayal only a few years earlier, Romy was making herself dangerously vulnerable. She'd given up everything for him, and in return she'd had her heart broken. To top it off, none of Romy's Hollywood efforts were successful enough to allow her to fully cross over, and so, without Alain, she had nowhere to go but back to the Germany she'd forsaken. While there, she married and had a son, David, and she was now in the process of resurrecting her career. With *What's New Pussycat?*—the first feature film written by Woody Allen, then a rising star, and starring Peter O'Toole, Peter Sellers, and Capucine—Romy had launched a comeback that now landed her in a role opposite Alain, the very man who'd made a comeback necessary in the first place.

"Sometimes you have to follow your nose," Romy liked to say, "even if it means it gets broken."

She'd brought David, her son, with her to Saint-Tropez, and it was a joy to watch them together. It was not lost on me that, of the women my age, most were now mothers. Claudia, Penny, Nathalie. The anchor that this gave their lives illuminated the lack of any anchor in mine, but I was only happy for them. Especially Romy. Motherhood animated her in a way that nothing else had, and the bond between her and David was tender and deep. David was angelic and energetic, and when I played "Hey Jude" for him, he loved it as only a three-year-old can love something, wildly and unreservedly. We played it over and over, and I have the most beautiful memories of us dancing and laughing as we sang out the na-na-nas.

Since she's also in the film, Jane Birkin was there, her signature straw basket perpetually in the crook of her elbow. Since her divorce from John Barry, she'd been cast opposite Serge Gainsbourg in the French film *Slogan*. They'd fallen madly in love and were about to scandalize all of Europe with his song "*Je t'aime moi non plus*." In it, Jane's audible breathing and cries of pleasure build up to an orgasm. Predictably, the song was denounced by the Vatican and was banned in multiple countries across Europe. All of this was a coup for the album, though, and Serge is on the record as calling the pope "our greatest PR man."

Filming of *La Piscine* got underway, and it was evident that Alain had no interest in treating Romy badly. In fact, it was the opposite; the romantic love may have ended, but we could all see that he loved her dearly, that they loved each other, and that out of the ashes of their relationship, something new was now emerging.

With Romy's permission, I made plans to return to London. But before leaving, I met Alain for a drink. He was tanned and attractive, and it seemed to me that, at that very moment, his beauty was peaking.

"You were good to Romy," I said.

He laughed.

"Are you surprised?"

"No," I said. "I know how it is between you."

Alain might have been unpredictable, but he was not unreliable. He and Nathalie were still trying to untangle themselves from each other. They were in the process of divorcing, but because of Anthony, their lives were still intertwined. She continued to live in the house, and they were both intent on preserving some semblance of family.

"And you, Caroline, there's something going on with you?"

"What do you mean?"

"It's love, isn't it?" He laughed, knowing he'd caught me off guard.

"No. Maybe. Do you know something?"

"Only what your eyes tell me."

I sipped my drink and looked away.

"Anyway," I said, looking back at him, "he's married."

"Is he French or English?"

"Does it matter?"

"It matters."

"He's English."

He sighed. "That is more complicated. For the English, everything is more, I don't know, consequential."

"So what advice do you have for me?" I asked with a smile.

"Me? Who am I to give advice? I always dare everything in love. And look." He shrugged and held out his hands. "On the other hand, who am I to withhold advice?"

"*Et alors*," I said with a laugh. "So then?"

He looked me in the eye and, in a subdued and solemn voice, said, "Open yourself to the gentle indifference of the world, Caroline."

It was a line from Albert Camus's *The Stranger*. Robert Bolt had had me read it during our affair on *Zhivago*. A pivotal book in Alain's life, it explained, at least in part, the ease with which he dismissed the opinions of others. An existential masterpiece centering on a senseless murder, Meursault, the protagonist, resents society's insistence on manufacturing meaning in a meaningless universe. With its argument that this compulsion estranges us from our true identities, *The Stranger* is a challenge to its reader—and to Alain specifically—that the ultimate, and perhaps only, certainty is the experience of one's own reality.

"You're saying it doesn't matter what happens?" I asked.

"I'm saying it's you who decides what matters," he said.

I left him with a hug and a promise to continue our conversation. I then took a taxi to the Nice airport, remembering that it was there that Françoise Dorléac had died. On my flight home, I reflected on Romy and Nathalie and Alain, about the elasticity of the bonds that tie some people together. But were they even people? They seemed, to me, more like archetypes, vital expressions of the times. Alain was French masculinity, proud and determined to restore dignity; Romy was old-world royalty, a princess dropped into radical modernity; and Nathalie was the voice of countless women, raw femininity loosed on the patriarchy.

When I got home, my Englishman took me to a nearby pub for dinner. I told him about *La Piscine*, and our conversation slowly made its way around the industry. We talked about Julie Christie and Vanessa Redgrave, Albert Finney and Jack Nicholson. My Englishman wanted more than anything to direct feature films. He had it in him. The vision and voice; the rare quality of originality. But life got in the way. He had his family and his job and the problem of not enough time. And so it was mostly something he talked about, a dream for another day.

That night, as we lay in bed, a soft light came from the hallway. He propped himself up on an elbow, and I could see in his eyes that he was not looking at me but seeing me. In turn I tried to see him: he'd married so young, and his life was so full of hustle and responsibility, and he was sometimes overwhelmed by a fear that he might never get to live enough or create enough or love enough. His dreams and fantasies haunted him because he was so terrified of always having to imagine them and never getting to remember them. But I was the exception he allowed himself; I was both fantasy and memory, and because of that, his gaze would fall on me, and it would stay on me even as I looked away self-consciously.

His expression changed as his eyes shifted downward. He traced a finger from the notch in my clavicle down my sternum and then, following the bottom of my rib cage, to the line dividing my hip from my thigh. If I lifted my knee, I could have pinched his finger in its crease.

"This is my favorite part, this line from the outside to the inside."

"It's skin."

"It's more than that."

His finger moved along it lightly.

"If wanting and having could be one word, it'd be something like that."

I've often wondered why a man sees magic where a woman sees skin. And I've thought that maybe it's an important distinction: a man learns to know himself—what he wants and what interests him—and from this knowledge his power is sourced. But a woman learns to understand herself—what and why something is wanted from or of her—and from this understanding her power is sourced. Maybe one knows and the other understands.

My Englishman never spent the night with me. At the end of our evenings, he always went home to his real life and always left me to mine. And I never minded—except that one night. Just that once, I wished he had slept with me until the morning.

Twenty-Six

I'd told myself it wasn't love with the Englishman. Then, when I admitted that it was love, I told myself that it wouldn't last. But the thing about love is that once it comes into the world, there is no forcing it back out. As weeks turned into months, I stopped telling myself that I knew what it was, and I accepted that it was an important, and very secret, part of my life. But a secret molds itself to its holder. Like metal poured into a cast, a secret takes the form of what is already there: insecurity, vulnerability, weakness.

When the d'Amicos returned from Castiglioncello, where they'd gone to escape the August heat, I made a long overdue visit to Rome, and as I got out of the taxi on Via Paisiello in front of the d'Amicos' building, I had the unmistakable feeling of returning home. With the d'Amicos, you can be gone a day or a decade and it is as if you never left.

Suso, Silvia, and Caterina hugged me warmly, and Maso greeted me with a kiss on both cheeks.

"*Benvenuto,*" he said, smiling.

Then Lele made a show of kissing my hand.

"Our American daughter has returned."

Seated across from me at lunch was Masolino and, beside him, Benedetta, the woman he'd married. She was attractive and elegant, and I could see that they were good together. Then I found myself studying Masolino. His shoulders were now full, his jaw sturdy, and his brow, inherited from his maternal grandfather, strong. The effect was a sharpened gaze and an aura of authority that obscured the boy I'd loved. And this seemed like it had been inevitable all along; the man across from me was always who Masolino was going to become. He'd found his path early, and perhaps it was the illusion that we were searching for one together that undid the future we might have had together.

After lunch, Silvia and I walked over to Piazza di Spagna and sat among the tourists on the Spanish Steps. She'd begun an affair with Alfredo Giannetti, a prominent writer and director who'd won an Academy Award for writing the screenplay for *Divorce Italian Style*— and she was in the feverish throes of new romance.

"Do your parents know?" I asked.

"You know how Rome is—people know but they don't know. Besides, I'm not a girl anymore who has to ask for permission."

"Is it love?"

"Of course it's love! People talk of love as something scarce, as if love will run out if you love too much or too frequently. *Ma perché?* No, for me, love is easy."

"And if he doesn't love you back?"

"I love him because I love him, not because he loves me."

A few years later, she would begin another affair, this one with the great director Roberto Rossellini. It would be deeply important to them both and would last until his death.

Was it true that there was enough love? That you could love and love and it would never run out? Or that you could love without needing to be loved in return? Beneath these abstract questions were questions that I not only struggled to answer but also struggled to ask. Did my Englishman love me? For how long could we keep on? For how long could I love him?

Back at the flat, I found Suso sitting in the corner of the couch, her Olivetti on her lap. Her most recent project was another collaboration with Visconti, this one about Ludwig, the nineteenth-century king of Bavaria.

"How is London?" she asked. "Do you like it?"

"Exciting things are happening."

"And are you fulfilled?"

"I think so, yes."

She looked at me and I felt vulnerable. She was seeing something, reading something.

"Carolina, do you know why Rome is Rome? Do you know why Rome came to dominate the ancient world?"

"I don't know," I confessed.

"Rome became Rome," she said, "because of its genius."

"I don't understand."

"What was the genius of Rome? It was that Rome is in the middle of Italy and Italy is in the middle of the Mediterranean. Does that make sense? Rome had a climate suitable for agriculture. It was also on the Tiber, which was important for trade. And it was close to the sea but inland, protected from pirates and naval attacks. That was Rome's genius. It was because of those qualities that Rome became Rome and was able to dominate the ancient world."

"But how is that genius?"

"Today, genius means what—an exceptional talent?"

"Something like that."

"But in ancient times it was believed that every person was born with a guiding spirit, with a genius that attended them in their life. This spirit determined their essence and their qualities. If they had an exceptional talent, it was because of their genius. But with time this changed, and genius came to refer to the talent itself and not to the spirit responsible for the talent."

"But you don't believe in spirits in that sense, do you?"

"I believe that genius is not what you do but what is there already. As in the case of Rome, it's the qualities that account for the outcome. *Allora*, take Visconti. What is Visconti's genius?"

"His direction, of course," I said. "His ability to re-create authenticity and to make important films."

Suso shook her head.

"No; Luchino's films *express* his genius, but they aren't genius itself."

"What, then, is his genius?"

Suso shrugged nonchalantly, as if the answer were plain to see.

"It's all that is innate in him and all that is unique to him—that is Visconti's genius."

"But everyone has that, no? Everyone has things that are innate and things that are unique about them."

"*Esattamente giusto.*" There was intensity in her expression. "And that is what I'm saying to you. Mind your genius. *Listen within and mind those things that come together in you and only in you.*"

All my life I'd thought of genius as a word reserved for the Einsteins and the Mozarts, the da Vincis and the Michelangelos. Could it be that everything and everyone was possessed of genius?

I left Rome the next day for Madrid to see Geraldine, and as the plane moved out over the Mediterranean, I watched the land disappear from view. Beneath us were small, inconsequential islands and the vast expanse of the Tyrrhenian. Then the pilot pointed out Sardinia, blue and sprawling, to the west. And as we soared past it, all I could think about was how things came to be. Everything exact. Everything as it must be. Everything bursting with its own genius.

With the success of *Zhivago* and *Peppermint Frappé*, Geraldine was finding her voice and coming into her own. The stability of her relationship with Carlos Saura also gave her confidence and a disarming combination of alacrity and grace. We were to go out for dinner with a visiting friend of theirs, a writer from Mexico, but Saura was detained. While we waited, Geraldine poured glasses of cava and we sat in the sitting room. After bringing me up to date on *La Madriguera*, the film she and Saura were beginning, she cocked her head and looked at me.

"Do you ever think about babies?"

"I think every woman does at one point or another," I said. "Why? Are you and Carlos . . . ?"

"It's come up."

Saura had two sons from an earlier marriage, and so Geraldine came to the matter from a different angle. Still, that neither of us had our own children gave us something in common, and as we sipped on our cava, we talked about pregnancy and relationships and the trade-offs between career and family.

The writer from Mexico turned out to be Carlos Fuentes, a novelist of international renown. He was waiting for us at the restaurant off Plaza Mayor, and after hugging Saura and kissing Geraldine, he held my hands in his and made a point of looking me in the eyes. Then he introduced himself and kissed me on the cheek. He was tall and handsome, dressed in boots and a leather jacket, and he had the gravity of someone to be taken seriously.

We sat down and conversation quickly turned to Czechoslovakia, where Fuentes had gone to observe the Soviet suppression of the Prague Spring, which had been a popular movement to reform hardline Communist policies in Czechoslovakia that had been met with over half a million Soviet troops and tanks. The crushing Soviet response had left scores of civilians dead, hundreds more injured, and had caused tens of thousands more to flee to the West.

"Deeper into the darkness we go," said Fuentes ruefully.

Saura took a sip of beer.

The Soviet invasion of Czechoslovakia
(Bettmann © Getty Images)

"Is a Communist regime like theirs any worse than an authoritarian regime like ours?" he asked.

"It's the horseshoe," Geraldine remarked, drawing a horseshoe in the air. "Extremists are more similar than not."

The son of a diplomat, Fuentes was born in Panama; he moved to Ecuador when he was two and to Washington, DC, when he was four. He spent his grade school years there before moving to Chile and, at age sixteen, "home" to Mexico. He spoke half a dozen languages and was comfortable anywhere on the planet. But he was Mexican through and through, with roots reaching back in time to Spain and to the Mediterranean. It was a nomadic existence that resonated strongly with me.

"What makes you Mexican?" I asked. "I mean, if you didn't live there until you were sixteen?"

We were multiple bottles of wine into the evening, and a warm familiarity was drawing out more personal conversation.

"Well," Fuentes said, "the US is a country of victors; Mexico is a country of survivors. So, for one thing, I have Mexico's tragic conscience.

But I wouldn't change that because we have some advantages over our neighbors to the north."

"Like what?" asked Geraldine.

"For one thing, we accept death. Americans accept violence but they cannot accept death. In Mexico, we give life to the past so we can live into the future."

It was not lost on me that his sentences were sometimes beautifully lyrical.

"Also, the US has yet to deal with 'the Other.' Indians. Blacks. Immigrants. In that sense, America is not yet a modern country, and I can say with some confidence that dark days lie ahead for the Americans."

It was perhaps a more ominous note than he'd intended, and he tried to salvage the mood.

"But if you ask me how I know I'm Mexican, it's because I dream in Spanish." Here his eyes lit up mischievously. "And because I can only make love in Spanish."

Saura roared with laughter and Geraldine slapped his forearm in mock outrage.

"Geraldine," cried Fuentes, "is French your language, or is it English? Saura will tell me. And what about you, Carolina?"

We tumbled out of the restaurant at midnight. Still laughing, we decided to walk through the city center. Saura and Geraldine led the way, pointing out fountains and monuments. Between Fuentes and me there was an obvious attraction, the kind that electrifies eye contact and, like a wave of energy, forces you to look away.

At the end of the night, we said our goodbyes, we exchanged our addresses, and we promised to stay in touch.

"Carolina," he said, "our lives are now marvelously and perilously tied together. Someday you and I will talk, and we will try to understand how and why things happen as they happen."

After kissing me on each cheek, he gave me a lingering hug, allowing the attraction that had been in the air between us to be transmitted.

When I returned to London, Suso's words returned to me: *mind your genius*, she'd said. But what was my genius? It was so easy to see the genius of those around me. In addition to an auspicious background, Geraldine was possessed of a piercing innocence and curiosity, of extraordinary talent and beauty. No wonder David Lean had cast her in *Zhivago*. No wonder she was personally and creatively intertwined with one of Spain's great filmmakers. Fuentes too. He was from a political family, and he had a cultural fluency unlike anything I'd encountered. Of course he wrote novels; he had the genius for it.

When my Englishman came over, I was eager to discuss all of this with him. But when I opened the door for him, I saw that he was bleeding. It wasn't the first time. He'd gotten into a fight at the pub—a slight he couldn't abide—and he'd gone in like a wolverine. I sat him down and fussed over him, carefully cleaning his scrapes and wiping away the blood.

"Did you win?" I asked.

"If it's a matter of who lost the most blood, then no; I lost badly."

I smiled and turned to rinse the cloth in the sink. He followed close behind me and, as I ran the water, I felt him against me, his mouth on my neck.

"I want to talk," I said.

"About what?"

"I want to talk about you. About your genius."

"I haven't any of that," he said, pulling me closer to him.

"But you do," I protested. "And you have to mind it."

I turned around, and he took a step back and leaned against the counter. Then I told him about my conversation with Suso, about how genius wasn't an expression of the extraordinary but, rather, described what was exceptional about the ordinary.

"It's to do with essence," I said, adding that everyone has genius. "It's here now. Yours and mine."

He looked into my eyes, and I could see he was taking the conversation seriously.

"Then, tell me," he said, "what is my genius?"

"You are brilliant and you are good," I said, touching the scrape on his cheek. "And you feel so much. That I know."

He stepped toward me, and I wanted him to see in me what I couldn't see in myself; I wanted him to say something tidy and profound—about my character, about my potential, about what my future would be.

Instead, he took another step forward and now we were as close as we could be without touching. The intimacy between us grew thick, and I could feel the essential part of me engaging with the essential part of him. This was his way of answering me, his way of letting me know that words would only diminish what he had to say.

Twenty-Seven

When Nathalie called, her voice was shaking and she could barely speak. All I could make out was that someone had been murdered, and that she was on her way to London.

She arrived in the evening, exhausted and in a state of shock. I drew a bath for her and sat beside her as she soaked. Gradually, I was able to piece together what had happened. The body of Stefan Markovic, one of Alain's bodyguards, had been found in a public dump on the outskirts of Paris. Alain was still in Saint-Tropez shooting *La Piscine* with Romy, but both he and Nathalie were persons of interest. After two days of grueling interrogation, she'd been allowed to leave. The story was now breaking, the press were in a frenzy, and Nathalie needed sanctuary.

"Do you know who murders people?" she asked, spitting the words out. "Men, that's who. It's men who assault; it's men who torture; and it's men who murder."

"But, Nat, you adore men."

"Of course, I adore them. And they're also impossible!"

The phone rang in the kitchen and I went to get it. On the other end was the grave voice of a French investigator demanding to speak with Nathalie. In order to leave France, she'd been forced to give them my number. I put the receiver on the counter and went back to the bathroom.

"It's the police," I said. "They have some more questions."

She sat up in disbelief and leaned over the side of the tub, straining toward the door.

"No, they *don't*!" she shouted past me, loud enough for the investigator to hear. "Tell them to *Fuck! Off! Merde!*"

Stefan was like Ivan, another of Alain's bodyguards. Unlike Ivan, he was handsome and charming. But over time his charm faded until, eventually, his relationship with Alain turned cold. It was rumored that he'd resorted to blackmail, that he had a habit of setting up surveillance cameras in bedrooms and that he had in his possession compromising images of everyone from Alain and Nathalie to Madame Pompidou, whose husband, Georges, was the prime minister and a favorite to succeed de Gaulle as president of France.

After her bath, Nathalie put on a robe, and I wrapped her in a blanket and sat her on the couch with a cup of tea. For a long time, neither of us said anything.

Finally, she spoke.

"I slept with him, you know. Once. Alain made sure I was home with Stefan when he announced on television that our marriage was over. Yeah," she sighed, "Alain arranged it like that. *Ces connards.*"

Then she took a sip of tea and seemed to soften.

"I only wish Alain could find enough love," she said. "The whole world loves him. You love him and I do, even now. But he's wild, and I don't know if a wild thing can know love."

Nathalie stayed with me for several weeks. It was an intense time, not only because of the investigation swirling but also because 1968 seemed determined to leave nothing unbroken, nothing unexploded. American cities were literally burning while, in Mexico City, hundreds of students and civilians were massacred. Closer to home, the Troubles were taking vicious hold of Northern Ireland. It felt like the planet couldn't take any more, like we had barreled past a tipping point and were now plummeting into the abyss.

While Nathalie was visiting, the Englishman kept his distance. And, by the time she returned to Paris, the holidays were bearing down. Alone in my flat, I felt a pang of loneliness. Christmas decorations were springing up around London, and a part of me hoped he would call or maybe just show up at my door one night. But he was with his family, and I wouldn't see him until the new year.

Since Penny had left the company, I'd brought on a young American named Allen Burry. Through Lee Solters, the publicist I'd met in Los Angeles, we'd been hired to do publicity for the London and Paris premieres of *Funny Girl* in January. This meant that, apart from Omar, we would be responsible for handling the inimitable Barbra Streisand as well as Ray Stark, the film's formidable producer. *Funny Girl* had opened in New York to smashing critical and commercial acclaim. Barbra Streisand, who was until then completely unknown outside of theater circles, became an international sensation overnight. The film would go on to receive eight Oscar nominations, with Streisand winning best actress. And, for his part, in the role of gambler and con man Nicky Arnstein, Omar had somehow found a still higher register of success and celebrity.

The media frenzy surrounding *Funny Girl* was fueled considerably by the enormous controversy of Omar and Barbra, an Arab and a Jew, falling in love in a major motion picture. After the Arab-Israeli War the previous year, in which Egypt suffered a humiliating defeat, tensions in the Middle East were dangerously high. For Omar and Barbra—whose affection for each other was as present off camera as it was on—to kiss on-screen was received, among some factions, as insensitive at best and as nothing short of treasonous at worst. A furious uproar filled with ugly accusations led to Omar's Egyptian citizenship nearly being revoked.

Of course, the controversy only benefited the film, and as the London premiere neared, the city filled with excitement. With Omar and Ray Stark to look after, I had Allen focus on Barbra, who, it turned out, was not the diva I was expecting. Surprisingly shy, she had a two-year-old son back in the States whom she missed immensely, and the punishing interview schedule took a toll on her. I was grateful for Allen's gentle touch and the grace with which he guided her through the media frenzy.

Barbra, Omar, and Princess Margaret at the Funny Girl *premiere*
(Photograph by Les Lee/Hulton Royals Collection © Getty Images)

The premiere was a dazzling evening. The red-carpet screening was followed by a gala attended by a host of celebrities and dignitaries, including Princess Margaret and her husband, the Earl of Snowdon. Extravagant gowns and sleek black ties were everywhere, as were camera flashes and crowds of fans. And, inside the theater, with the lights down low, there was the hushed magic of the movies. To forget about politics, to be transported to another world, to imagine yourself a different person: it was a soaring high that lingered long afterward.

In Paris days later, we produced another magical evening. What I remember most vividly is standing next to Barbra at the top of the steps outside the Royal Opera House as the crowd pushed in around us. There were journalists and photographers, television crews and hordes of fans, all of them walking a line between enthusiasm and incivility. There was something lawless about it, a terrifying feeling of individuals ceding control to the crowd and the crowd taking on a life of its own. The shouting grew louder, the aggression more desperate, and Barbra began to tremble. I could feel it in my shoulder that was touching hers, yet when I looked at her face, it was calm, consummately professional.

It's like that with celebrities. Or at least it was with Claudia, Omar, Romy, Geraldine, even Alain. They all had a sixth sense, an understanding that the outside—their appearances and their images—belonged as much to the public as it did to them. For my part, I never forgot that; even with those I considered friends, I never forgot that I was a part of the public and that as a publicist my job was to help them with what was on the outside, with the parts of them that belonged to us.

After the premieres, my Englishman was eagerly awaiting me in London. The new year was underway, and we quickly fell back into our obsessive patterns, stealing whatever time we could as if it would make up for all we'd lost over the holidays.

I wanted to tell Penny. It was an important part of my life, and I felt that, in the name of friendship, I owed it to her.

She invited me for tea, and I might have brought it up, but it turned out that she had news of her own. "As you know," she began as she filled our cups, "I've been quite keen on further studies. Well, I've given it a great deal of thought and I think I might do a course in psychology."

I wasn't expecting this. A part of me still thought she would come back to the company. But the more she expanded on her interest in psychology, the more sense it seemed to make. She'd always described herself as a listener and not a talker, and I could absolutely see that she had both the personality and the intellect to be a wonderful psychologist.

"I'm thrilled for you," I said. "Really."

"You're not disappointed?"

"Of course I am. But only selfishly."

The significance of Penny's news unsettled me. She was minding her genius. She was nurturing it and allowing it to blossom. In contrast, a married man was moving ever closer to the center of my life. She was pursuing a new dream; I was sinking deeper into an old one. With this realization, I felt the coils of a dilemma slip around me. I could want the Englishman away from me or I could want him with me; either way, it was around him that my wants were wrapped. And if I did nothing, if I left our entanglement to time, the dilemma would constrict more tightly around me and a solution to it would move further away.

Sometime later, Omar was back in London following his tour to promote *Funny Girl*. He'd invited me out for an early dinner and stopped by my flat to look through some press clippings I'd saved for him. Then, as I finished up some paperwork at my desk, I poured him a whiskey, and he took up a game of bridge against phantom opponents. It was a wordless interaction, the choreography of which we'd perfected over years of relationship.

But it was interrupted by a phone call from Jon Bradshaw, the American journalist who'd gotten himself stabbed in the back in southern Africa and who'd kept me up all night after the premiere of *Charley's Aunt* in Manchester.

"Who was that?" asked Omar after I hung up.

"Just a friend looking for some trouble."

I told him about Bradshaw, about his interest in gamblers and outlaws, mercenaries and gangsters.

"Call him back," insisted Omar.

"Yeah?"

"Let's have dinner at the races. I need the amusement and so do you."

Bradshaw rode with us to White City Stadium, and Omar took immediately to Bradshaw's devil-may-care attitude. Omar did well with sensitive types, but he really loved men with big personalities, men who lived large. Peter O'Toole and his ilk. Men like that gave Omar cover, permission to let loose in a culture that might otherwise single him out. And not only was the feeling mutual between Bradshaw and Omar, but Bradshaw was roundly impressed that I'd delivered up a delicious evening with one of the biggest movie stars in the world.

Both men fancied themselves serious gamblers, and a playful competition immediately began. I sided with Bradshaw because I didn't think anyone could beat Omar. I was right. Omar won every one of his races. The alcohol flowed, and between races the men told their stories of conquest and adventure, each one-upping the other.

"I was out with O'Toole," Omar began, smiling at the memory. "Bastard calls me Cairo Fred. Anyway, we're somewhere in Hollywood, out all night, and Peter takes us to see Lenny Bruce. Now, if O'Toole's a ten on a scale of crazy, Lenny's a thousand."

I watched Bradshaw lean forward, the pleasure of anticipation already challenging him to top Omar's story when his turn came.

"Peter and I are blind, falling-down drunk and ready for bed when Lenny pulls out his heroin. He starts shooting up, and we're making a terrible racket. Then there's a knock on the door and Lenny, who still has the syringe in his arm, mind you, stumbles over to the door. Do you know who it was?"

"Who?" Bradshaw said, smiling.

"LAPD. Batons out."

"No!"

"So off to jail we went."

"But you got off?"

"The studio sent a brigade of lawyers. At first, they were going to keep Lenny, but O'Toole just kept shouting, 'I'm not going anywhere without my friend Lenny Bruce!'"

Bradshaw's laugh was deep and infectious. I'd heard the story before and always chuckled at the thought of Omar, bewildered and swept up in O'Toole's carousing.

The silence was Bradshaw's to fill, and he didn't need prompting.

"Lenny Bruce should spend some time with Nguyễn Cao Kỳ."

"Who?"

"He's the prime minister of South Vietnam; a bit of an unguided missile. I was in Saigon on assignment, back when things were really heating up."

It was common for journalists to show up in war zones outfitted in camouflage, ready to roll around in the dirt, but Bradshaw's technique was different. He'd arrive in a brown velvet Carnaby Street suit and quickly figure out how to share a bottle of whiskey with the highest ranking official he could find.

He went on to entertain us with a story about a wild night that almost landed him in the hospital and that, if not for the status of his companion, would certainly have landed him in jail. But more than the content of the story, what I loved was Bradshaw's telling of it. It was adventurous and entertaining to him, and so it was also adventurous and entertaining to us. By the end of the evening, Omar was left howling with laughter, and I was left wishing Bradshaw might hang around London a little longer this time.

After Omar's driver dropped him at his hotel, Omar asked his driver to take us home. Bradshaw came with me to Connaught Place and walked me to the front door.

"Where to next?" I asked. "Mongolia? Madagascar?"

"Kingston. I'm doing a story on some Rastas."

"Jamaica?"

He nodded.

"Ever been?" he asked.

"Not yet."

"You should go. It's the most beautiful island on Earth."

"Well, good luck, Jon Bradshaw."

He kissed me, not on the cheek, but on the forehead. Innocently though, with a smile. Then he vanished.

Up in my flat, I sat with Roger and wondered if maybe there was something between me and Bradshaw, if maybe Bradshaw also felt the thing that I felt. These thoughts merged with thoughts of the Englishman, and I found myself musing about choosing and being chosen, about wanting and being wanted. To want, it seemed to me, is a simple kind of power since it's grounded in one's own desires. In contrast, to be wanted is a different kind of power because it's grounded in the desires of others. The problem with the Englishman was that I was never able to untangle his wants from mine or my being wanted from his. Between us there seemed to be so much of both, and when you are what someone else wants, how can you know what you want?

When I ran into the Englishman's wife at the supermarket, everything changed. I was in the dairy aisle when she came around the corner. I recognized her from her visits to the set of *Zhivago,* and impulsively, I ducked out of view. She had no way of knowing of the affair, and I needn't have hidden from her. But there I was, crouching behind a display of cheese, paralyzed by guilt.

When the Englishman next came over, I was reluctant. I told him about seeing his wife and immediately regretted it. He looked at me and there was a change in his eyes.

"We've known this from the beginning," he said carefully.

I went to him and pressed my body against his. And then we went to the bedroom, neither of us daring to speak—he because I'd invited his wife into the room with us and me because I knew we had arrived at the end.

Twenty-Eight

I f discord was entering my life, it was disappearing from Nathalie's. She'd appeared in several films that year, and she and Alain had arrived at a functional equilibrium; they were divorced but still a family, independent but not autonomous. Meanwhile, she'd begun one relationship with the director Louis Malle, my longtime friend, and she'd begun a second with a young Italian man named Andrea.

For Anthony's sake, it was important to both Nathalie and Alain to spend their holidays together, and with the year and decade ending, Nathalie had rented a chalet in Wangen, Switzerland, for Christmas and New Year's. She'd invited Louis to join them, and while it might have seemed ill-considered to celebrate the holidays with her ex-husband and current boyfriend, what really stretched credulity was that Andrea, whose family owned a hotel in Wangen, would also be on hand.

When she invited me to come along, I looked at her in disbelief.

"Do you and Alain still . . . ?"

"Sometimes."

"But Louis is . . . ?"

"He's the man I'm with, absolutely."

"And Andrea . . . ?"

"We like each other. He's young, you know; it's just something fun."

"And Alain? He's okay?"

"He respects Louis, of course, and he likes Andrea."

"But Nat . . ."

"Relax, Caroline! They'll behave. Everything will be fine."

I wasn't so sure. But where Nathalie went, adventure followed, and I readily accepted the invitation. The 1960s were almost over, and I was grateful to celebrate the beginning of a new decade amongst friends. Also joining us was Georges Beaume, Alain's manager and Anthony's godfather. Nathalie had already been to the chalet to set it up and to get Anthony and Loulou, Anthony's nanny, settled. She'd then returned to Paris so we could travel together. But, as it turned out, Louis was unable to arrive until the day after Christmas, and so Alain chartered a plane for himself, Nathalie, Georges, and me to fly from Paris to Basel, the nearest airport, on Christmas Eve. From Basel, we needed to catch a train to take us into the mountains.

A heavy snowstorm delayed our departure, and we didn't land in Basel until well after dark. This put Alain on edge. He'd been filming *Borsalino* with Jean-Paul Belmondo that morning and was exhausted. To make matters infinitely worse, the trains had stopped running. I thought Alain was going to explode. But Nathalie, miraculously, arranged for a private train to take us the rest of the way.

Arriving at the Wangen station, the snow continued to fall heavily. The world was white and uniform, its beauty smudged only by our delirium. Luggage in hand, we set out from the station single file with Nathalie in the lead. This seemed to be going well enough, but only Nathalie had snow boots and, with our civilian shoes now soaked, Alain's frustration began to boil. When Nathalie stopped to get her bearings, I could see him working hard to stay calm.

"Where is it?" he asked in a controlled voice. "Where is the chalet?"

"It must be that way," Nathalie said, pointing uncertainly down a street that, buried beneath snow, looked identical to all the others.

"Aren't those our tracks?" Alain asked heatedly, pointing to a line of troubled snow that had obviously been made by a group of people walking single file.

It became evident that the disorienting whiteout had confused Nathalie and that she had no idea where the chalet was. Georges and I exchanged nervous glances. We'd witnessed plenty of spats between Alain and Nathalie, and for all our sakes, we prayed the chalet would materialize. But for what felt like an hour, we followed Nathalie down street after street until we inadvertently arrived back at the train station.

At this, Alain could take no more, and he exploded. He shouted at Nathalie and she shouted right back at him. Without office walls to reverberate around, their voices were swallowed up in the falling snow. Then, in an effort to somehow distract them, Georges and I began throwing snowballs at a nearby tree, seeing who could hit it first. Noticing this, Nathalie and Alain, still shouting, now started throwing snowballs at each other. When Georges hit the tree, I shouted in delight, and somehow this dispelled the tension. Suddenly we were all laughing at the absurdity of solving a conflict with snowballs.

We eventually found the chalet, and Alain made a fire while we changed into dry clothes. By two in the morning, presents were under the tree and we'd gathered around the fireplace, champagne glasses raised. As the room warmed, the intensity of the day and of the city melted away. In place of traffic and sirens, there was the crackling of the fire, and in place of Paris's smog, there was the clean mountain air. Between Nathalie and Alain, all was forgiven. She kissed him and he kissed her back, and when they went to bed, his arms were around her.

Andrea, hair dark and curly, facial hair scruffy, came over the next morning while we were having breakfast. Alain puffed up his chest and reached out his hand. His job was to not be threatened, and he managed it well. When Nathalie kissed Andrea and brought him coffee, Georges and I held our breath. But there was no explosion in the offing, no tense exchange, and no male display of ego. Instead there was a kind of deliberate tenderness, a peace actively pursued.

After breakfast, Andrea offered to show Nathalie his hotel, and they excused themselves as Georges retired to his room.

I was left alone with Alain.

"How is your Englishman?" he asked. "Do you still see him?"

"I'm trying not to."

"But you do?"

"I do."

He leaned back in his chair.

"Do you understand it, Caroline?" he asked.

"Understand what?"

"Attraction. Can you explain it to me? Why are we attracted to this person and not that one? Why now but not later? Or later but not now? At least love doesn't come and go. But attraction is what—a craving? An appetite? It's like hunger; it happens by itself. But does a hungry man ever say he isn't hungry when he is? No. Yet everyone—*everyone*—lies about attraction."

"Even Nathalie?"

"*Mais oui*," he said. "Even Nathalie!"

"I think," I ventured, "that if we were always truthful about attraction, there would be more heartache."

"But there would be more freedom."

"More loneliness."

"More connection."

"I don't know," I said. "Maybe it's dishonesty that makes us civilized. Without it, maybe we become like the animals."

He sighed and looked at me wistfully.

"Sometimes I wonder where is the nobility in being unlike them."

When Louis arrived the next afternoon, Nathalie ran to him. Her happiness was so visceral that, in spite of themselves, even Alain and Andrea seemed pleased to see him. That she was so open and so sincere made it difficult to remember why I'd had any reservations in the first place. Louis got settled in his room, and then Nathalie took him for a walk.

Since Alain had to fly back to Paris in the morning, he spent the afternoon playing with Anthony. Meanwhile, the rest of us sat around a bottle of wine and reflected on the decade that was about to end. It had been a decade of change, a decade of asking questions that were more interesting than the available answers. Why are women unequal? Why are races segregated? Why do ideology and religion lead to war? Why is sex so regulated? As the decade progressed, the drumbeat of these questions grew louder and louder until it became evident that the answers would have to be made up, dreamed into existence by the same people asking the questions. God would have to be reimagined. Tradition too. And patriotism, gender, and family.

That night we ate dinner together, all of us, and there was something enchanting about it. I watched Nathalie, the way she shone, the way she meted out her affection in perfect proportion: Alain, her ex-husband and the undisputed alpha; Louis, a gentle artist and someone in whom she was genuinely interested; and Andrea, so young, so eager for a kiss and a smile.

After dinner, Nathalie joined me by the fire. We sat close together as the men smoked at the table behind us.

"*Joyeux Noël, chérie*," Nathalie said. "Are you happy?"

I nodded.

"I'm happy," I said, reflecting on what a beautiful and supremely French Christmas it had been.

"To a new year, *mon amie*."

"And a new decade."

Nathalie smiled and threw a look over her shoulder.

"You see how they are?" she said in a low voice. "I told you they would behave."

"You," I said. "I don't know how you manage."

She waved this away.

"I lost a daughter by trying to please people. Always there will be those who don't like you. What I know is that no one knows better than anyone else."

It was impossible not to compare myself to Nathalie. She had three lovers who all knew about each other. I, meanwhile, was someone's secret. That I was a secret was also my secret, and that was unbearable. How confusing it all was, love and sex and marriage. Divorce was easier in Paris than in Rome, but France nonetheless shared Italy's Catholic aversion to it. As a consequence, family mattered more than fidelity. And, as in Italy, France skewed pragmatic when it came to sex. This was in contrast to Protestant England, where access to divorce had a tendency to sacrifice marriage in order to preserve the sanctity of sex.

Later, we poured Courvoisier into brandy glasses and passed them around. Then Nathalie walked Andrea to his hotel. When she returned, she sat with Louis on the couch. Across from them, Alain read Anthony a book. Snow began to fall and a deep sense of calm and quiet surrounded us. When it was time for bed, Nathalie kissed Louis on the mouth and followed Alain and Anthony into their room. Louis soon went to bed, and I followed Georges out onto the balcony. There was no sound at all, and the world around us was white with moonlight.

Georges rubbed his hands together and I sipped my cognac.

"Did you think it would be like this?" he asked.

"Christmas?"

"No, this. Europe. All of it."

I knocked snow from the railing and watched it float down to the ground below.

"No," I said. "This is better."

Alain returned to Paris the next day, and with Andrea celebrating New Year's Eve with his family, Nathalie, Louis, and I set out for Klosters, a town ninety minutes away, to visit Louis's friend Peter Viertel, an accomplished writer who, by age twenty, had already written *Saboteur* for Alfred Hitchcock, adapted Irwin Shaw's *The Hard Way*, and completed a novel, *The Canyon*. Viertel later adapted both *The Sun Also Rises* and *The Old Man and the Sea*, and if all of that weren't impressive enough, he was married to Deborah Kerr, star of *Black Narcissus* and *From Here to Eternity*.

We left Wangen well after dark and were immediately caught in a snowstorm. There was no way we were going to arrive in Klosters before midnight, and so we stopped to telephone our hosts. Then, as we inched along the Walensee, Louis looked at his watch and then at Nathalie.

"Kiss me, *ma chérie*."

"*Pourquoi?*"

"Because the sixties are finished," he said, smiling. "It's a new decade."

I awoke late the next morning and walked over to the main house, where I found Deborah Kerr cooking an enormous brunch. With her blonde hair swept back and her attractive, no-nonsense face elegantly framed by a button-down blouse, she was a vision of classic Hollywood beauty. Louis appeared soon after and was followed by a very groggy Nathalie, who sat down beside me.

After a moment, I noticed that Nathalie was fixated on Deborah.

"Excuse me," Nathalie said. "Has anyone ever told you that you look just like Deborah Kerr, the actress?"

Louis and I both kicked Nathalie under the table, but she continued.

"You know who I mean? From *Casino Royale* and *An Affair to Remember*. Or was it *The End of the Affair*?"

Our hostess smiled.

"I was in both pictures, dear."

"*Merde*," was all Nathalie could think to say.

I arrived back in London invigorated. I'd begun the previous decade in Rome. At the time, I'd just broken up with Paul and had moved into my own flat. To stay in Europe, I'd hoped I might teach English or find work modeling. Since then ten whole years had passed. I'd been Carolina and then Caroline, and now I was back to Carolyn. In some ways, I'd become a different person. My relationships had fashioned my life into something my younger self would scarcely have recognized. But in other ways, nothing had changed. I was still someone who looked to others, someone who was susceptible to their desires and impulses. Still, it was a new year and a new decade, and I was excited for a new beginning.

Twenty-Nine

But much can be lost in the translation of intentions to actions. What makes sense when you are in a chalet in Switzerland does not always make sense when he is there, at your door, his smile sly, his eyes mischievous. Because you sometimes forget that you are interesting and attractive and valuable. And it can feel good to be reminded that those things are not forgotten by someone you also find interesting and attractive and valuable.

After seeing his wife at the supermarket, I knew I needed to end my affair with the Englishman. Shame and guilt were worming their way into my conscience, and this brought with it a cruel but exhilarating game of power. The Englishman knew I wanted it to be over and also knew I was unable to end it. He'd show up at my flat and I'd turn him away. Then, a week later, I'd invite him over because the combination of time and taboo had once again turned my conviction into capitulation.

All because we had the problem of love. We had let love into the world, and now we were unable to dispose of it. We were like murderers unable to hide the body. There was blood everywhere. Evidence everywhere. It was a matter of time until we were discovered, and so we kept going back to each other for want of knowing what else to do.

Work was my only reprieve from this torture. I had more than I could handle and had recently brought on another publicist to ease the burden: Sue Barton, the woman who, in her robe, had accepted the flowers on Omar's behalf when I showed up at his flat for my first day of work. The company had steadily built up a reputation with the industry PR companies, and through the New York–based publicists Pat Kingsley and Lois Smith, we were hired to oversee publicity for the London premiere of Robert Altman's *M.A.S.H.* We hadn't heard of Robert Altman, but Pat and Lois were important in the PR world, and I readily accepted the contract.

When I walked into the dining room of their rented flat, Robert— Bob—was on one side of the table, a large breakfast laid out before him. Opposite him was Kathryn, his wife, a single hard-boiled egg perched

Nathalie, Maria Schneider, and Carolyn at a Pink Floyd concert
(Photo by Odile Montserrat)

atop an egg holder in front of her. Bob dominated the room and exuded both a warmth and wisdom that wordlessly established a gentle authority. He'd flown dozens of missions during World War II, dropped hundreds of bombs, and was extremely opinionated when it came to war. All of this was visible in his eyes, which flashed back and forth between fierce and friendly. And Kathryn was every bit his equal. She'd been a showgirl and knew a thing or two about entertainment. Beneath her smile and charm was someone who knew what she was doing. She believed in her husband's talent, and she knew that in *M.A.S.H.* they had a game changer.

The remarkable thing about *M.A.S.H.*—a savage and irreverent comedy set in the Korean War but that was, in fact, a commentary on Vietnam—was that it was a studio film. But it was unlike any studio film I'd seen. Whereas the studio formula depended on a handful of evergreen themes—the triumph of good over evil, the supremacy of love, patriotism, the call of duty—in *M.A.S.H.*, all of this was subverted, if not outright mocked. This was not a movie that used big stars and targeted a broad audience, rather it was a disregard for those conventions entirely. And the filmmaking was gleeful and unhinged. The characters talked over one another, and you could feel the improvisation, the maverick filmmaking—the fingerprints, in other words, of the French New Wave.

It was a smashing success. *M.A.S.H.* won the Palme d'Or at the 1970 Cannes Film Festival and received five Academy Award nominations, winning an Oscar for best screenplay. As a cinematic event, it was revolutionary; it reached back through the French New Wave, Italian neorealism, and classic Hollywood and was an early indicator that the cinematic zeitgeist was now migrating back across the Atlantic.

The new generations had no interest in lavish musicals and historical epics, and Hollywood had seemed to run out of ideas. Exploding out of this downward spiral was Antonioni's *Blow-Up* in Europe and, in the States, Arthur Penn's *Bonnie and Clyde*. Seemingly overnight, a cohort of low-budget, director-driven movies filled with lowlifes and antiheroes were green-lit and rushed into production. Suddenly, the so-called New Hollywood movement was the hottest thing in cinema.

With Americans infiltrating the ranks of global auteurs like Carlos Saura, Luis Buñuel, and François Truffaut in making politically engaged and commercially viable work, there was a scramble to advance more high-minded projects. And Carlos Fuentes—the novelist I'd met in Madrid and found so intriguing—was among those eager to translate his work to film. We'd stayed in touch, and much of our correspondence was about getting his scripts into the hands of people who could help. This changed, though, when he wrote to let me know he would be returning to Europe. As his departure from Mexico neared, the tone of our letters veered toward the romantic.

Mexico City, Oct, 4, 1969

Dear Carolyn,

I'm off to New York for ten days. Sign contract with Commonwealth for film rights of my novel "The Death of Artemio Cruz", ditto for staging of my play by The Washington Players, plus book of literary essays, sundry assignments with magazines, etc. I'll be there from Friday 10, at the Algonquin. If you know of anybody interesting I should see, drop me a line at Brandt & Brandt, 101 Park Avenue. N.Y.C. Also, I'll phone you in any case, and especially if by that time I've had news from Buñuel. I do know he's been having a dreadful time bickering with the Spanish censorship; finally, they&ve relented and he will be shooting "Tristana" in Toledo, as were his wishes. Since I know the way he plunges into a project to the exclusion of everything and everybody not directly concerned, it will be an act of absolute friendship if he writes. I'm rather sure that, nevertheless, he will. My novella "Birthdays" appears in Mexico at the beggining of November, and that will clear the property rights once and for all.

I do miss you and think about you, more than you can imagine. Sometimes, it puzzles me.

Much, much love

A letter from Carlos Fuentes
(Carolyn Pfeiffer archive)

"You looked so beautiful that distant night in Madrid," he wrote. "How is your life? Mine is not happy; something broke and I deeply feel something lost forever, and it hurts very much. My marriage is in shambles and I do remember you constantly. Is your mirror still my memory?"

"I received your beautiful letter," I wrote back, "and I carried it around all week in my handbag. As you know, I thought you were smashing."

"I do miss you and think about you, more than you can imagine. Sometimes, it puzzles me."

"I can't wait to see you," I wrote. "I think I have been waiting for you to come back since that long-ago night in Madrid."

When he arrived, we met for a drink. Maybe we were both nervous, worried we would fall short of the other's memory or expectation, but the easy cadence of our written flirtation didn't translate into comfortable conversation. And so we hunted about for an access point, both of us anxious to find something to talk about.

We found it in the person of Irwin Shaw, the novelist and American expat. Fuentes was friends with Shaw, and he chuckled sympathetically when I told him that Penny and I had met him for brunch when I first arrived in Europe and that Shaw had chided me for not eating fresh asparagus with my fingers. Silly as it was, the humiliation still stung.

"I have a story about Shaw," Fuentes said. "Do you want to hear it?"

"Of course," I said, happy that conversation was flowing more freely.

"The thing to remember about this story is that I'm extremely allergic to cats."

Fuentes went on to explain that Shaw had once offered his flat in Paris to him for the summer to use as a writing retreat. To accommodate his allergies, Shaw had his housekeeper take his cat with her on her vacation. This left Fuentes with weeks of uninterrupted time to write. When the housekeeper returned with the cat, Fuentes left by train for Barcelona the next day.

"So, that's the story," he said. "I had a productive time; very little sneezing."

"Wait!" I cried. "That's it? Where's the rest of the story?"

"Ah, yes, there is one more detail," he smiled. "When I got to Barcelona and opened up my suitcase, guess what I found inside?"

I covered my mouth.

"No."

He nodded, laughing.

"Yes."

"The cat?"

"Irwin Shaw's dead cat," said Fuentes. "It was an unfortunate case of curiosity killing the cat."

It was enough to break the ice between us. In the dim light of the restaurant, we talked eagerly, leaning nearer to each other. Then he touched my forearm, and moments later, when he suggested a nightcap, I made it uncomplicated.

"I have a cat," I said, "so we can't go there."

The next day we rendezvoused with Saura, Geraldine, Guillermo Cabrera Infante, and Guillermo's wife, Miriam, in Cambridge. Octavio Paz, the Nobel laureate and lion of Mexican letters, was there in residency, and we'd been invited to visit with him. Paz was politically courageous, culturally proud, transnationally engaged, and a mentor to a generation of writers, Fuentes included. But what I loved about Octavio Paz was not his politics but his poetry.

My favorite is "Two Bodies," which begins:

Two bodies face to face
are at times two waves
and night is the ocean.

It is a simple, piercing meditation on relating differently to different people in different contexts, and about relating differently to love itself. I took it to heart—a poem about me, about Carolyn, Carolina, and Caroline.

With Fuentes I was Carolina, and it was true what he'd said that night in Madrid, that, for him, Spanish was the language of love. This allowed me to see a side of him that I would never have otherwise seen. And I thought maybe there are only three places where the true self is unable to hide: in dreams, in prayer, and in love.

From Cambridge, we went to Austria to attend the Vienna Festival where Fuentes had a play premiering. Leonard Bernstein, the prolific and prodigiously talented conductor and composer who was not only the music director for the New York Philharmonic but who also composed the music for *West Side Story*, had been invited for celebrations to commemorate Beethoven's two hundredth birthday. He invited Fuentes and me, along with the playwright Adolph Green, to accompany him on a walk, and I remember the feeling of being in the company of giants. It was the same feeling I'd felt with Irwin Shaw and Ginette Spanier, and when the conversation turned to pop music and Bernstein dismissed the Beatles as a flash in the pan of musical history, I again felt an impulse to accept his judgment just as I'd accepted Shaw's. Fuentes and Green then nodded their agreement, and we walked for a few steps in silence.

But I couldn't bear it.

"Respectfully, I disagree," I said.

"You do?" asked Bernstein, taken aback.

"I do," I said. "I think that in a hundred years, people will still be listening to the Beatles."

I could have said two hundred and would still have been right.

From Vienna, Fuentes and I went to Venice, where Visconti was in production on *Death in Venice*. My friend Silvana Mangano was starring in the film, and I would handle the London premiere when the time came.

Set in 1911, *Death in Venice*, tells the story of an aging composer who visits the Grand Hotel des Bains, a hotel on the Venetian Lido, a sandy hotel-lined barrier island that helps to shelter the city from the Adriatic.

In the story, based on novelist Thomas Mann's own visit to Venice, the city is being overrun by plague. Against this backdrop of death and decay, the dying composer looks out on the Lido and catches a glimpse of Tadzio, a youth of breathtaking beauty.

The production was filming in and around the Grand Hotel des Bains, the same hotel used in the novella and the same hotel in which Thomas Mann had stayed. When Fuentes and I arrived, we were told the crew was filming on the beach, and we set out to find them. Walking toward the set was like walking back in time. Old rowboats were lined up on the beach, and actors in stunning period dress were sprinkled throughout the crew. Men wore light linen suits, and women, shaded by exquisite parasols and elegant veils, wore flowing muslin dresses of white and ivory.

I hugged Silvana, who with her classic beauty was a kind of Italian Ingrid Bergman, and introduced Fuentes to Visconti. When shooting wrapped, Visconti invited us to dinner. A water taxi took us to the historic city center, and we found a restaurant away from the gondolas and throngs of tourists. Fuentes loved Mann's novella and deeply admired Visconti's work. As he was also interested in adapting plays and literature for film, he had a lot of questions.

"A novel changes with every read," Visconti explained. "That is so, isn't it?"

Fuentes nodded and Visconti continued.

"The experience of a novel depends on the reader, who that person is and what they imagine in their mind. But the experience of a film depends on the director. Nothing is left to the viewer, and so a director must be *intransigent*."

It was a word Luchino liked a great deal. This concept, the idea that a novel changes while a film doesn't, was something I'd understood instinctively but had never heard articulated so plainly. It made me think of Bolt, the way his ideas became words instead of images. And of Fellini, who thought first and only in images. Does the writer engage a different part of a person than the filmmaker? Or is the difference collective, to do with the sharing of experience?

As Fuentes had to return to Mexico, we left the next day for London. He was afraid of flying, and so from London he needed to get to Southampton. I went with him to the train station, and it was there that we said our goodbye. Neither of us resisted, and I think I knew that, somehow, our friendship would never recover from our romance, that some things really are better imagined.

As I once again pulled Roger onto my lap in my empty flat, I knew that, as a short-term solution, my tryst with Fuentes had not solved the longer-term problem of the Englishman. Like the proverbial moth drawn to the flame, I continued to be drawn to the Englishman.

What's so interesting to me about this as an age-old metaphor is that we infrequently consider the flame from the perspective of the moth. Why do we never ask what's in it for the moth? Why do we never ask *why* the moth is drawn to the flame? One theory is that the moth is drawn to the flame not because of the allure of heat and danger, but instead because the moth mistakes firelight for starlight, a flickering flame for an optical infinity. Before humans lit up the night with electricity, and before that with fire, the only light at night was from the moon and the stars—light sources that are permanent and unmoving. And because you can move toward these optical infinities forever without ever drawing closer to them, they provide vital navigational bearings to all manner of beings.

But now our nights are illuminated, and the light of electricity has obscured the light of the stars. What is reality and what is illusion? And how can any of us find our way? I didn't call the Englishman, though. I needed the affair to be over, and I didn't want to find out that he had reached the end of our story before me. I was barely able to handle being loved by a married man; I couldn't bear to not be loved by one. Still, when I didn't hear from him, I grew anxious. Maybe he'd taken another lover. Or maybe his wife had found out about me, and they were working through what that meant for their marriage, for their family.

When he finally knocked on my door, I was happy to see him and was relieved that he wanted to see me. But the time had come. If I was to end it on my terms, it had to be now. If I ended it, I could take the memories and I could still hold my head high. If I didn't end it, he would eventually stop knocking. And, if that happened, then I would resent him and I would resent all of our time together.

I stood in the doorway gathering the resolve to stand my ground. But in his eyes was the mischief I loved, the desire I desired.

"It has to be over," I said. "You see that. I know you do."

He could hear the indecision in my voice.

"You're wrong," he said. "It doesn't have to be over."

"If I don't end it, then you will have to. And if you end it, it will be unfair to me."

"I don't have to end it."

Here I said his name, the melancholy of my voice pleading with him.

"Carolyn," he said, "let me take you somewhere, a weekend away. Dover. Bath. Anywhere you want."

A hopeless sadness filled me, and I asked simply, "And then what?"

For us, in that moment, those words were insurmountable. Every conceivable answer returned us to our despairing, solutionless present. I went to him, and I leaned my forehead against his. There were no words we could say; there was nothing with which we could clean up the mess we'd made. He didn't hug me and he didn't look at me and he didn't walk away. And so it ended like that, quietly. I stepped back into my flat, and when he still didn't look up, I closed the door.

Thirty

was numb, indifferent even to work, in which I'd always been able to lose myself. And the project before me—Cinema City—was both ambitious and important. Organized by the British Film Institute's National Archive and sponsored by the London *Sunday Times*, Cinema City was a month-long film exhibition commemorating the first seventy-five years of cinema. To be held at the Roundhouse in north London, it was a massive effort to raise funds to transfer iconic films from nitrate to safety stock. Among the films to be preserved were Harold Lloyd's *Safety Last!* (which famously depicts Lloyd hanging from a clock face over New York City), *The Kid Brother* (a film that hadn't been shown in London in forty years), and Charlie Chaplin's *The Circus*. Screenings of these foundational works were to be hosted by an impressive lineup of film legends, among them Harold Lloyd, Marlon Brando, Richard Burton, Clive Donner, Gene Kelly, Joseph Losey, Shirley MacLaine, Norman Mailer, Louis Malle, James Mason, André

Previn, Elizabeth Taylor, Dimitri Tiomkin, François Truffaut, Luchino Visconti, and Franco Zeffirelli.

I worked closely with my friend Marion Rosenberg, who had recommended me for the job. We'd already done a lot to bring the project to fruition, but as my malaise deepened, I struggled to engage.

I was sitting at my desk staring at the phone when a knock on the door sent a shot of adrenaline through me. I was certain it was the Englishman, and I considered not answering because I had no interest in getting mired down in conversations about feelings, his or mine.

Still, I opened the door.

Instead of the Englishman, it was Penny, a bright smile on her face. She was eight months pregnant, radiantly so, and I felt like a storm cloud in comparison. She coaxed me downstairs and across the street to the park. We found a bench, and I held her hand and helped her ease down to a seat.

"Remember our first time here?" Penny asked.

She was talking about my visit to London with Claudia, who was meeting the queen. At the time, Penny had just learned that her boyfriend, Richard, had been killed in the Amazon. It was a lifetime ago.

"We were just girls," I said nostalgically.

A moment passed, and with her hand on her stomach, she looked at me.

"I want to ask you something," she said solemnly.

"Anything," I said.

"Will you be the baby's godmother? I want you to be in this child's life, well, forever."

"Yes, Penny. Of course. I'm . . . I'm honored."

"This one's going to be special," she said. "I'm sure of it."

Beneath our happy exchange was the unexpected gravity of a formal bond, a commitment that transcended affection, goodwill, and even friendship. As I lifted Penny onto her feet and as we walked back through the park, I felt something protective, not quite maternal, glow warm within me.

Benjamin was born a month later. At his christening, I held him close and marveled at his angelic fingers. His birth touched me not only because he was my godson but because it underscored the fact that gone, now, were beginnings. Completely. Penny was done with her childbearing, my company was operating at full throttle, and I'd now lived in London longer than I'd lived in New York, Rome, or Paris.

I had no desire to leave. I was embedded in community and in deeply meaningful relationships. Around this time, my friend Bianca, whom I'd met through friends of friends, moved in with me. She'd just moved out from the flat where she'd lived with the actor Michael Caine who'd recently appeared in *Alfie* and whose career was exploding.

Marisa Berenson, Carolyn, and Bianca Jagger
(Carolyn Pfeiffer archive)

Bianca was beautiful, with perfect skin and an intrepid fashion sense. She was also a creature of the night and was friends with everyone from David Bowie to Elizabeth Taylor and Manolo Blahnik, the shoe designer. One evening we had friends over for drinks. I'd just put on

Let It Bleed, the Rolling Stones record, and had gone to the kitchen to refill drinks when I heard the music cut out midsong.

Confused, I returned to see what had happened. Holding the offending record was Mick Jagger, red lips lit up with a smile.

"Dreadful taste you've got, love."

Bianca, of course, would go on to marry him. Their wedding, based on the oceans of press and paparazzi present, might have passed as the rock and roll event of the decade. Mick hired a 747, and we all flew down to Saint-Tropez for a few days of revelry and sun.

The wedding of Bianca and Mick Jagger
(Express/Archive Photos © Getty Images)

Cinema City got underway in October. The exhibition opened with a screening of Mike Nichols's *Catch-22*, attended by Princess Alexandra and by Harold Lloyd, who, with Buster Keaton and Charlie Chaplin, is one of cinema's all-time great comedians. Among the films presented were short silent films, early one-reel dramas like *The Life of Charles Peace* (1905), which not only features one of the first executions by hanging in cinema but was precisely the sort of film that led to the emergence of theaters in the first place.

Cinema City brought a carousel of actors and directors to London. I became friendly with Norman Mailer. He'd gone through a filmmaking phase and had produced several eccentric experimental films. His fascination with images came close to equaling his fascination with words. He was well into a book project entitled *The Faith of Graffiti* and would later ask me to handle publicity for the book's London launch.

The spotlight then shifted to François Truffaut. I'd known him for so long, and I'd handled the premieres of *The Wild Child* and *Two English Girls*, yet he was only now becoming comfortable with me. He really was impossibly shy. As an example, his affair with Jeanne Moreau was characterized by an exchange of feverishly impassioned letters. To punctuate this torrent of erotic handwritten fervor, they would then meet once a week for lunch at Brasserie Lipp, and they would sit side by side and pass their time together in absolute silence.

When I asked François what he wanted to make next, he confided that he was toying with an idea of a movie about making a movie.

"For me," he explained, "there is no difference between living and filmmaking. I know art should come from life, but for me it's the opposite. For me, to make a film about making a film is to make a film about life."

The result, *Day for Night*, would come to be known as one of the most beloved French films of all time.

Cinema City overlapped with a month-long newspaper strike, but I did my best and, in addition to publicity, I recruited talent—Malle and Truffaut, Visconti and Zeffirelli—and attended to some of the exhibition's logistical details. Just as my work on *Zhivago* had expanded my professional responsibilities beyond those of an assistant, I was again taking on responsibilities beyond my job as publicist. In fact, it occurred to me that my work on Cinema City was not unlike the work of a film producer, who in simple terms is responsible for combining talent, resources, and material. For the first time, I realized, I was catching glimpses of a life beyond PR. Maybe Suso was right. Maybe in the building of relationships I was also building the skills and the connections to produce actual movies.

Franco Zeffirelli, Luchino Visconti, and Carolyn at Cinema City
(Carolyn Pfeiffer archive)

It made me think of all the movies that had not yet been made. Someone needed to make them, and I thought it might as well be me. But which would I want to produce? What genre? What themes? And who were the filmmakers I'd want to champion? Invariably, my answer to this last question was always the same: my Englishman. *Maybe I could call him,* I'd think, *just to talk business. Yes, I could ask if he had a script ready. I could discuss his vision with him, get a sense of what he wanted to accomplish with the film, tell him I believed in him. And then we could take our project out to financiers. We could begin recruiting talent. We could . . .*

No. It was a lethal daydream. There was no "we." That was over now, and I needed for it to stay that way. So I made a concentrated effort to push him from my mind, to turn him from *my* Englishman into *an* Englishman like any other.

In time, days went by without me thinking about him. Then entire weeks. Finally, he rarely crossed my mind at all. Like footprints washed away by the tide, there was no evidence that our affair had ever happened.

Except that, a kept secret is not the same as something that never happened. Rather, a secret lies dormant, an unexploded ordnance, a bomb that, without notice, might detonate at any time.

Some months after Cinema City, Geraldine invited me to go with her to the United Artists screening room where her father, Charlie Chaplin, had arranged to have some of his early films projected. In the room was just the family: Charlie, Oona, Geraldine, a few of her siblings, and me. Geraldine and I sat behind Charlie and Oona, and my view was framed by the outline of his right ear and of her left. I remember the silence, of not watching but of absorbing his films. And I remember the way he turned to Oona so that his profile was silhouetted against the screen as he spoke softly into her ear. He was telling her the stories behind the movies. The ruined takes. The on-set miracles you would never believe. It was an intimate and important experience, and I reached over to squeeze my friend's hand in gratitude.

The next day, I took Geraldine with me to the Altmans' flat. Bob had arrived to prep his film *Images*, which was to shoot in Ireland. He was enamored of Ingmar Bergman's *Persona*, which inspired a number of his films and which, in turn, would influence David Lynch's *Twin Peaks* and *Mulholland Drive*. Altman loved to discover new talent, and their flat, a magnificent building that would eventually become New Zealand's embassy, was always filled with the young stars of the day— Shelley Duvall, Elliott Gould, Julie Christie.

On the night I took Geraldine, John Williams was there, as he was composing the score for *Images*. I introduced Geraldine to Kathryn and then to Bob. And then, before we left, Bob pulled me aside and told me he was going to cast Geraldine in his next picture.

"Do you have a title?" I asked.

"I'm calling it *Nashville*," he said. "We'll see."

Altman would indeed cast Geraldine in *Nashville* and, in fact, would go on to cast her in a half dozen others. That I was able to introduce Geraldine Chaplin and Robert Altman suggested a degree of stability in my career. If I still felt like a minnow in a shark tank, at least I no longer felt at risk of being swallowed up at any moment. One reason for this might have been because of how surprisingly small the London "scene" actually was. Though there were different crowds—music, film, theater, photography, art, fashion—for all of so-called Swinging London's influence, everyone knew everyone else.

My friend Richard Perry, the music producer, would invite me to sit in while he recorded Ringo or Harry Nilsson. Or I'd drop by the studio of David Bailey, the photographer, as he shot Jean Shrimpton or Catherine Deneuve. To be an effective publicist, it turned out, required a fair amount of social crossover.

Jane Birkin continued to be a friend. She and Serge Gainsbourg were still together, and she'd recently given birth to their daughter, Charlotte. They lived in Paris, but when Jane was in London, we'd meet for coffee or go for a walk down Kings Road. I remember walking with her to her mother's house in Chelsea. She had Charlotte in a pram and had wheeled it up a few steps to the front door stoop. Alas, she'd neglected to put on the pram's brake, and when she turned to dig in her straw basket for her keys, the pram rolled down the steps and fell over. Poor Charlotte tumbled onto the sidewalk and let out a mighty scream but, thankfully, was no worse for the wear.

A newcomer to our London milieu, Alice Cooper soon came on as a client. He was in England with his band to launch *Love It to Death*, his first European tour. Born Vincent Furnier, the Godfather of Shock Rock was then in his early twenties and was still working out his image and how he might most effectively scandalize the middle classes. He

Carolyn and Alice Cooper at a London fair
(Carolyn Pfeiffer archive)

already had Kachina, the first of many large boa constrictors that were central to his act. I admired the band's manager, Shep Gordon, who had a brilliant mind for publicity and a playful approach to business that camouflaged how deadly serious he was about both publicity and business. I joined them for the ten-city tour, and Shep and I became quite skilled at convincing airport officials to let us sneak Kachina through customs.

And then we'd watch as Vincent would transform into Alice just as Claudia had transformed into La Cardinale and Alain had transformed into Delon. But, for me, the metamorphosis was complete; there was no more discovering a new version of myself and no more learning to fit into a new world. I was just me. I had a home and a career and a community. At long last, I belonged.

So why did I feel melancholy? It was December when Shep and Alice returned to the States. The holidays were settling up on the city, and I remember that there was something lonely in the air. It was the feeling of having enough and of still wanting more, of being worried that the bone-deep sensation that still more awaited me out in the world would never, ever go away. Would I always be restless? Would I always feel like something was missing?

I spent Christmas with Penny and her family. It was a gathering of generations: a big meal full of sibling disputes and the meltdowns of overstimulated children. I was so grateful to be a part of it. And at the end of the night, I smiled, gave my gifts, and said my goodnights.

Carolyn on tour with Alice Cooper
(Carolyn Pfeiffer archive)

At my flat, I poured a sambuca and thought of North Carolina. I thought of what it means to be from a place, of what it means to leave that place and to cede it to memory. Leaving home can seem brave. You do it because you want to find out who you are. You rid yourself of everything familiar so you can uncover what is uniquely you. But what you don't comprehend is that you can't take yourself with you. If you do, then there you are—same you, different place. You have to let go; you have to leave yourself behind. You can't hold on to pain or to love or to ideas of how life might have gone. You have to leave all of those things behind. If you don't, then they come with you and they exist in the present where they clutter and conflict with what is. And, when that happens, you discover that independence and loneliness are the same. Freedom and captivity too. That's the danger of change: it creates versions of yourself that might have been. And unless you let them go, they haunt you, each with wrongs you can never right.

My sambuca was almost empty when there was a knock on my door. I opened it to find my Englishman standing before me. It was surreal and not in keeping with the flow of events, the flow of my life, but there he was. He wasn't sober and he wasn't drunk. His was a happy and full life, but he sometimes felt crowded out of it. And now he was here, with me, his face an endearing combination of ecstatic and despairing.

I wanted so badly to send him away. I wanted the love between us to stay in the past, its secret to stay buried. But I also wanted to let him lay me down on the bed, let him lower his weight onto me, let him look into my eyes and whisper all that he missed, all that he wanted. I looked at him for a long time, and then I chose once more to own what wasn't mine.

Thirty-One

The days that followed were not like other days. I felt a lightness inside me, a gentleness in the world around. The thing with my Englishman was over, truly over, and I was at peace.

But one afternoon, fatigue overwhelmed me. I'd awoken that morning to a finicky appetite and tender breasts, and as I lay down to rest, it occurred to me that I'd felt this way once before.

I couldn't shake the sensation that invisible forces were at work within me, and a doctor soon confirmed what I already knew. I was unmarried, I wasn't in a relationship, and I was pregnant.

Back at Connaught Place, I methodically made tea, and sat by the window overlooking Marble Arch. When the emotions came, it felt like all of them at once. Anger and disbelief, fear and shame.

I'd wanted one last time, one last moment of impulsive, uncomplicated intimacy. And I'd wanted that moment to not connect to the moments that came before or to those that came after. I'd wanted the photograph and not the film, the waterfall without the river.

How alone I felt. Not lonely, but alone. Distinct, bounded, cut out from the world around me. Because what was happening was happening to *me*, to *my* body, to *my* future. I pulled Roger onto my lap, and looked down at Bayswater Road. So many people, each one going somewhere, doing something, on their way to see someone. A group of teenagers huddled together. A man with a briefcase walked past them, an umbrella in his hand. Two women strolled nearby arm in arm. People at a distance are comforting. They accomplish. They endure. They find a way.

I was single, and single women weren't supposed to have babies—least of all babies fathered by married men. But I wanted this baby and, like the people on the street below, I would find a way.

I asked the Englishman to meet me, but not at my flat. Already something territorial within me was awakening. We met in the park, and without preamble, I told him I was pregnant and that I was keeping the baby.

He may have wanted to express fear and vulnerability, but instead he tripped over apologies and curses, over disbelief and offers to pay for a solution.

"You will destroy your life," he cried, "and you will also destroy mine."

I wished I could explain to him how I knew, in every cell of my body, that impossible things sometimes become possible and that possible things sometimes become inevitable.

"I'm having this child," I said. And I then made a promise that I have never broken: "I will never name you as the father. You have my word."

He was quiet for a long time, until at last he spoke.

"I love you."

He wasn't saying those words because they were what he wanted to hear in return; he was saying them because it was how he felt and because he wanted me to know.

While it may have been welcome, my pregnancy was not convenient. I was just then expected in Germany where Romy had been cast as Empress Elizabeth in Visconti's *Ludwig*. It was the same character

Romy had been stuck with as a teenager, but now, with the passage of time and with Visconti's magisterial direction, she was eager to bring a definitive performance to a historical character she knew so well.

In her very first scene, Romy was to ride a white Lipizzan stallion sidesaddle around a tented ring at night while exchanging coquettish dialogue with Helmut Berger, the titular Ludwig. Her outfit, created by Piero Tosi, was laboriously constructed and included a dress, riding coat, top hat, and a mesh veil pulled over her face. She looked magnificent. And with the meticulous production design, the regal stallion, and the dashing Helmut Berger, the scene was absolutely breathtaking. But Visconti was asking for a lot. And underneath Romy's clothes, the intricate corsetry bit into her. She was also having a hard time riding sidesaddle, hitting her marks, and pulling off the effortless seduction Visconti demanded. Take after take was interrupted either by Visconti, who was increasingly dissatisfied, or by Romy, who was increasingly exasperated.

Finally, he pushed her too far.

"It's not you doing the work, is it?" she shouted as she jumped from the stallion. "You don't know what you are asking!"

She then ripped the veil from her head and flung it down. I followed her out of the tent and found her hyperventilating, barely able to speak.

"I quit," she panted. "I'm leaving."

She then told me to inform Visconti, her agent, and the financiers who had put up the money contingent on her involvement in the picture. The problem was that if she quit, not only would the film collapse, but she would be legally vulnerable. And so filming shut down and a standoff began. We were all staying in the same hotel, but Romy refused to speak to Visconti and Visconti refused to speak to Romy. For several days it went on like that. Intermediaries went back and forth, but neither would budge. I watched from the sidelines, sad because I was so fond of both of them and because I knew that deep down they loved each other.

Then, remembering a story I'd heard about producer Sam Spiegel making peace between a warring Marlon Brando and Elia Kazan on the set of *On the Waterfront*, I spoke separately to Romy and to Visconti, and I insisted to each that the other was eager to meet and to resolve the conflict. Neither Visconti nor Romy was willing to go to the other's room, but they agreed to meet at the hotel bar. It was neutral ground, and it would be just the two of them.

The rest of us hovered anxiously down the hall and were jubilant when, after half an hour, Romy and Visconti appeared arm and arm. The next day we all went back to work. It was a meaningful victory for me. I'd just had a hand in keeping a Luchino Visconti film afloat, and I couldn't help but wonder if moviemaking might actually be somewhere in my future.

Before returning to London, I whispered to Romy that I was pregnant and that, like her, I would be a mother. She wept; I knew she would. David was her everything. I think by that point in her life the world disgusted her. I think she no longer believed it had anything of true value to offer. Just games of accomplishment, asinine ways of manufacturing status and importance. But what took place in a woman's body, what transpired between mother and child—those were things in which she still believed.

When I got home, I told the other mothers—my own, then Suso, then Penny, and then Nathalie and Geraldine.

My mother said, "Sug, say the word and I'll come to England."

Geraldine said, "So, a Pfeiffer, then?"

Suso said, "Your genius has prepared you for this."

Penny said, "Our children will be like us, friends for life."

Nathalie said, "You'll make a terrific father."

I was worried that news of my pregnancy would cause me to lose work, but no one that I cared about minded that I wasn't married. In April, Kathryn and Bob Altman came to London. Bob's film *Images* had been invited to screen at Cannes, and they'd come early to promote it. With the influence of European cinema so evident in his work, Bob's popularity in Europe was growing rapidly. It was often wondered why the United States hadn't produced a Federico Fellini or an Ingmar Bergman, and with *McCabe & Mrs. Miller* and now with *Images,* it was a role Bob seemed destined to fill.

I went to meet them at their flat and, when Kathryn offered me a cocktail, I demurred.

"I have a little production of my own," I said, putting my hand on my stomach. "It's a solo production, though. No coproducer on this one."

Kathryn immediately hugged me, and Bob roared with laughter.

"From what I can tell," he said, "there's no wrong way to bring a movie into the world, and, my Lord, there's certainly no wrong way to bring a baby into the world!"

He lifted his glass, and they toasted my health and the health of my baby.

"Listen," he continued, "this year, instead of staying at a hotel in Cannes, we're getting a yacht. Why don't you stay with us?"

When Shep and Alice Cooper returned to London for the School's Out tour, Shep, in his gentle way, was excited for me.

"We can always use another roadie," he joked.

I was helping Shep promote the tour, but we weren't seeing the kind of response that Alice Cooper's fame should have commanded. The band was scheduled to play Wembley Arena, a ten thousand–seat venue, but they were still unknown in England, and a few days before the event, only five hundred tickets had sold.

With the concert looming, we intensified our efforts. Shep was of the opinion that anything we could do to antagonize parents would result in good publicity for the band. With this as our guiding principle, he and Derek Taylor, the Beatles' publicist, came up with a marketing stunt that was quite literally designed to stop traffic. After hiring a two-sided billboard truck, Shep and I looked for a provocative image we could blow up and parade through the streets of London. Alice had recently been photographed by Richard Avedon, the most famous fashion photographer in the world, and the result was Alice, naked, save for a boa constrictor wrapped strategically around his middle.

Then, the day before the concert, we had the truck drive around London for hours, past Buckingham Palace and Parliament. Then, as it was wading through the thick traffic around Oxford Circus, the busiest intersection in London, the truck conveniently broke down. At this, I notified the photographers on Fleet Street as well as the television stations, omitting, of course, that Shep had given strict instructions to the driver not to move the truck no matter what. For two hours, the traffic at Oxford Circus came to a complete standstill. Traffic backed up. The police came. Helicopters circled. And Shep and I watched it all on the evening news in Derek Taylor's office.

Alice Cooper billboard breakdown in Oxford Circus
(Photograph by Tom Hanley © Tom Hanley Photography Ltd)

The next day, headlines read, "Ban Alice the Horror Rocker," and suddenly everyone in England was talking about the Alice Cooper concert. Indeed, it promptly sold out. One prominent moral watchdog, Mary Whitehouse, would not let the matter alone. Her determined efforts to bring attention to the moral corruption Alice was unleashing on England's youth were so successful that it became a major news story, with photographs of Alice appearing on the front page of every paper. No longer a curiosity buried in the culture section, Alice Cooper was international news. Shep couldn't contain his gratitude and sent Mary Whitehouse a bouquet of flowers every day for a week.

As summer stretched on, my stomach stretched out into the world. I'd been thin my whole life, but now that was changing. My body had taken over or, rather, had been taken over; I'd become a vessel, the project of some other intelligence. I first felt the kicking of my baby while lying in bed early one morning. Not recognizing it at first, I thought nothing of it. Then it happened again, the flutter of little limbs. And I knew that I was not alone in my bed.

With Penny as a mentor, mine was a happy pregnancy. She'd developed a serious interest in homeopathic medicine and organic living and took me shopping for vitamins as she talked to me about the baby food that she made from scratch. One of Penny's favorite salons belonged to Madame Lubatti. She was famous for her facials, and she sold handmade cleansers and lotions out of her flat with the help of her assistant, Eileen Malone. When Madame Lubatti retired, she left the business to Eileen, who then left it to Jo, her daughter, who went on to establish it as Jo Malone, the cosmetic empire of today.

Penny also connected me to Sir George Pinker—Mr. Pinker—who'd delivered Princess Margaret's children and who would go on to deliver both Prince William and Prince Harry. He was a pioneer in the field of obstetrics, and there was no one better in all of England to handle my delivery.

Confident that I was in good hands and that there was nothing more I could do to prepare for my baby's arrival, I spent the last days of my pregnancy working as much as I could during the day and watching as much of the 1972 Summer Olympics as I could in the evening. I'll never forget the excitement of watching Mark Spitz win seven gold medals, every single one with a world record. For the 100-meter free-style event, in which he almost declined to compete, I was lying in bed and peering over my enormous stomach as if spying on the television. I'd found a lavender ribbon on the couch beside me and had absently wrapped it around my stomach and tied it in a bow. As the race began, the excitement was too much, and I struggled to my feet. Standing there by myself, lavender ribbon still tied in a bow around my stomach, I cheered Spitz to victory.

The Olympics were overshadowed by what would come to be known as the Munich Massacre, but by then my baby was on its way. Penny took me to the hospital. And what happened after that was the work not of me but of my body. The intelligence that had overseen conception now brought the project to conclusion. Contractions. Dilation. Crowning.

Finally, the soft cry of a newborn.

Mr. Pinker placed my daughter in my arms, and I felt her skin against mine and I looked into the cloudy gray of her eyes for the very first time.

"Welcome," I whispered.

And I had the sensation that this bundle of vulnerability, this miracle of life, that only moments before had been inside me, was not separate from me. Though I held her in my arms and though she was her own finite and complete being, every part of her was nonetheless a part of me.

If pregnancy can turn one into two, childbirth can turn two back into one.

Thirty-Two

As I looked at my daughter, her head still conical, her face tranquil, I was sure of two things. First, that nothing in my life would be the same. And second, that I was happy. Everyone had told me that giving birth would be special, beautiful, unlike anything else. But those were just words. And words can't love, or smell, or touch.

Penny was beside me on the hospital bed, smiling a big smile. I'd talked about names with her, but now, as I stared down at my child, it seemed too soon to give her a name, to differentiate her and make her distinct.

At last, I looked over at Penny and saw the serene blue eyes and knowing smile of someone who'd already experienced what I was now experiencing.

"Here you go," I said. "This is Lola. Lola Suso."

I handed Lola to Penny, and I loved the sight of them together. What, anyway, is family if not people who love each other and who band together to manage the transition from one generation to the next? In that moment I had so much love in me. So much. For my family across the ocean. For my family in Rome. For the one in Paris. And for the one gathered around me in the delivery room. For a single mother, I was drowning in family.

Penny arranged to have a midwife stay with me. She was an older woman, someone who had seen it all. She helped me get settled and find the rhythms, to feel the simple symbiosis that binds mother and child. And then she left, and it was just us, Lola and me. I spent hours on end looking at her. Just looking. At the intelligence and the wonder in her eyes. At her mouth that would smile and then frown as different noises floated up from the street. Everything new. Everything fascinating. In Lola's face I could see the past, my mother and grandmothers; and I could see the present, me and her; and I could also see the future—almost—the girl and the woman waiting within her. Her face was an infinity, something I could stare at forever, move closer to forever, and I knew that as long as I held her, as long as I kept my eyes on her, I would never lose my way.

I was staring at her like this when there was a knock on my door. I opened it to see the trunk of an elephant peeking out of a gift bag. And holding the bag was my Englishman. Seeing Lola, he stopped cold.

And then he reached out a finger and slipped it into her little hand.

"Luminous Lola," he whispered.

He looked from her to me, and between us was an understanding of such profundity that I had to look away.

"She's breathtaking," he said.

"Yes," I said quietly.

I handed her to him, and he kissed her head and inhaled her scent deeply.

Looking at me, he said, "You're a mother."

"Of a daughter," I said.

Over the weeks that followed, work dragged me back into the professional world and I eased into a routine. I'd hired a nanny, Irene. She was from a village in the Welsh countryside, and I liked the decency and simplicity she'd brought with her to the big city. Whenever work beckoned and couldn't be put off, she'd take Lola across Bayswater Road to Hyde Park or play with her in the little nursery while I worked at the dining room table. Weekends were mostly mine, though, and Lola and I would wander down King's Road, go to parks, and visit other children. We took weekend trips, had friends over, and generally adjusted to life as a little family.

Carolyn and Lola in Hyde Park
(Photograph by Anthony Wigram)

Motherhood changed me; it made me a link in the chain of life. This sense of lineage, of connecting past and future and of contributing to something beyond oneself, comes through many experiences, but it came to me through motherhood, and it grounded me as nothing had before.

In addition to Penny, I'd asked Geraldine to be Lola's godmother and I'd asked Omar and Alain to be her godfathers. With my family in

America, I wanted to create a vast and deep network of support and love for her here in Europe. It was also for that reason that I'd chosen Lola's middle name: Suso. For the life I was living and for the life I anticipated for my daughter, connecting her to these people who had meant so much to me was the fullest measure of security I could give her.

Lola's christening in the Church of England was an intimate and joyful service. Something important happens when adults gather around a newborn. In the ritualized cadence of song and prayer, of vows and fellowship, there is an invocation of the sacred. At the center of this solemn ceremony, I think, is innocence. Because innocence is the one thing that we can all measure ourselves against. We gather around a child with hope and with love, and we commend ourselves to each other and to this innocent baby whose journey in life is now beginning.

Lola's christening with Omar, Penny, Alain, and Carolyn
(Photograph by Terry O'Neill)

After the service, we had cake and champagne back at my flat. We passed Lola around the room as Terry O'Neill took pictures and Allen Burry helped me make everyone feel welcome. It wasn't my whole life all in one place, but it came close. Geraldine was filming in Spain, but Penny was there along with a dozen other close friends. Omar and Alain had come from Paris, and I'd never seen either look more handsome.

Alain, Lola, Carolyn, and Omar at Lola's christening
(Photograph by Terry O'Neill)

That December, Lola and I flew home to spend the holidays with my family. Crossing the Atlantic this time felt exploratory and new, as if I were again reaching out to a new world. As I carried Lola down the jetway at the Greensboro airport, I saw my father smiling and waving. And then I saw my mother, who was in tears even before I reached her.

"Oh, Sugar," she cried. "Give her here."

As I gently handed Lola to her, I felt my father's arm around my shoulder.

"Attagirl," he said.

Carolyn and Lola
(Photograph by Steve Shapiro)

I sat with Lola in the back seat of my father's sedan and watched as city gave way to countryside. I smiled. My little English baby was here, in rural America, with horses and tobacco fields and backcountry roads. At our house, my father held Lola high. She giggled and he smiled up at her proudly. But it was my mother who would not be separated from her. She hummed and sang and whispered happy nothings to her. When I sat beside her and Lola on the couch, she smiled at me.

"There's nothing like it, is there?" she said.

My brother, Bill, was there with his family. His daughter, Heather, was a year older than Lola. With my great-aunt Caroline still living in the old Cardwell House, and with relatives all around, that Christmas we were four generations gathered together.

It was heartwarming to see some of my childhood friends. Thomas, good to his word, had become a doctor and had moved away. But Nancy Lee was there and so was Patsy Cox. We'd ridden horses together as girls, and now we were all mothers. Patsy had two sons, a husband, a career, and a household to manage. And David Spear was there. He

Liza Minnelli and Carolyn with Lola and Irene in Positano
(Carolyn Pfeiffer archive)

was the boy who'd always seen things I never did—the reflection of the sky in a rain puddle, the tracks of a deer in the mud. He'd grown up, become a father, and was preparing to take over the *Madison Messenger*, just like he said he would.

I walked with him on the roads we'd explored as children, along the Dan River and past the rolling hills with their histories and their secrets.

"It looks so different," I said.

"Different how?"

"More beautiful. Was it always like this?"

"It may seem different to you," he said with a laugh, "but it's the same old Madison."

Back in London, the mellow pace of Madison and the lackadaisical days of new motherhood began to fade away as the new year got busy. We took on PR for Paul McCartney and Wings. We did the London opening of Robert Altman's *The Long Goodbye* as well as that of *The Way We Were*, Barbra Streisand's new movie opposite Robert Redford. I was asked by David Puttnam, a successful producer and good friend of Terence Donovan's who would go on to become a member of the House of Lords, to join him and a few others to form a company that focused on athletes as clients. In those days, when an athlete's career ended, they had nothing to fall back on. This company, the first of its kind, secured opportunities to continue earning money through commercials, product endorsements, and other means that are now commonplace.

We also took on PR for the inaugural issue of *People* magazine. Working with Tessa Kennedy—whom I'd first met at that long-ago dinner with Penny and Grace Coddington—we assembled an impressive group of people for a photo shoot to commemorate the launch: Princess Firyal of Jordan, Tatum and Ryan O'Neal, Dewi Sukarno, Marisa Berenson, Joan Collins, Alice Cooper, Fiona Lewis, and Ron Cass.

For the cover of the new Alice Cooper album, *Billion Dollar Babies*, Shep insisted that a baby and $1 million in cash were needed, and he tasked me with finding both. Any misgivings I might have had about volunteering Lola were quickly assuaged. I trusted Shep, and I greatly admired the photography of my friend David Bailey, who was to shoot the cover. I liked the idea of Lola notching her own little footnote in rock and roll history.

Finding $1 million in cash in a country whose currency was the pound sterling was infinitely more difficult. But I eventually found a bank willing to lend us the money. When the armored car showed up at David's studio and the security guards marched in with the money, we were giddy with excitement. None of us had ever seen a million

Mike Hewitt, Richard Chamberlain, Lola, and Carolyn
(Carolyn Pfeiffer archive)

dollars cash before, and we imagined it would be enough to fill a swimming pool. Crowding around the table as the money was unloaded, I remember thinking to myself that a million dollars doesn't take up much space at all. In fact, I found the pile of bills rather anticlimactic. In the disappointing silence that followed, my eyes found Shep's, and I could see that he was thinking the same thing. We started to chuckle and we both looked over at Alice.

"Well," Alice cried, "where's the rest of it?"

Those busy days overflowed with laughter and friendship, and also with long hours of hard work. Though I sometimes left before Lola woke up in the morning, I made a point of always being home for bedtime. I'd read to her and sing lullabies as she drifted off to sleep. Watching her slowly close her eyes, I'd remind myself to not let the time pass too quickly.

I purposefully built a community around us, as I wanted Lola's early memories to be filled with the women who'd meant so much to me. With Penny and her three children, we spent a week in a village outside Saint-Paul de Vence, in the south of France. While walking through a cherry orchard of the most astonishing pink, her children darted through the trees, and we took turns carrying Lola. Nathalie and I took our children to Alain's villa in Aix-en-Provence, a charming town north of Marseille. We spent the time floating in the swimming pool, praising Anthony for his cannonballs, and marveling at the way Lola was beginning to assemble words into complete sentences.

When Suso came to London for meetings, we met in St. James's Park. Suso held Lola on her lap, and we watched the pelicans—whose ancestors were first introduced to the park in the 1600s.

"*Cara* Lola," Suso said, "we have loved your mother and now we will love you."

Seeing Lola with Suso, after whom she was named, brought something full circle. I promised to bring Lola to Rome to meet the rest of the family.

Between Lola and work, keeping my head above water wasn't easy. The first issue of *People* hit newsstands in early March 1974. By that time, we'd also taken on publicity for a revival of Tennessee Williams's *A Streetcar Named Desire*. Hilly Elkins, a prominent theater producer, hired me since we'd already worked on his film *A Doll's House*. I leapt at the opportunity not only because I loved *Streetcar* but also because none other than Tennessee Williams himself was coming to London to support it. Nearly twenty years had passed since *Streetcar* and *Cat on a Hot Tin Roof* had earned him the reputation as one of the world's great playwrights, but his later work had not resulted in the same level of recognition. Thus, he was unusually invested in the London production and hoped it would mark a comeback for him.

At a welcome reception hosted by his friend Marguerite Lipman, a Southern woman who'd married an Englishman, I fell under Tennessee's spell. His smile came easy, and his lilting Southern accent coaxed my own out of hibernation. But despite his energy and force of personality, to me it seemed that his laughter came too readily, that perhaps it was deployed as much as a defense as a response. Indeed, as I spent more time with him, I came to understand that a terrible darkness was at his heels and that he was right then clawing his way out of the depths into which his demons had driven him.

Abused as a child, Tennessee also developed a severe case of diphtheria, the complications of which left him unable to walk for two years. He was then discovered to have a heart condition and told he would never live to forty. On top of that, when his sister, Rose, slid into mental illness, she was lobotomized. All of this tormented him into adulthood even as he rose to fame. But with the death of his lover a decade earlier, he'd begun to unravel. Convinced that what had happened to his sister would also happen to him, and suffering from society's repression of same-sex attraction, he fell into depression and deepening drug and alcohol abuse.

According to many, Tennessee Williams, more than anyone else, is responsible for our image of Southern women as resilient and strong, beautiful and resourceful. Certainly, with Blanche duBois, *Streetcar*'s tragic protagonist, he created an archetypal heroine, a fantasist who is beaten down by the world and yet refuses to relinquish her vision of life as beautiful and the future as full of promise. Delusion, the play seems to suggest, is sometimes the only way to endure reality.

Opening night was triumphant, a success beyond what Tennessee had imagined. And as I watched Claire Bloom transform into Blanche, the love that Tennessee had for Blanche, and for all his Southern women, felt personal. Some will say that Tennessee's genius was his writing, but I think it was love. Love is what drew him to write about the unstable, the flawed, the broken, and the damned, and love is what rendered them noble in his writing. But writers sometimes give too much of themselves to their characters. They go too deep, identify too much. In this, they take empathy to a dangerous place. They walk for too long in the shoes of others and their own foundations begin to flicker.

When I first met Luchino Visconti, I was so intimidated that I couldn't think of anything to say to him. That was when Suso explained to me that the outside of a person tells you what defenseless thing lives within. That's how I think about Tennessee—as someone whose torment on the outside was a testament to the love on the inside. Isn't that how it is with all of us? Penny, buttoned up and proper, was playful and uninhibited. Romy had a regal, impenetrable facade because of the vulnerability she guarded within. Geraldine was delicate and dignified because she was still working out her own power. Claudia was a dove on the outside, a falcon within. And Nathalie, so driven and relentless, needed love and affirmation. Finally, there was me—chameleon-like, always fitting in on the outside, while on the inside, I was always searching, always moving forward.

We were just girls, all of us.

I thought about these things after Tennessee left London, about the way a person comes to be, how they are formed over time even as they carry something eternal inside. Gathering Lola in my arms, I held her close. For a baby, it's different. For a baby, that beautiful internal quality is still on the outside. There is no inside or outside; there is no separation anywhere—there is only what is.

Thirty-Three

'd never felt more connected, more right with myself and with the world. Life's current was with me, and I was aware only of a sense of flowing, of being.

We took on publicity for the film adaptation of *Steppenwolf*, the Hermann Hesse novel. This required me to visit the set, which meant occasional early mornings and late nights.

In April, Nathalie came to visit. By now, instead of my flat containing an office, it had become an office that contained a spot of living space. I needed more room and had already found a little two-story house in Battersea. It was a far cry from Alain's *hotel particulier*, but the idea— living upstairs and having an office downstairs—was the same.

One day, having visited the new house, I returned home late in the afternoon to find that Lola was fussing. Irene, her nanny, hadn't been able to calm her, and Nathalie was pacing with Lola in the living room.

"What's wrong, my sweet baby?" I cooed as I touched the back of my hand to Lola's forehead.

She was warm, and it was so unlike her to fuss like this, so I called the doctor. After describing the symptoms, the doctor assured me that it was nothing and that a little Tylenol would help her sleep. Sure enough, she quieted down. After reading her a book, I put her in her crib, and she was soon fast asleep.

Nathalie was leaving early in the morning, and so we soon went to bed. Because there was nowhere else for Nathalie to sleep, she shared my queen-sized bed with me. We slipped under the covers, and I turned off the light. Our voices lowered to a whisper, our words became infrequent, and then there was only silence. I liked the presence of her near me, and the even rhythm of her breathing soon lulled me to sleep.

We awoke early the next morning, and as Nathalie got ready to leave, I checked on Lola. She was still sleeping, and so I chose not to wake her. Irene was in the kitchen making tea and said that Lola had slept the whole night. Encouraged, I asked Irene to call me at noon with an update. I then hugged Nathalie goodbye and got myself ready for the day.

Walking into the studio, I watched as the crew trickled in and started working. For me, the time leading up to the first shot of the day is a small but deep pleasure. Though it can be intense, there is an elegance, a kind of collective intelligence in the way so many people arrange themselves in preparation for the work to come. Like ants or bees, there's a hypnotic sense of collaboration, of the way small tasks can be added together and that, from them, something greater can emerge.

I was in this state of quiet reverie when a production secretary came running in from the office.

"You have a call," she said in a voice ominous with concern.

On the other line was Irene, panicked, sobbing, fear ripping through her voice.

"She won't wake up. I can't wake her up!"

I don't remember what happened next, what I said or what I did. I don't even remember how I got to Great Ormond Street Hospital, where Irene and Allen had rushed Lola. But I remember running down a long corridor, pushing past doctors and nurses. I remember coming upon Lola as she was being hooked up to an assortment of machines. And I remember hearing Irene, somewhere in the room, shouting, "She's her mother!" over and over.

As I approached my baby, a doctor intercepted me.

"What is it?" I asked in a quivering voice. "What's wrong with her?"

"We don't know yet," came his stoic response.

His passivity was infuriating, and I moved past him, to Lola. The sight of her little body lying unconscious on the bed filled me with indescribable terror. I had so many questions, and they weren't being answered fast enough. "Can she hear me?" "Is she in pain?" "Someone please tell me what's wrong with her!" I tried to stay calm, I really did. I tried to let them do their jobs, but I had stopped breathing.

Then I heard the doctor saying that Lola's brain was swelling and that there was too much pressure in her brain. They needed to drill holes in it, he said. It was the only way to ease the pressure. The room began to swim, and a knot began to form in my throat.

"What is it?" I begged. "What's wrong with her?"

"A virus," he said. "We think it's meningitis."

The doctor was looking at me, asking me if I understood about the procedure, about the drilling. I tried to say yes, I understand. But my heart was pounding, and all I could do was nod.

I was in the waiting room when Penny arrived. She rubbed my shoulders, and even though I could hear her talking to me, I couldn't make out any of her words. I just sat there, detached and numb. When the procedure was over, I went to the recovery room. When they left me alone with Lola, tears flooded my eyes as I looked down at her. Her little head was completely bandaged, but she was still so perfect.

"Baby," I said, taking her hand. "Mama loves you."

But her fingers wouldn't curl around mine.

"I am here," I whispered. "I am with you."

I wanted love to save her. I thought that if I could love her enough, if I could somehow transmit all the love in my body into hers, then the infection would be turned back. But that didn't happen. Instead she just lay there peacefully, and I stayed with her like that, her hand in mine. Until they told me it was over.

Penny held me tightly. She said things about the pain being gone, about peace. I loved her for holding me, but I just couldn't . . . I couldn't hear; I couldn't understand. I still thought that maybe there was a chance. Maybe the doctors were wrong. Maybe it could somehow be reversed.

The worst thing is that you have to choose a moment to let go. As long as you hold on, you're connected, but when you let go, you fall into the abyss. I squeezed Lola's hand for a long, long time, and then I let Penny take me home.

We buried Lola in a small cemetery on the edge of London. My mother and brother flew over to be with me, allowing me to face the reality that I was no longer a mother from the safety and refuge of knowing I was still a daughter, still a sister. Is it possible to convey the depths of emotion that a baby's casket is able to conjure? There is a bottomlessness. There is a ferocious desire for what is to not be. There is a simple, gutting, irreversible injustice.

It is surely the greatest of all pain.

When my mother left, I went to Italy. Silvia and Silvana Mangano took me to the healing waters at Montecatini, the baths featured in *8½*. I don't remember where I heard it, that when an elephant is sick, her friends come alongside her and, shoulder to shoulder, steady her on her feet. They do not leave her side until she dies or regains strength. This is how I felt. It wasn't that my friends were supporting me; they were keeping me alive. I'd been to Montecatini before, a decade earlier. Then we had come for art. Now I came for health and healing; I came for life.

Silvia d'Amico, Silvana Mangano, and Carolyn in Montecatini
(d'Amico family archive)

I don't know what it is about Italy. It was there that I knew I had to leave my job with Claudia. It was also there that I knew I had to begin a new life in London. And now, again, that familiar feeling began to stir once more.

As the months passed, the feeling grew. I once again felt restless, the desire to jump from this rock to another. Sometimes you jump so you won't be haunted by what might have been; other times you jump so you won't be haunted by what already is. I jumped from rock to rock to be free. From the beginning, that was the reason. Freedom. From boundaries and from prejudice. It was the same now. I jumped to be free. From the haunting. From the finality. From the love I felt for Lola.

The rending thing was that I didn't want to be free of her. That was the dagger—that my freedom from her was bitterly unwanted.

And unwanted freedom feels nothing like freedom.

Thirty-Four

My flat felt like something from the past, a place in which I'd
once lived. London, too, began to feel like something that
once was. Without the instinct to provide stability, to build
a place where a child could thrive, faraway horizons beckoned once
more. I kept handling premieres and events, but the dull pain of loss
wouldn't go away.

Nashville brought Kathryn and Bob Altman back to London. We
got to talking, and Bob suggested I join him at Lion's Gate, his production company in Hollywood. Some weeks later, Shep also came into
town, and we went out to dinner. He was doing well and was thinking
about launching a film company.

"Need any help?" I asked. "I think I need to go home."

"You should run it," he said. "We should work together. Think of the
trouble we could cause."

We talked about it long into the night.

I packed up my things. I gave Roger and my business to Allen. And then I said my goodbyes. If you worked in entertainment, a reason to be in New York or LA was easily found, and so my permanent goodbyes were few. But it was different with my Englishman.

We met in Hyde Park, and I hugged him and we rocked back and forth for a long time. We pulled apart but still our foreheads touched. What is there to say when you love someone you should never have loved?

Find your way. Live your life. But also—remember me! Remember this! This moment! This place! Remember this thing that happened between us! Though it be lost to age and to time, let you and me always remember that we once loved each other and that from that love a child was born.

On the afternoon of my flight, Penny took me to the cemetery to say goodbye to Lola. It's a peaceful place with a schoolyard nearby. As I stood over her grave, I could hear the joyful sound of children at play. Their happiness warmed me even as it made me cry. I did nothing to stop the tears. Because Lola's death wasn't anyone's fault and because I had no other response to it. I was crying for the tragedy of it, because I had no protection to give her, because terrible things can happen at any time.

You want, in those moments, to be one of those happy children at play in the schoolyard. You want for there to be a world of adults able to provide solace and explanation, to give you narrative and to buffer you from the indifference of the universe. You want there to be someone able to sponge up the sorrow, to absorb it back into something contained and logical. You want, in those moments, to not be grown up, to not have the knowledge that you must wrestle alone with all that is.

I laid a rose on Lola's grave and rested my hand on her little pink headstone. Here, again, I had to choose the moment to let go.

Catharsis is a curious thing. It is not, in my experience, that a reset is possible. Rather, catharsis has a transformational quality. It allows hurt to exist within a complex sense of fullness. And, in fullness, there is something that hints, ever so slightly, at contentment. Catharsis introduces a distance between you and the thing inside you that won't stop hurting in a way that threads the pain into your constitution. The pain becomes a part of you, and you stop wanting to excise it, to wish it away. And as it becomes a part of you, it stops being apart from you.

Through the oval window of the Pan Am 747, I looked down at the vast blue of the Atlantic Ocean. It was the same ocean that had carried me to Europe fifteen years earlier. Then, there was a gaping space between the girl I was and the woman I wanted to become. I'd wanted adventure; I'd wanted to make my mark. But what did I know of myself? Of the world? I leaned my forehead against the window, and I thought about being out of place in Rome. Even with Claudia, I'd been a visitor in her world. With Alain, the same. I thought of Omar, of Cairo, Belgrade, Madrid. There was revolution all around me, but I was always apart from it. In London, too, even as it convulsed with change, it was something others were doing.

I looked at the gentle arc of the horizon and I smiled softly at the girl I used to be, at her longing for the faraway. I felt her, still inside me, still yearning, still restless. And I knew she would be with me always. I leaned back. I couldn't wait to get to America. Because if you never leave home, you will never have a home to return to. And if you never go home, the revolution will never be your own.

Epilogue

Some years later, I met Jon Bradshaw for dinner. He was the enormous-hearted journalist I'd first met on the train to Manchester, the one who'd pop into my life without warning only to disappear from it just as quickly. He was the one I'd never stopped thinking about.

After dinner, as he held the restaurant door open for me, I felt the palm of his hand, gentleman-like, on the small of my back. Outside, the night was cool, the Los Angeles traffic subdued.

"My hotel is that way," said Bradshaw, nodding his head.

"My house is that way," I said, nodding in the opposite direction.

I always knew Bradshaw would turn up in my life again. He was based in New York and had been living with Anna Wintour, the promising young magazine editor. But their relationship was ending and his visits to LA were becoming more frequent, and, at least to me, it seemed like the affection between us was thickening into attraction.

Carolyn and Sam Shepard on the set of Far North
(Alive Films archive)

Since returning from Europe, I'd been living in Los Angeles. Alive Films, the company Shep started and that I ran, fit neatly in the New Hollywood movement. I brought my experiences in Rome, Paris, and London to my role as producer and executive, and so the films we worked on were necessarily informed by the French New Wave and by Italian neorealism before it. We brought many groundbreaking films into the world, and we championed many beloved filmmakers. At one point, I was the only woman in Hollywood able to green-light a movie. The *Wall Street Journal* dubbed me a "mini-mogul."

Waiting for Bradshaw to speak, I think I already knew what was going to happen.

"What would you think," he said, "if I got my things from the hotel?"

I just slipped my arm into his and we walked to his room. He quietly packed his suitcase, and as we were driving to my house, it felt like we had been together all our lives, as if our togetherness had always been and would always be.

Carolyn, Shep, and Alan Rudolph on the set of Roadie
(Photograph by Joyce Rudolph)

He returned to New York the following day and, a week later, moved in with me for good. The chaos of his creativity complemented the curiosity of my ambition and brought symmetry to the life we were beginning together. His books covered several walls, floor to ceiling, and his art and paintings folded nicely into those I'd collected over the years. The clickety-clack of his typewriter added a seductive staccato to the endless ringing of my telephone, and his evening whiskey contrasted nicely with my vodka and water. His short, sandy-blond hair offset the dark strands that fell over my shoulders, and the contours of his body aligned perfectly against the contours of mine.

Bradshaw loved Jamaica, and when he took me there for our first Christmas together, I fell in love with it too. We married at the headwaters of the White River in Ocho Rios, and we bought a Great House high in the hills of Saint Ann. In California, we adopted our daughter,

Shannon Frances. Named after my mother, she wasn't yet six weeks old when we welcomed her into our family.

Carolyn and Bradshaw's Jamaican wedding
(Photograph by Nathalie Delon)

The years that followed are among the happiest of my life. Motherhood returned me to a state of wonder as Shannon reminded me of the way in which the oneness of life is so obvious to a child. Our home teemed with animals, with dogs, cats, and birds, and when we took our evening walks, I felt a wholeness within that I didn't think would ever again be available to me. Sometimes Shannon toddled ahead and sometimes Bradshaw carried her on his back, and, in those moments, I came to trust that even Lola's death was a part of a mysterious current of life by which all things exist.

We began to have history, Bradshaw and me. He wrote article after article for *Esquire* and other top magazines, and he finished a biography about the tragic life of torch singer Libby Holman. Meanwhile, the movies I worked on grew more ambitious. One of them, *The Whales of August*, starred Lillian Gish and Bette Davis and would premiere at the Cannes Film Festival, the screening attended by Princess Diana and Prince Charles.

After my tumultuous years in Europe, I believed that, with Bradshaw and Shannon, with our little family bound tightly together, I'd at last arrived at a serene stretch of river. I was sure that the rapids of self-discovery and young adulthood were behind me and that the waters ahead would be tranquil and untroubled.

But one lazy Saturday morning, a car screeched to a halt in our California driveway. Our friend was driving, and Bradshaw was slumped over in the passenger seat. They'd been playing tennis and he'd collapsed on the court. We called an ambulance, but it was too late. The heart attack had done its damage.

He was forty-eight years old.

Instead of the quiet waters I'd hoped for, I was suddenly in free fall, hurtling down a waterfall. Isn't that how it always is? Waterfalls, moments of immense and irreversible change, appear without warning. You come upon them before you can process what they are, before you can prepare yourself for the drop. And, suddenly, you're in it—you're falling, sinking, drowning. And then, because you have no choice, you let go.

I have so much to share about Bradshaw, about our life together, and about all that has happened since, but I'll save that for another time.

For this story, what matters is that Bradshaw changed me, first because I loved him and again because I lost him.

I'd been a single parent before, and I'd been tasked with that role once again. Shannon, our daughter, was only three when Bradshaw died, and to provide the stability we both needed, I chose to leave Hollywood and move to Jamaica permanently. Once there, I started a business outside of film, and I devoted myself to our new life. But the cinematic zeitgeist was evolving beyond the New Hollywood movement, and the advent of digital filmmaking was just then dawning. Despite living in the deep rural countryside, I was again pulled into it, and I produced several films in Jamaica, among the first digital features ever made.

This led us back to Los Angeles, where Shannon began high school and where I began a career in academia, first at the Los Angeles Film School, then at the American Film Institute Conservatory, and finally in Austin at the University of Texas. In these positions, I started programs and mentored students, crafted curricula and recruited established filmmakers to share their stories, to record their oral histories. Then, with Shannon on her way to a career in social work, I left academia and moved to Marfa, in Far West Texas.

Surrounded by a panorama of mountains low on the horizon, Marfa is a place where Mexico and the United States meet and where artists and ranchers live side by side. Along the main street is the Hotel Saint George and the Paisano, where James Dean, Elizabeth Taylor, Rock Hudson, and the cast and crew stayed during the filming of *Giant* in 1955. There is a single blinking traffic light, a gas station, and some excellent restaurants that are only open sometimes. By the side of the road a few miles up Highway 90 is a Prada storefront stocked with Prada shoes. The door is locked, and no one is there. There isn't a building around, and it's supposed to say something about context.

In moving here, I have returned to producing films and seem to always have multiple projects in various stages of development and production. But I was also inspired by the oral histories I'd organized, and I'd started to think about putting something of my own life into writing. I wanted to write about film and filmmaking, about the way the filmmakers that came before me connect to those following behind. More personally, I wanted to write about daughters and mothers. I wanted to tell the story of being a daughter and becoming a mother, and I wanted to do what I could to strengthen the connection between my own daughter and my own mother. For this work, Marfa has proven ideal.

I live on the outskirts with unobstructed views of the prairie. The sky above is a waterfall of darkness cascading down through layers of indigo and periwinkle and evaporating into a plane of white weightlessness. Red-tailed hawks soar overhead, javelina and antelope come and go, and coyotes are never far away. There are foxes and bobcats and, everywhere you look, jackrabbits. Every now and then I see them popping up one at a time, rabbits like popcorn shooting into the air. And then, low in the tall grass, I'll see a coyote stalking and lunging and waiting. The days are hot and the nights are cool, and I like nothing more than sitting on the porch as the sun sets. You can hear for miles, and in the dusk there is a quality in the light that I have never experienced before.

As I look out across the prairie, the fullness of the empty desert envelops me and, as the wholeness of the world is restored, so, too, is the wholeness within. And there is once again no here and no there, no me and no not-me. There is only what is.

Acknowledgments

Our debts and acknowledgments are many.

First and foremost, we thank our intrepid agent, Jeff Silberman, who read an early draft and came on board, heart and soul. His steadfast support, counsel, and encouragement have meant everything to us.

We are very indebted to Andrea Fleck-Nisbet, who brought the project to life, and to Matt Baugher, whose passion and vision made it a reality. This would never have been possible without you and we are deeply grateful.

Thank you to the rest of the HarperHorizon team: to Amanda Bauch, whose gentle guidance and sharp eye helped us over the finish line; to Meaghan Porter, for her tireless work and support (and for coming up with the title); to Mike Bzozowski, for guiding us through the legal process; and to Verônika Shülman and Erin Brown for seeing us through important phases of our journey. We are most grateful to Kevin Smith, Kara Brammer, Hannah Harless, and Belinda Bass for their expertise in introducing the book to the world, to Richard Ljoenes for the brilliant cover, and to Jeff Farr and his team at Neuwirth & Associates for overseeing the production process with efficiency and quality.

We also thank our friends who were on hand with advice and assistance when we needed it, among them Thomas Schatz, Deborah Eisenberg, Glenn Horowitz, Patricia Louisianna Knop, Marcia Newberger, Valerie Breuvart, Richard Maxwell and Tory Vasquez, John Salvetti, Rodrigo Lopresti and Maayan Laufer, and Michael Donaldson.

Finally, thank you to the readers and researchers who gave generously of their time: Shannon Kelly, Joanne Oh, Briana Pagano, Jill Zimmerman, Katie Yockey, Caroline Fairey, Megan Barnard, Tara Dugan, Oliver Hughes, Vanessa Chandler, and Abigail Henkin.

GREGORY & CAROLYN

. . .

Carolyn, I have loved walking for a while in your always fearless, always formidable shoes. In them I have learned courage and grace and the importance of always moving forward.

Cassia and Luce, you enchant this world just by being in it. Such magic you possess. Such beauty. And Jenny, most of all. For the countries and the continents this project has spanned. For the life we have lived and the life we have shared in the course of its making.

GREGORY

. . .

My first debt of gratitude goes to Gregory Collins, who suggested this book and then dove in to make it happen. His interest, talent, and patience were unparalleled. I could not have asked for a better partner.

Heartfelt thanks to the many friends and loved ones who helped us pin down dates and details from the years covered in the book. I am particularly grateful to my "bestest" friends Penny Wigram and Nathalie Delon for tugging at their memories. They are gone now, and I miss them more than I can ever say.

Big thanks to my dear friends Geraldine Chaplin and Patricio Castilla, who helped find images and always gave support. I am especially thankful to Lionel Wigram, who was always there when I asked him to read and confirm things as he recalled them. My profound gratitude to Masolino d'Amico, Silvia d'Amico Bendicò, and Caterina d'Amico, whom I consider family, and my dear friend Marianne Frey Giannoli. All of them patiently searched their memories whenever I asked.

Thank you to my close friends and filmmaking partners Shep Gordon, Alan Rudolph, Allen Burry, and Marion Rosenberg, who were wonderfully generous as I peppered them with emails and phone calls. My childhood friend David Spear was instrumental in helping re-create the Madison of my upbringing, and I'm very happy that we are still pals after all these years.

I am indebted to Jim Fissel, my neighbor and friend, for his willingness to scan the many old photos and handwritten notes I dug up over the writing of the book. Special thanks to all my Marfa friends, especially Rob Wiener, Eileen Myles, Martha Hughes, and Jim Martinez. Your encouragement and counsel has been deeply appreciated.

Finally, I am most grateful to my beloved daughter, Shannon, who was supportive every step of the way, and to my newfound stepson, Rick Guest. Bradshaw died without knowing he had a son. Thank you for finding us and thank you for being family.

CAROLYN

About the Author

CAROLYN PFEIFFER is a pioneering producer in the world of American independent film. Having run two successful film companies, Alive Films and Island Alive, and having worked with directors like Alan Rudolph, Sam Shepard, Mary Lambert, and Wes Craven, Carolyn was dubbed a "mini-mogul" by the *Wall Street Journal*. Carolyn was also the founding president of the Los Angeles Film School, vice chair of the American Film Institute Conservatory, and the founding president of Burnt Orange Productions at the University of Texas.

But her early years—which prepared her for this trailblazing career and which are recounted here—tell the story of a free spirit from North Carolina who, at twenty, booked a one-way ticket to Europe, where she lived in Rome, Paris, and London, and where her formative experiences, filled with love and loss, introduced her to a cast of characters ranging from Federico Fellini and François Truffaut to Tennessee Williams and the Beatles, and where she came of age on the sets of films like *8½*, *The Leopard*, and *Doctor Zhivago*—among the most important films ever made.

Born and raised in Kenya, East Africa, GREGORY COLLINS is a writer and filmmaker whose work explores connections across and between cultures and people. www.acrossandbetween.com